Survival in the Trenches of the NFL

Joe Klecko
Joe Fields
and Greg Logan

William Morrow and Company, Inc.
New York

Library of Congress Cataloging-in-Publication Data

Klecko, Joe.
    Nose to nose: survival in the trenches of the NFL / Joe Klecko,
Joe Fields, and Greg Logan.
        p. cm.
    ISBN 0-688-05281-9
    1. Klecko, Joe. 2. Fields, Joe. 3. Football players—United
States—Biography. 4. New York Jets (Football team) 5. National
Football League. I. Fields, Joe. II. Logan, Greg. III. Title.
GV939.A1K52 1989
796.332′092′2—dc20
[B]   89-35071
                                                                 CIP

Printed in the United States of America

First Edition

1 2 3 4 5 6 7 8 9 10

BOOK DESIGN BY WILLIAM MCCARTHY

Joe Klecko

To my loving wife, Debbie, and my sons, Michael and Danny,
for allowing me the freedom to be the pro football player
I wanted to be

Joe Fields

To Kay, Christopher, and Sean,
for all the time you spent alone

Greg Logan

To my father, John Paul Logan,
a passionate fan

Contents

The Beginning
of the End

As they stepped over the collar of dirty snow surrounding the matted brown grass field at Cleveland Stadium, none of the New York Jets gave more than a passing thought to Joe Klecko, not even his best friend, Joe Fields, who was absorbed with the coming battle. In football, the injured get left behind like so much dead weight, and it is left to the doctors to clean up the mess while the army marches ever onward. It was January 3, 1987, and a broken-down Jets team was about to play a divisional playoff game that would turn out to be the third-longest game in National Football League history. The winner would advance to the American Football Conference Championship Game, and the core group remaining from the Jets team that four years earlier fell one step short of the Super Bowl knew this probably would be their last shot to grab the diamond ring.

Klecko ached to be with his teammates and defend his piece of ground in Cleveland Stadium, but he and his plaster-encased left leg were confined to his house, a contemporary design of natural wood and stone set atop a bald hill in the farm country northwest of Philadelphia. Just two weeks earlier, Dr. Bart Nisonson had cut open Klecko's left knee, which already was missing the anterior cruciate ligament because of a previous injury. Nisonson took what was left of the damaged cartilage and somehow patched it together, using a five-inch bolt to hold everything in place. Klecko sat with his wounded knee propped up in front of

9

the television set in his thickly carpeted den. A magnificent southern exposure afforded him a view of the wooded hillside across the snug valley below. But Klecko's gaze remained fixed on the television screen, and he turned inward, feeling as desolate as the barren cornfield that lay to the west of his house.

Keeping her distance, Klecko's wife, Debbie, watched her husband suffer through the game, and she could see his anguish. "I was kind of scared, and I know he was that day," she recalls. "He was sitting there steaming. In some ways, it probably made him want to come back even more."

A combination of anger and despair over his fate welled up within Klecko. The same body he had built into such a dominating force now had betrayed him for the second time in his career. He had made a phenomenal recovery from traumatic knee surgery once before when he ruptured the patella tendon in his right knee in the second game of the 1982 season and came back in time to take part in three playoff games the same season. That injury forced some adjustments. In 1981, Klecko was the consensus NFL defensive player of the year and led the league with 20½ sacks from his position at right defensive end, but the knee injury cost him some of the speed that, together with his quickness and strength, made him almost impossible to handle at end. Klecko evolved into a defensive tackle in the four-man line and then into one of the most punishing nose tackles ever to play the game, and along the way, he became the first defensive player ever to make the Pro Bowl at three different positions.

The move to nose tackle in 1985 turned Klecko back into "Mr. Dominance," as he thought of himself at his best, not in terms of sacks but in the sense of controlling games the way he had in 1981. He felt like the young Joe Klecko again. "I was going like a bear in '85, and I was having a better year in '86 when I got hurt," Klecko says, thinking back on the injuries that cursed him. "I guess I felt cheated. I always wondered what I would have been like if I had been injury-free after 1981. I probably hurt myself by playing hurt at the start of the 1982 season instead of waiting it out. I can't imagine what it would have been like to just train in the offseason without rehabilitating an injury."

Without his determination to play with pain and injuries that would have sidelined most other players, Klecko would not have been Klecko. He was a heroic figure in 1981 when he played most of the season with a foot injury that required him to spend every day but Sunday on crutches. But he was thirty-three years old now, and Nisonson practically had to reinvent Klecko's left knee during surgery to give him any kind of chance to play again.

Ordinarily, the 6-foot-3, 265-pound Klecko presents a hard exterior suitable to the reputation of a player who once was known as the strongest man in the NFL. He's built like a baby bull, and when he sees red, he charges about snorting and puffing like one. But when he returned home from the hospital two days before Christmas, Debbie and Klecko's sons, Michael and Danny, who were eleven and six years old at the time, saw a different man from the one who always was so strong and full of bluster. It was Klecko's habit to shield his family from whatever pain he was feeling with a shrug and a show of confidence, but not this time.

In his depression, Joe Klecko let down his guard and cried. "Debbie saw me cry, and Danny did, too, which I never wanted to happen," Klecko says. "I can't imagine myself being like that. I don't like for anyone to know me like that; it's like a flaw in the armor. I get around my kids, and they bring out the sentimental side in me. They're the only ones who can do it. It was pretty hard to be around them with my leg in that condition. It was like, 'Am I not going to be able to do this for them?'

"I know it shocked Danny when he saw me cry because he brought it up later. I hope it's something he forgets. I told him I was just kidding."

The truth was that Klecko was worried he was kidding himself with thoughts of another comeback. That much was obvious to Debbie and the kids and five or six friends who dropped by the house to watch the Jets' playoff game in Cleveland with him. Upset that he had allowed himself so much as a moment of self-pity, Klecko substituted a simmering anger for his fear and doubts about his future. As the game progressed and the outmanned Jets fought their way to a 20–10 lead with barely four minutes left in regulation time, Klecko immersed himself in the television images without saying a word to his friends, who were uncomfortable spectators to what was taking place on their side of the screen. While he was rooting for his teammates to win, Klecko knew the army was leaving him behind, and that was painful.

"It was real hard to watch, real bad," Klecko says. "It was eating me up. Knowing what a difference I would have made if I were healthy, we wouldn't have had any problems putting pressure on their quarterback, Bernie Kosar. I got very mad while I was watching the game, especially when Mark Gastineau got a stupid penalty for hitting Kosar near the end of regulation. That killed us."

Somehow it figured that Gastineau, whose unthinking play and self-promoting sack dance had galled Klecko for years, would be the one to give the Browns the break they needed. Buried at his own 18-yard line and needing 24 yards for a first down, Kosar threw an incomplete pass on second down that just about would have ended the Browns' hopes—except that a late blindside hit by Gastineau drew a personal foul penalty that gave Cleveland an automatic first down. That gaffe began the rally that enabled the Browns to tie the Jets, 20–20, and send the game into overtime.

If only he had been healthy, Klecko thought, he might have made the difference. But the cast on his left knee was telling Klecko something else that day: "I was thinking how much I would have loved to have been there, and I was worried I might not ever play again. It was very depressing."

In Cleveland, where an arctic wind was churning up whitecaps on nearby Lake Erie, the mood was equally grim on the Jets' sideline. What had begun as a wonderful year—*the year!*—had turned into a death march as the Jets' 10–1 start collapsed under the weight of the mounting injury toll. The Jets finished the regular season with five straight losses, and these were not generic, hard-fought losses. The average margin of defeat was 36–12, which made for an experience that was embarrassing and humiliating in the extreme. The dizzy downward spiral abated just long enough for the Jets to catch their breath with a 35–15 wild-card playoff victory over Kansas City, but the decline had been so unimaginably precipitous that it was clear professional careers were on the line from coach Joe Walton on down.

Center Joe Fields felt the pressure and anxiety as acutely as any of the Jets. He had suffered a sprained knee in the second week of the nine-game winning streak that gave the Jets the best record in the NFL when they hit the 10–1 plateau. By coincidence, Fields timed his return to the starting lineup with the 45–3 loss in Miami that stunned the Jets and sent them into their five-game free-fall. Three weeks into the losing streak, Walton threatened Fields, a two-time Pro Bowl selection, with the loss of his job. It was shocking because Fields was known to his teammates as "The General" for the way he had taken charge of the offensive line since becoming the starting center in 1976, his second year in the league.

Linking Fields's return to the losing streak was a tenuous proposition at best, considering all the injuries to key players on defense and offense. He played poorly the game before Walton threatened to replace him, but Fields's knee still was less than 100 percent sound and he was beset by business and personal problems, including serious medical problems affecting the handicapped son, Christopher, whom he and his wife, Kay, recently adopted. Walton's turning the spotlight of blame on Fields came not only as a surprise but an insult. It was the first time his leadership role on the Jets ever had been questioned.

"Everything bad that could happen to me was happening all at once," Fields says. "When Walton told me he was thinking about replacing me, that was the culmination of it. The fact the team was going bad just intensified it. Then, in the playoffs, I had to play against two All-Pro nose tackles, Bill Maas of Kansas City and Bob Golic of Cleveland. After the Kansas City game, our left tackle, Jim Sweeney, got the award for offensive lineman of the week because we ran a lot to his side. He told me, 'I don't deserve this. The guy I played against wasn't half the football player as the guy you played against. Here, take this.' "

Like everyone else on the Jets' offensive line, Fields was a physical wreck by the time he stepped on the field at Cleveland Stadium. His knee still was bothering him, and two weeks earlier, he'd needed a painkilling injection in his back just so he could bend over to snap the ball. In the first quarter against the Browns, he separated a couple of ribs but kept on playing despite the jarring pain of every collision. But when running back Freeman McNeil scored a touchdown to give the Jets a 20–10 lead with 4:14 left to play, a spot in the AFC title game suddenly was within reach.

"I remember coming off the field after Freeman scored the touchdown, and I yelled, 'Don't get loose. There's still too much time,' " Fields recalls. "I was really scared we would sit back and Cleveland would come back and beat us. That's exactly what happened."

Starting with the penalty on Gastineau and aided by some questionable play-calling decisions by Walton, the game began to ebb away. Kosar was spectacular, passing for 489 yards, and the Browns outgained the Jets by nearly 300 yards, 558–287. It was amazing the Jets held out as long as they did. Quarterbacks Pat Ryan and Ken O'Brien were sacked a total of nine times, in part, because four of the Jets' five interior offensive linemen were playing hurt. At 2:02 into the second overtime period, Mark Moseley kicked the field goal that beat the Jets, 23–20, and ended the game more than four hours after it began.

It took all the energy the battered Jets had left to pick themselves up out of the mud and drag their bodies back to the locker room. The loss to the Browns was all the more crushing because it mirrored the Jets' collapse at the end of the regular season. "After the game, I was very depressed," Fields says. "I sat in my locker with my shoulder pads and jersey on, the last one to get undressed. They set up a stand in the locker room for the post-game TV show. I put a chew of tobacco in my mouth and just sat there and reflected on the season and that game and thought, 'Shit! Man, did we blow it for good. I might not get another chance.' We'd gone 10–1 and then lost 6 of the next 7. Whenever there's something like that, you really don't know what the coaches and front office are going to do the following year. At that moment, I first thought my career might be over, but I wanted to continue to play."

As the locker room began to empty, right guard Dan Alexander, who had lined up next to Fields and lockered next to him for the previous ten seasons, said in a quiet voice, "Come on, Joe, get dressed."

"Well, I may have played my last game as a New York Jet," Fields replied, "and I just want to spend a little more time in the uniform."

The fears aroused in Fields and Klecko by their first face-to-face confrontation with retirement were a bit premature only in the sense that they still were on the roster when they reported for training camp in 1987. But both were certain the end of their lives as Jets now was under consideration by the decision-makers. What they didn't realize was how little input they would have into the decision. Klecko's rehabilitation was on schedule for his return in November, but there were obvious questions about whether his left knee would hold up. Fields's vulnerability was not so apparent, but when Walton switched him to guard in training camp, his anxiety began building again. The Jets were a losing team, not the 11–7 playoff team of record but a 1–6 team preparing to make changes.

"You learn to live with the physical pain every day—shoulders, elbows, and knees that always hurt," Fields says. "As the weather gets colder, those aches and pains grow worse. Then you start losing, and you have to deal with the mental pain. All mistakes become ten times worse. That mental anguish is much tougher than the physical part.

"When you're young, you figure you'll get it next year. As you get older, you don't know if you're going to get a chance. If the team has gotten to the point where it hasn't been able to make that push at the end, they categorize you when you hit a certain age, say thirty-two or thirty, and they really examine you with a critical eye. The things Joe Fields is criticized for doing, a younger guy wouldn't be downgraded. That's because they were looking to replace me. It was tough on me mentally. My first year, there were four new faces on the football team, three rookies and a guy from Denver. We were 3–11, and Lou Holtz took over as the coach my second year. He brought in twenty-five new faces. When we lose, that's always in the back of my mind."

"You last a long time and do well, and there's never a question mark about coming back the next year," Klecko adds. "When those question marks start coming up, you always want to do it your own way. You don't want somebody to tell you that you have to retire."

Klecko and Fields were the pillars—one on the defensive line and one on the offensive line—around which the New York Jets were built in the post–Joe Namath era that ended in 1977. That was the year the flamboyant quarterback who "guaranteed" the Jets' victory in Super Bowl III was traded to the Los Angeles Rams after he failed to reach agreement on a contract for his final NFL season. It also was Klecko's rookie season. Fields had arrived in 1975 in time to witness the final chaotic days not only of the Namath regime but of general manager and ex-coach Weeb Ewbank. In his first two seasons, Fields played for four head coaches, including Holtz, who returned to the college ranks with one game left in a 3–11 season in 1976 to take the Arkansas job. He went on to coach Notre Dame to a national championship a dozen years later.

The blue-collar image evoked by Klecko and Fields was miles

from that of "Broadway Joe." Klecko was driving a tractor-trailer rig when he was discovered playing semipro football for the Aston, Pennsylvania, Knights. He went to Temple University in Philadelphia to serve the four-year apprenticeship he needed to gain admission to the NFL and was drafted in the sixth round. Fields was a fourteenth-round draft pick from Widener College, a Division III school in Chester, Pennsylvania, a suburb of Philadelphia that happened to be Klecko's hometown. More than down-to-earth, they were bedrock.

Namath had given the old American Football League a glamorous presence in New York when it was most needed, but the team around him fell into disrepair over the years. What Klecko and Fields brought to the Jets was the necessary backbone to help make them a contender once again. Walt Michaels, who became head coach in Klecko's rookie season, recognized those qualities early on and eventually named Fields his team leader on offense and Klecko his team leader on defense. They performed in those roles for a team that made the playoffs four times in six seasons from 1981–86 and often was described in the early 1980s as "the most talented team in the NFL."

Those Jets were their team just as the Super Bowl III champions were Namath's. The close and enduring friendship that developed between Klecko and Fields reinforced the tone they set in the locker room and on the field. At first, they shared obscure roots in the game, a hard-nosed work ethic and a lineman's taste for hand-to-hand combat. Over the years, they came to share a house during the season, and they worked to build a joint business with assets worth more than eight million dollars. Together, they lived through a period of mind-boggling growth in salaries, and they saw how it changed the game and the nature of many of those who play it.

The money they were going to make in 1987 was unbelievable to them—$812,000 for Klecko and $467,000 for Fields—but it wasn't the driving force behind their desire to continue playing and risking their limbs. Their business interests would sustain them. More important, it was the life of a professional football player that Klecko and Fields didn't want to give up until they felt ready. Money never could buy a place for them in the middle of the arena; only youth and health and desire could do that.

"It's the spectacle of pro football that is so exciting," Fields explains. "Even though I'm not into the fans, they generate a tremendous energy and electricity that feeds your emotions. The contact gives football players a chance to release those emotions, that pent-up anger. I'm not going to miss the injuries, but in a strange way, I will miss the contact because contact is football. That's why an offensive lineman likes to run the ball; we get to deliver the blow."

The vast majority of NFL players don't last past their thirtieth birthdays, but it wasn't a barrier to Klecko and Fields, both of whom turned thirty during the 1983 season. In fact, that was the year Klecko came back from the ruptured patella tendon to make the Pro Bowl at defensive tackle. By the time training camp began in 1987, he was convinced he could come back from his second major knee operation, although he didn't expect to be the same dominant player right away.

Describing how he would recognize the end when it came, Klecko said, "I don't want to be abused. I don't want to go out on a football field when I can't win one-on-one."

There's a theory that the player is the last to know when it's time to quit, but as he labored through the 1987 season at the unfamiliar left-guard position, Fields expected it to be just the opposite. "I'll know it before anyone else because I'm the one feeling it," he said then. "I'll know when my techniques aren't there, if my hands aren't where they're supposed to be or I don't take the right steps to get someplace and my head isn't where it's supposed to be. I'll know if I'm getting rag-dolled, just not being able to do the physical things the position demands. When I can't play center anymore, I'll think it's time.

"But I firmly believe I still can play. I'd like to start and finish my career with the New York Jets. It would be hard for me to go someplace else, but if they say, 'We want you to retire,' I'll tell them I'm not retiring. I've still got football left in me."

In terms of their feel for the game, Klecko and Fields always thought of themselves as players in the traditional mold, guys who loved to fight like hell on the field and then laugh about it over a couple of beers. That was their heritage. Klecko's father, Joe Sr., even had been a local hero during the thirties and forties in Chester's sandlot football leagues. When the Eagles were home on Sundays, he took his two sons to the Polish-American club, where they boarded a bus that took them to Franklin Field for some raucous times. It was his dream just to meet a pro football player, and then he raised one.

A truck driver and a fourteenth-round draft pick from a Division III school. Having made it to the NFL from such unlikely circumstances, Klecko and Fields appreciated their chance to live the dream, as a child would. At the same time, they understood the brutal physical reality of the game and reveled in their ability to survive "in the bubble," as Fields describes the area where the linemen do battle while the game swirls around them. Add the camaraderie and the spectacle, and the mix is addicting.

Klecko and Fields still had football in them. Faced for the first time with the prospect of a retirement Walton seemed to be mapping out for them, they tried one night near the end of the 1987 season to imagine what it would be like and to explain why it would be so hard to leave the game.

"The biggest thing I'll miss is the guys," Klecko said. "You are a family. I literally live with Fields during the season. There's a special way about that. The other part is winning and the gratitude that comes with that. It's a feeling the fans really like you because you do well.

"I never knew how important football could be to people. At Temple, I played in front of four thousand fans in Veterans Stadium. I could hear my father in the stands yelling, 'Go get 'em, Joe!' I really feel like the fans in the stands are my friends. After every home game, I go to my fan club outside and have a great time with them. Win, lose, or draw, I visit them. I've sat in that parking lot for hours. I like the people to ask you about this guy and that and what goes on. It's kind of neat. I'll really miss those times.

"There ain't nothing like when you go out in front of a packed house for a big game and they announce your name. There ain't nothing like it in the world. People talk about their kid being born as a rush. Well, this happens every Sunday. That's what makes it great. It's an unbelievable feeling. Of course, you think about the money. But I always revert back to being a young kid and thinking how many people would love to be me, not Joe Klecko, but an athlete. The mystique of being a professional football player has a lot to do with it."

Adulation was part of the package for Fields, too, but since offensive linemen rarely are the focus of the crowd's attention, he couldn't drink as deeply from that cup as Klecko. For him the thrill lay in the ritual of preparing for battle and the satisfaction of knowing he could handle the best any man had to offer.

"I love this life," Fields said. "It's so much fun. It's hard to imagine doing anything else. Being in the locker room is like coming home from a long trip. There's no place like it. It's a part of me; it's what I do. When the days get warm, I start to feel training camp coming, and I go out to run. It's like when they're getting ready for breeding season and the bucks are starting to rut. When spring comes, it's time to get ready to play football. When summer comes and everybody else is going to the beach, it's time for hard, serious work."

The thought of those sixteen Sundays a year always was sufficient to keep Fields going season after season while others fell by the wayside. Among his contemporaries, only place kicker Pat Leahy, who joined the Jets a year before Fields, had outlasted him. Out of superstition, as well as friendship, they always sat together on plane trips.

"What you think of most are the tremendous highs you get from this game," Fields said. "There's hills and valleys. The valleys always seem to be much lower, but when you're on the hill, it's all worth it.

"Before every game, I walk down that field. Klecko used to walk with me until I took him out in the snow one time in Denver. I walk to the opposite goal line and just look up in the empty seats. I always say a little prayer and thank God for the opportunity to be there and play football, and I say to Him, 'Please don't let me be embarrassed today by getting beaten by my man. Don't let me embarrass myself, my family, my friends and teammates, my coaches.' I walk back down the field, and I picture what's going to happen. I get to the fifty-yard line, and I picture what it's like to be at the fifty; I get to the forty, and I picture the nickel defense in front of me as I'm going back into the locker room. I can feel the emotion and excitement of being in the game right then. It actually has a calming effect on me because I'm very hyper until I do that. The game has started for me. I'll miss that. I'll miss Sunday afternoons."

As they counted down the Sundays during the 1987 season, Klecko and Fields, so long in control of their careers as Jets— their team, the team they had led for so long—felt it all slipping away. They thought of where they had come from and how much of themselves they had given. And they hoped the men who ran the Jets would remember, too.

Fields, Fourteenth Round, Widener

In the words of Buffalo nose tackle Fred Smerlas, the AFC East division was the "home of the great centers" in the 1980s. After a decade of going nose to nose with them all, Smerlas described in an interview the problems of wrestling twice a season with the likes of Miami's Dwight Stephenson, New England's Pete Brock, and Ray Donaldson of Indianapolis. Then, he came to Joe Fields of the Jets. "My nemesis," Smerlas called him.

"A magician in his prime, Fields did it with mirrors," Smerlas told *Sports Illustrated* magazine. "He was the craftiest guy in football. The first time I played him, he looked tight, short, small. 'Hey,' I thought, 'I'm going to kill this guy.' I tried to ram him, and he wound up on the side of me, on top of me. I punch him, he punches me. This guy doesn't look like a tough guy, but I can't lay a glove on him. He yells, 'I'm still here, you sonofabitch!' He was right. I couldn't figure out that guy's style. No one could."

The story epitomizes Fields. It wasn't simply that no one could dissect his style or use leverage to the same advantage as Fields; it was more a case of not being able to picture him as a pro football player. At 6-foot-2, 253 pounds, he was just barely big enough to play the position in the NFL. Imposing he wasn't. From his youngest days, Fields always looked a little soft around the edges. Put him in overalls and a flannel shirt, and he could pass for the Cornhusker mascot of the University of Nebraska, a real farm boy type. Except he wasn't massive enough to attract the interest of a football factory of that magnitude. No matter how much weightlifting he did, Fields never developed the hard finish of the seasoned bodybuilder, the sculpted look. He was still the lump of clay.

The truth is there was little else Fields could do athletically with any degree of success. His sister Cheryl, who is four years older, always could make him mad by beating him in a footrace. "He was chubby and quiet, and he loved to play for hours with his toy soldiers," Cheryl says. "Joey was pretty much a straight-A student, which is one of the reasons he was so valuable in football."

Fields demonstrated a couple of other distinguishing characteristics as a youth. "Joey didn't exude much self-confidence, but he had bulldog tenacity," says Fields's father, Joe Sr., who worked twenty-five years as a trooper with the New Jersey State Police. "He was an average athlete, but he had intensity, the ability to think on his feet, and desire."

In short, Fields was a classic overachiever who was underrated for most of his athletic life. He found his niche as an offensive lineman through the process of natural selection. As a kid playing pickup games, Fields says, "Usually, I was the last or next-to-last guy picked until I was older and was doing the picking. In fifth grade, I was twenty pounds overweight for midget league tackle football, so I signed up for Catholic Youth Organization touch football. I played guard my first year and center my second year. I just took it for granted they put roly-poly kids in the offensive line. It didn't bother me. I played Little League baseball, but I just wasn't a good baseball player. I don't think I was much better at football; I just think it was the only thing I really could play. I wasn't that good a football player, even in college."

For a long time, Fields had a hard time picturing himself as a talented football player, so he directed much of his energy toward the accumulation of the capital necessary to maintain a basic teenage life-style in Deptford, New Jersey, which is located in the southern part of the state a short distance from Philadelphia. A newspaper route and a job behind a counter at a local delicatessen provided the funds to operate a car, and he paid his own tuition at Gloucester Catholic High School. Joe and Helen Fields made a point of instilling a strong work ethic in all four of their children, and young Joe was a willing hand. There were many times he gladly chose work over playing sports. The three eldest Fields children, Cheryl, Joe, and sister Sandy, also learned to become more self-reliant because their parents devoted much of their time to the care and nurturing of their youngest child, Robert, who was born with Down's syndrome.

"I had a tough life myself as a kid growing up in the Depression," Joe Sr. says. "I always believed good, honest work is a source of discipline. The life of a state policeman was tough on the kids. It was like a military life. I'd work a three-day shift and get two days off, work another two days and get one day off. I hardly ever was off on the weekend. It was a life of discipline."

As a joke, Fields's father once wrapped a snow shovel as a Christmas present. "Joe thought it was a guitar he wanted, and when he opened it, his face just fell," Joe Sr. says with a note of regret. "It wasn't a very good joke. Joey got the guitar, but he never learned how to play one song on it."

Both of Fields's parents were happy to see him play football, but they didn't expect anything to come of it. Fields's sophomore season ended abruptly when he tore the anterior cruciate ligament in his right knee. The doctors told him there was nothing they could do for it and put the leg in a cast for seven weeks. Since there was very little emphasis on weightlifting in 1968, his rehabilitation consisted of nothing more than a little running. Amazingly enough, the knee would remain relatively stable through another twenty years of football, but when he came back a year later, Fields didn't last through his junior season.

"I was working at a couple of jobs and got banged up at the end of the year and just stopped playing," Fields says. "I wasn't starting, and my heart wasn't in it. I'd get done with football practice and work in the delicatessen at nights. I never even thought about playing college football, not even in my senior year."

As a senior at Gloucester Catholic, Fields was the starting center and defensive tackle on a 3–5–1 team. He earned the nickname "bologna brains" from his coach because he was knocked out and suffered concussions twice that year. After the season ended, Fields visited Randolph-Macon College in Virginia and Pennsylvania Military College, as Widener was known at the time, with a teammate who was being recruited by both schools. But he enrolled as an accounting student at Rutgers-Camden—which had no football program—because it was inexpensive and he could live at home.

Even after Widener coach Bill Manlove called to say he could arrange a student loan and a job to help Fields pay the tuition at the Division III school, which does not offer athletic scholarships, Fields was lukewarm to the idea. He only went to Widener because his mother insisted on it.

"Joe said he'd had enough football," Helen Fields recalls. "He didn't want to go because he had a job and didn't want to change his life. I told him he always liked football, and it would be good for him to live away from home."

At that stage of his athletic career, Fields was a football player only a mother could love. He arrived at Widener as a 6-1, 185-pound center, which was small even by Division III standards. But once he was at Widener, which had a highly successful program under Manlove, Fields began to work seriously at football. Unlike many of the skill positions, such as running back, where the best players often rely more on intuition and instinct to make moves that are impossible to explain, a good offensive lineman sometimes can be fashioned from the spare parts in the athletic stockpile. Fields wasn't much to look at, but he turned out to have a workhorse of an engine under the hood.

"An offensive lineman is an offensive lineman because he can't play anything else," Widener offensive line coach Neil Taylor says. "It's a trickling down kind of thing. But it takes a special kind of person who is very self-satisfied when things go well because they get a pat on the butt and that's about all. When I talk at banquets, I talk about my definition of success. The two things I think are most important are striving for excellence and staying positive. I tell our recruits the guy that most exemplifies that is Joe Fields. When he was a freshman, Joe weighed a hundred eighty-five pounds and ran the forty-yard dash in 5.3 seconds, but when he was a senior, he was six-foot-two, two hundred and fifty-five pounds and ran a 5.0 40. He got bigger, faster, and stronger, and it was all his work, nothing we did. Nothing was going to get in his way. He led by example even as a sophomore, and when he got more confidence, he began to verbalize it.

"Joe was as good a technician as I've ever had here because he worked on it. He could block a nose man easily because he was very good at making a quick snap and getting off the ball. He wheels off the nose man to get in the best position to block him. Joe finessed opponents, and that's what made him so good at shielding his man away from the quarterback in the pros. To be honest, I didn't think Joe had pro potential at all. I knew he was good, but the inkling came when he was a junior and the scouts showed a little interest."

Widener was 8–1 in each of Fields's three seasons as starting center, and in his junior year, NFL scouts began to come around to watch halfback Billy "White Shoes" Johnson, who was drafted in the fifteenth round by Houston and went on to a long pro career as a kick returner and wide receiver. One scout, Carroll Huntress of the Jets, told Fields, who weighed 218 at the time, he had a chance to be drafted if he could gain about forty pounds without losing any speed.

"I just ate like crazy and would lift at night and run at night," Fields says. "It was tough, but when I got to two-fifty, I still could run a 5.0 in the forty-yard dash. Carroll came to see me after a game in September of my senior year. He said I looked good, but he wanted to know if I could long-snap."

Long-snapping is a specialized art that has enabled more than one player to have and sustain an NFL career. It's the ability of a snapper to look back between his legs to fire an accurate spiral on punts and placekicks and still lift his head up in time to block before it gets knocked off. The irony was that, as good a center as Fields was at Widener, coach Manlove never had trusted him to do the long-snapping because he was too inconsistent. When Huntress asked for a demonstration, Fields was wearing a suit because he had just returned from dinner, but he found a ball and snapped into a net well enough to satisfy the Jets' scout.

"When Carroll left," Fields says, "he told coach Manlove, 'I'm looking at three centers, Joe, a kid from Michigan State, and a kid from Ohio State. I think Joe is as good as any of them, if not the best.'"

In 1975, the draft lasted seventeen rounds (it was cut back to twelve rounds in 1977) and was spread over two long days. On the first day, the big sports story in the Philadelphia area was that Temple quarterback Steve Joachim was not picked until the seventh round, an occurrence one of the local sportscasters termed a disgrace. By six o'clock in the evening of the second day of the draft, Fields still had not been selected.

"I was in my room at the fraternity house playing darts with a teammate, Bill Stahl," Fields remembers. "I figured the draft was over, and I was a little depressed. The phone rang in the hall, and Bill answered it. He said, 'It's a secretary from the Jets.'

I shot my last dart and ran to the phone. Charley Winner, the coach, came on the line and told me he was sending an airline ticket and wanted me to come up to New York that week. I was chosen in the fourteenth round, the three hundred forty-ninth player overall."

By contrast to the fanfare for Joachim, who didn't last long in the NFL, Fields's selection merited just a note in the newspapers and TV sports reports. That was understandable. Even though they knew the scouts had expressed some interest, the members of Fields's own family still were shocked by the news. "It was a surprise," says Fields's sister, Cheryl. "Everybody said Joey wanted to be a millionaire, but nobody thought it would be this way." After signing for a $3,000 bonus and a first-year salary of $17,000, neither did Fields.

On his first trip to New York, Fields was told to wait at the Philadelphia airport for rookie guard Joe Wysock, a fifth-round pick from Miami, so the two could catch the same flight. Widener quarterback Kenny O'Brien (no relation to the Jets quarterback of the same name) accompanied Fields to the airport. The two of them were sitting in the terminal when O'Brien said, "There's Joe Wysock."

"How do you know?" Fields responded.

"Turn around and look," O'Brien said.

Recalling his astonishment at the sight of another rookie who already had the look of a pro, Fields says, "Here was one of the biggest human beings I ever saw. He was six foot four, two hundred seventy-five pounds, and he was a weightlifter with these huge arms. He was wearing a black fur coat, a huge coat that made him look enormous. I remember looking at Wysock and thinking, 'What am I doing here? If all the offensive linemen are like this, I don't have a prayer. I'm two hundred fifty pounds, but I'm not two hundred fifty pounds like this guy is two hundred fifty pounds. What are the defensive linemen like?' "

Jets general manager Weeb Ewbank, who had retired from coaching after the 1973 season, made it clear to Fields in his first rookie minicamp that he had to make the team as a long-snapper. Because it was raining outside, Ewbank held Fields's first audition for the job in a hall outside of his office in the Jets' training complex on Long Island.

"The first one I snapped to Weeb went over his shoulder and knocked a couple of pictures off the wall," Fields says. "He called someone else to come over and catch them. I snapped a couple, and he said, 'Yeah, you can snap.' That was about it. Preparing for my first season, my dad would catch about a hundred to two hundred snaps every night. I had to snap twenty-five in a row perfect before I'd quit."

"We'd argue a lot," Joe Sr. says of those practice sessions. "I was hard on him if every snap wasn't perfect. He'd take his ball and go home, but he'd come back the next night and snap for almost two hours. I'd tell him, 'Okay, this is a Super Bowl snap.' "

Training camp began just after the Fourth of July holiday in Fields's rookie season, more than a month before the first exhibition game. Joe Wysock never participated because of a knee operation, which meant all his weightlifting went for naught. At least the injury saved Wysock the torture of a month of twice-a-day blocking drills against veteran defensive linemen. Rookie offensive linemen thought of themselves as "wasted meat" because they had to run repeated trap plays on which they got beat up by veterans who knew what was coming. In those days, defensive linemen were permitted by the rules to deliver head blows that gave offensive linemen an understanding of what it felt like to be the clapper in a bell.

"You got a lot of headaches pulling and trapping against those guys" Fields says. "Billy Newsome and Richard Neal knew how to stop those traps with a headslap. I never got headslapped at Widener, but on the first day of Jets training camp, an old veteran named Jim Bailey headslapped me and almost knocked me out. He went right by me."

Describing an offensive lineman's perspective on the abuse to which he is subjected, Fields says, "My vision's always a little blurred the first couple of days in training camp, and my hearing's not as good. All of a sudden, you get out of that. I believe your brain's not used to getting jostled around, but the more hitting you get, the brain adjusts. I call it 'game vision.' Suddenly, you can see and calculate and make decisions in the middle of the action, and your hearing gets very acute."

The nerves, however, are another matter. Arizona State University's Sun Devil Stadium in Tempe, Arizona, was the setting for the Jets' opening exhibition game against the Minnesota Vikings in Fields's rookie year. The game attracted an overflow crowd of about sixty thousand because it was the first NFL game held in the Phoenix area, and the crowd was in a special state of excitement because Jets quarterback Joe Namath ended a contract holdout a few days before the game and was expected to play.

When Namath showed up in camp, Fields was required to stay after practice to snap to him. When he asked Namath how he wanted the ball, the famous quarterback replied reassuringly in the southern drawl he acquired at Alabama, "You just put it up here, kid, and I'll get it."

But when the Jets walked out of their locker room at Sun Devil Stadium, Fields was taken aback by the crowd's response to Namath's presence during warmups. Fields was the only rookie playing on special teams because of his job snapping for punts and placekicks, but he never had played in front of such a large and loud throng. "The stands were packed, and people even were sitting on the hills behind the stadium," Fields says. "The place was flipping out, yelling for Namath. It scared me. I was dripping sweat because it was over a hundred degrees at game time. All my practice snaps were bullets, but I still was nervous as hell."

As he ran on the field for his first play in an NFL game, Fields told himself he wanted his snap to punter Greg Gantt to be the best snap of his life. Then, he bent over and fired a bullet that missed the target by a mile. "I snapped the damn ball way over Gantt's head," Fields says. "Just smoked it. Talk about a lousy feeling. Al Atkinson was the fullback. He told me to relax and not to worry about it. What a nice man he was. I snapped a couple more good, then I bounced one, and the rest were good."

Maybe his coaches at Widener had been right not to use Fields as a snapper. "I thought I was going to get cut," says Fields. "But Charley Winner said in the papers that week that he was going to give me one more chance. All week in practice, he would stand near me and stomp his foot and yell at me while I was snapping and try to make me nervous." The next week in St. Louis, Fields executed a perfect snap on the extra-point kick that won the game with less than a minute to go.

The Jets' third exhibition game was against the New York Giants at the Yale Bowl in New Haven, Connecticut. If the Jets' upset victory over Baltimore in Super Bowl III was the most important victory in club history, the second biggest victory was the one they scored over the Giants in the summer of 1969, validating the world championship they had won a few months earlier in the eyes of New Yorkers. Even though the Giants were down in the 1970s, they enjoyed the slavish devotion of their fans, who clung to the memories of the Giants team that won six Eastern Conference titles and one NFL championship from 1956–63. For as long as they have shared New York with the Giants, the Jets have been acutely sensitive to what they consider their treatment as "second-class citizens" by both the public and the media.

"In 1975, the Jets-Giants game was still a big game, and there was a lot of animosity between the old AFL and NFL guys," Fields remembers. "It was played like a regular-season game. I was doing a good job of snapping. Then, we got down around the twelve-yard line with about six seconds to go, and Pat Leahy came running in to kick the field goal to win the game. It was drizzling, and I asked for a new ball. I looked back through my legs, got the signal from Gantt, who was the holder, and snapped that ball forty yards over his head. I'll never forget it. The game was over, and we had lost 21–20. I was lying there on the field, and I didn't want to get up. Roy Hilton, a defensive end for the Giants, helped me up and said, 'No place to hide out here, son.'

"When I came off the field, my friend, Darrell Austin, was laughing at me and saying, 'I can't believe you did that.' There were about a hundred reporters waiting to talk to me in the locker room, and I'd never had one reporter talk to me in training camp. I went back to the dormitory at Hofstra University, where we trained, and packed my bags. The headlines the next day were stuff like: ROOKIE BLOWS IT. I felt like shit at breakfast. I could feel the other players staring through me, but they didn't make any comments. They all thought I was going to get cut because I was there to snap, and this was my second one over the head. When Monday came and I didn't get cut, the reporters asked Charley Winner why. He said, 'Well, if he does it again, we're just going to have to get a taller holder or a taller punter.' "

Despite Winner's vote of confidence, Fields remained skeptical about his chances of making the Jets and with good reason. "He would've been cut if we had anybody else to snap the ball," says Bob Fry, who coached the Jets' offensive line from 1974–82. "Guys on the staff were saying, 'Boy, he can't snap the ball. We've got to get rid of him.' Joe was undersized and had a baby face. He looked like he was about eighteen years old. You didn't realize how quick he was because he looked soft and pudgy. Joe was an excellent student of the game, and he had quick feet and could get into position to make a block. About Joe's third year, we realized he was good enough and strong enough to play in the league. Because of his quick feet, he had the knack of being able to center the ball and still get his arms under the nose man as he's head-butting him. He could stymie the guy, and a lot of times, he was strong enough to move the guy out."

But since no one expected Fields ever to do much more than long-snap, he never really had the chance to prove himself as a player in that first training camp. Like any other rookie, he kept a sharp eye out for "The Turk," which is the nickname given to the club official whose job it is to tell players they have been cut. The graphic imagery is meant to suggest a Turkish warrior wearing a turban and wielding a scimitar for the purpose of lopping off heads. Assistant coach Mike Holovak played that role for the Jets in Fields's rookie year.

"Holovak would come into the cafeteria in the morning and ask guys to come and see him after breakfast, and you knew they were cut," Fields says. "Mike Bartoszek, Tom Alward, Darrell Austin, and I were eating together one morning when they were getting ready to cut the roster to sixty. Holovak started coming toward us, and I just knew he was coming for me. He bent down at the table, and everybody looked. I couldn't eat; my stomach was in knots. He said, 'How you doing, Joe?' I said, 'Fine.' He said, 'You're looking pretty good,' and I said, 'Thanks.' And he left. The whole table was ruined. Everybody was saying, 'Damn it! Why does he do something like that?' The next week, Bartoszek and I were eating together, and Holovak came over and told Mike to come see him. Alward got cut the following week, so, it was down to just Austin and me as rookie offensive linemen.

"After we came back from our fourth exhibition game in Atlanta, Darrell and I were walking around the corner of the training complex the next day on our way to practice when we ran into the veterans we were trying to beat out, Warren Koegel and Roger Bernhardt. You could see they were upset, and I think Roger was crying. When they saw us, Warren stuck out his hand and said, 'Congratulations, Joe. They just released me. Good luck to you.' Roger said the same thing to Darrell. We kept walking around the corner, and Darrell and I both jumped up in the air, screaming, 'We made it!' Then, I started thinking, 'How can they get rid of us?' That's all I could think about the next week, but nobody came in."

There was one other way to keep Fields out of the NFL. The week before the last cut to the forty-three-man roster limit in effect at the time, the Jets traveled to New England to play their final exhibition game against the Patriots. But both teams voted the night before the game to call a wildcat strike. Their game was canceled, but no other NFL teams followed suit.

"At the strike meeting, Darrell and I said, 'Shit, we don't want to go on strike. We're going to make this team. What do you mean strike?' We voted not to strike and so did a couple of veteran offensive linemen, Randy Rasmussen and Gary Puetz. After the game was canceled, we went to the complex Monday morning and picked up all our gear. The Jets locked the whole team out. Everybody met at a bar across the street from the complex in the morning, and we practiced in the afternoon at a nearby park. On Friday, the Jets let us back in, and we practiced one day before the opener in Buffalo. We got our asses kicked, 42–14."

That made it official. Joe Fields was in the NFL. As improbable as it seemed, it said so right there in the game program:

No. 65   Joe Fields   C   6-2   253   R   Widener

Good-bye, Joe Namath

Joe Namath *was* the Jets. In fact and in fancy. The mention of his name instantly conjures up the familiar images: "Broadway Joe," Bachelors III, the Fu Manchu moustache, "guaranteed" victory in Super Bowl III, Lenox Hill steel derotation knee braces, blue eyes, hawk nose, dark hair flowing out from under the back of a white helmet with green stripes, the "quickest release in football," Johnnie Walker Red with a blonde back. That was the popular picture of No. 12, Joe Willie Namath of the Jets.

The first time rookie Joe Fields saw Namath, reality picked right up where myth left off. It was the week of the Jets' first exhibition game of the 1975 season. Namath had just ended a holdout before signing what would be his last contract with the Jets. "He pulled up in a limousine while everybody was practicing," Fields recalls. "That was the neatest thing I'd ever seen. I don't think I'd ever seen a limousine before then. Practice came to a stop, and he walked out onto the field and shook hands with the coaches and a lot of the veterans. I was a lowly rookie, and I was just in awe of the guy."

The Namath aura was very much in place, but it wasn't an act. There was no sense that anything Namath did was contrived to make himself appear larger than life. He lived the superstar role with a becoming grace in the eyes of the players. Namath had his run-ins with reporters and the Jets won more than they lost in just three of Namath's twelve injury-interrupted seasons with them, but those who worked with him believed in him and respected him.

"People think Joe Namath was hard to handle," says Bob Fry, who coached the Jets' offensive line from 1974–82. "He wasn't. He was a class guy, the easiest guy in the world to work with. The offensive linemen loved him. He respected the coaches, and he never really bucked the system or showed displeasure with it."

With his relaxed manner, Namath had a way of taking pressure off those around him and putting it on himself, and his confidence in himself was absolute. As a jumpy rookie, Fields discovered when he replaced injured Wayne Mulligan at center in a couple of games that Namath was not a demanding quarterback so much as a calming presence on the field. "For the limited time I worked with him, I don't think we ever had a fumbled snap," Fields says. "He didn't rattle. It was so easy to play for Joe. But I used to laugh about the fact he almost made more money in one game than I made in my first two years combined. I made thirty-seven thousand dollars [in base salary], and he was making about thirty-five thousand per game."

In the time Fields played with him, Namath did nothing to diminish his reputation off the field. Near the end of a long 3–11 season, the Jets had a chance to spend several days in San Diego before they played the Chargers in a Monday-night game. One evening, Namath walked into the hotel bar and sat down with a few of the older veterans.

"There were two women sitting at the bar," Fields says. "You could see they were attractive, but nothing special. Their hair was up, and they had glasses on. When Namath came in, they got up and disappeared. When they came back, their hair was down, the glasses were gone, and their faces were different, like they had put on more makeup. Next thing you know, they're talking with Joe. We had a few more beers and went back to our rooms. Joe didn't make curfew that night."

Ken Shipp, who had replaced Charley Winner as head coach with five games remaining in the season, decided it was important to show that the same rules applied to Namath as everyone else. Shipp benched Namath and started unknown J. J. Jones in his place. "The San Diego fans were upset because they wanted to see Namath," says Fields, who played most of the way at center that night. "Joe came off the bench in the second half and almost pulled the game out for us."

"Namath's life-style didn't have any effect on the team," Fry adds. "When Weeb Ewbank was the head coach, he accepted it. Joe could stay up past curfew as long as he was in the hotel. But he drew commotion. We had to have a security guard on his floor of the hotel because people would bother him all the time. Many times, we had to sneak him out the back way from the locker room in a car, and he would meet the team bus a block away from the stadium. But the thing about Namath is that he could handle all of it."

The Jets got off to a 2–1 start that season and then fell off a cliff, losing eight straight games. After the first six of those losses, Winner was fired. It seemed to Fields that Winner had lost control of the team somewhere along the line. Four games into the losing streak, the Jets held a stormy team meeting in their hotel the morning of a game in Miami against the Dolphins and coach Don Shula, who always inspired a mixture of hate and envy in his opponents.

"John Riggins was our fullback then, and he got up and gave this rah-rah speech because his school, Kansas, had won a big game the day before," Fields recalls. "It sounded like he was drunk, and everybody was looking at each other and thinking, 'What's going on? This is getting out of control.' Then, Winner got up and said, 'I'm tired of being second-best to Don Shula, and I'm tired of hearing Joe Namath's not as good as Bob Griese.' With that, Namath stood up and said, 'I don't take a backseat to nobody.' Winner says, 'Yeah, that's what I want to hear.'

"Then, we broke up into our little groups. The offensive line was at a round table with Fry, who never was a rah-rah guy. He comes over, and he's chuckling and says, 'What do you guys think?' One of our tackles, Gary Puetz, grabs a water glass and bites it and starts chewing. He says, 'I think we ought to go get 'em coach.' Fry cracks up and says, 'Then get out of here.' "

Riggins was in his fifth and last season with the Jets, who traded him to Washington in 1976. He was an enormous talent, but he definitely was the most off-the-wall character on the Jets. It was hard to tell if the drummer Riggins followed was a sixties dropout bent on self-destruction or just a lonely country boy who never was quite sure how to handle the success that was his.

Many of the things he did, such as wearing a Mohawk haircut one year, were meant to have a shock effect on those around him. But his erratic behavior hinted at deeper troubles.

"If you saw him dressing for a game," Fry says, "you knew he'd do a lot for you. He was well-liked by the offensive linemen because of the way he looked to run over defensive backs. The problem was to get him dressed. If he had a nick or a pull, he wouldn't play. The doctors would say he'd be ready to practice on Wednesday after a game, but he'd stay out two weeks. When he got the pads on, though, he was something to watch."

In marked contrast to Namath's limo, Riggins came wheeling into training camp in 1975 on a 750cc Honda motorcycle he had driven all the way from his home in Kansas. His complete wardrobe for eight weeks of camp fit in the saddlebags on his cycle. Darrell Austin, Fields's fellow rookie on the offensive line, got along well with Riggins. But even though Fields lockered next to Riggins at the Jets' training complex, he kept his distance from this strange personality.

"I was scared of him because there were times when it seemed like Riggins was completely over the edge," Fields says. "I never really knew him. John was the kind of guy, sometimes he would practice and sometimes he wouldn't. When we went out in shorts, he would come out and sit on his helmet. If he wasn't going to practice, he would wear real heavy work shoes like you wear in the winter to keep warm. They were like ski boots. Then, he'd pull his shorts up the crack of his butt. Some guys finally got him a director's chair and set it up on the side of the practice field.

"I remember the last game of my rookie year Riggins had a chance to become the first Jet running back to rush for a thousand yards in a season. He got to about nine hundred ninety-five yards, and he decided he wasn't going to play anymore. He just took himself out of the game and was sitting on the sidelines getting undressed, taking his pads off. Frank Ramos from the public relations department comes running down on the field and tells him, 'You only need five more yards.' He says, 'Nah, I'm not playing anymore.' Finally, Ken Shipp, the head coach, talked him into going back in. He rushed for ten yards and that was it. He was done playing.

"John was a hell of a player. When he turned the corner, defensive backs were afraid to tackle him. He was a beast. When he caught the ball, they'd almost want to get out of his way. I don't think people realized how great he was when he was with the Jets. He was nuts, but he was a hell of a football player."

When training camp opened in 1976, Riggins was gone, but that didn't mean the Jets lacked for entertainment. Coach Lou Holtz was recruited off the campus of North Carolina State, and he came to New York with the intention of infusing the worldly team of Broadway Joe with some of that old-time college football religion. What the heck, he must have figured, the pros are just big kids. Holtz brought along some other really neat stuff from the college ranks, such as the veer option offense. He gave his assistant coaches odd jobs, assigning one to be in charge of the training room, one to run the locker room, and one to handle hotel arrangements, apparently not understanding that pro clubs have other people whose fulltime job calls for them to manage those responsibilities so the coaches can coach. To make the atmosphere complete, Holtz also made a deal to draft two of his N.C. State players in the twelfth round, wide receiver Don Buckey and his brother, quarterback Dave. "The Buckey Boys," as the veteran NFL assistants on the Jets' staff referred to them with a smirk.

But it was the veer offense that really caused eyes to roll skyward in the Jets' camp. What a novel idea! Paying NFL quarterbacks to run option pitch plays, as if you could just throw in a third-string sophomore after the two senior quarterbacks got beat up in the first ten games. It was rather obvious the veer wasn't designed with Joe Namath's steel knees in mind. That left number-one draft choice Richard Todd, who played his college football at Namath's alma mater, Alabama, to run the veer. And, of course, Dave Buckey.

So, Holtz split the squad and put Todd in charge of the veer offense while Namath ran the pro set. Austin was the center for Namath, and Fields was the center for Todd. "What a mess that was," Fields says. "Holtz ran one of the most physical training camps I've ever been through. Everything was live action."

"We didn't throw a pass in practice for two weeks," Fry adds. "But to show you the kind of guy Namath was, he never said a word about it."

Along with the physical gauntlet he forced the Jets to run, Holtz went to work on the spiritual side of things, as well. Mo-ti-vation. "Holtz was a great speaker," Fields says. "He could captivate an audience. As part of his speeches, he would do magic tricks. Another thing Holtz did was show us how to line up for the National Anthem. We actually practiced it.

"After we beat Houston for our only victory in preseason, Holtz went around the locker room handing out sheets with the words to a Jets fight song he had written, and he wanted everybody to sing it. The older guys were saying, 'Fuck this! We ain't singing this bullshit.' "

Not that there were a lot of older guys left by the time Holtz finished putting together a team of NFL freshmen. Two days after the final roster cut to the forty-three-man limit in effect at the time, Holtz did an amazing thing. He trimmed the roster to thirty-five players, including just five offensive linemen. By the end of the week, Holtz had culled eight players from the waiver wire, who became known as the Hempstead Eight after the Long Island town in which the Jets' training complex is located. Completely unfamiliar with the system, the newcomers had to play in the opener at Cleveland, a 38–17 loss that set the tone for the season and was followed by a 46–3 loss at Denver and a 16–0 loss at Miami.

"I was so nervous for the first game at Cleveland that I threw up through my facemask going out on the field for the first time," Fields says. "I bent over to snap for the first punt, and it was dripping on my hands. That was the last time I ever ate a pregame meal. I had to take stomach tranquilizers back then, so, instead of having the pregame meal, I'd just eat a piece of toast and drink a cup of tea."

Four weeks into the season, the Jets were 0–4 and getting ready to play their home opener against Buffalo. For some reason, Holtz didn't attend the pregame meeting Saturday night, but Fields stepped into the breach. "Joe had gone to dinner with some friends that night and obviously had one too many drinks," place-kicker Pat Leahy recalls. "When Lou didn't show up at the meeting, Joe went up to the projector and turned on the film. He started hollering and screaming, 'Namath, call the defenses! Let's go and get it right!' Guys were howling. Then, we all wished Joe well in his new job Monday selling shoes at Thom McAn."

Despite the 3–11 record that season, the Jets still were a team that knew how to have fun. "We used to have great team parties," says Fields. "The guys in their first and second years would put their money in for a party, then guys who had just qualified for their pension, then guys in their eighth and ninth years. I remember going to parties at a place called the Anchor Inn and having all the lobsters and clams you could eat. We had a tight end named Willie Brister who would make ribs with this great sauce. Everybody on the team would come, black guys, white guys. Namath would come."

Naturally, Namath would charm all the players' wives in a way that made everybody feel comfortable with his celebrity. At a team Thanksgiving party in 1976, the celebrated quarterback made a point of introducing himself to Fields's wife, Kay. "You don't know me, but I know you," Namath said to Kay. "I thought it was about time I met you because I've been patting your husband's ass for two years."

"I think all the wives paid special attention to him," Kay says. "They would check out his girlfriends and what they were wearing. He was dating Randi Oakes, the model. I was impressed. She was very glamorous."

Fields adds, "About five years later at Richard Todd's wedding, Namath came up to Kay—and he hadn't seen her since that first meeting—and he said, 'Come on, Kay. Let's get up and dance and leave these stiffs.' He called me and Joe Klecko stiffs. He took her out and danced with her. Then, she introduced him to Debbie Klecko, and he danced with Debbie. He was just a super guy. He always came to all the team parties. The players thought he was a regular guy."

All things considered, it was a good time to be young and a Jet because of all the job opportunities. Austin was the starting center when the season began, but he was alternating with Fields. Early in the year, right tackle Robert Woods was injured. Right guard Puetz moved to tackle; Austin shifted to guard, and Fields became the starting center. When Woods came off the injured list in the fifth game, Holtz left it that way.

That marked the beginning of one of the longest runs by a player at one position in Jets history. But the Lou Holtz Show was not as long-lived. It closed in a matter of months to bad reviews that suggested he was out of his element in the NFL. Toward the end of the season, rumors began circulating about his imminent return to the collegiate ranks.

Holtz met with the team in the final week of the season to put an end to the rumors. "On Monday, Lou assured us he wasn't going to leave," Fields recalls. "He left on Thursday." Assistant Mike Holovak replaced Holtz for the final game.

During the offseason months that followed, it became clear that a much more significant era was about to end. Joe Namath, the player who put the AFL on the map and whose presence on Broadway helped speed the merger of the two leagues, was placed on waivers and signed a month later with the Los Angeles Rams.

From his perspective as a player, Fields says, "There was no feeling that Joe was too old to play. The feeling was, 'We've got Namath. All we have to do is support him a little bit.' The defense wasn't as good as it could've been, and that hurt us. We got bombed a few times and went downhill."

A decade later, when Fields and his closest friend, Joe Klecko, the leaders of the generation of Jets that succeeded Namath, were facing the end of their own careers, they often thought of Namath's departure from the Jets as the prime example of the organization's lack of feeling for its most valued players and the absence of any sense of tradition. Namath wanted to play one more year and then retire as a Jet, but the club wanted to retire him after the 1976 season with a big party. When Namath refused, the Jets traded him to the Los Angeles Rams.

"Namath made the New York Jets; he made the AFL," Klecko said one evening as he and Fields sat in the living room of the Long Island home they shared and discussed the moves the Jets were making to push them closer to the exit. "Why do you let the one man that made your franchise go to another team? There's no doubt that, in the NFL, you are treated like a piece of meat, big-time."

"Wouldn't it be worth it to keep a guy like that around one more year if you're talking about building tradition and excellence and loyalty?" Fields added. "If you kept Joe Namath on injured reserve, I don't think anybody would say he's healthy enough to play. Hell, he couldn't even run because his hamstrings were in such bad shape from all the wear and tear over the years. That was his problem more than his knees. He had a twelve-inch stride because his hamstrings were so bad. It seems you could let a guy who did so much finish his career as a New York Jet."

Klecko: Truck Drivin' Man

The houses on the street where Joe Klecko grew up in Chester, Pennsylvania, a working-class suburb hard on the southwestern flank of Philadelphia, all are exactly the same inside and out—two-story row homes built of red brick with three bedrooms upstairs and front and back yards slightly bigger than a postage stamp. Each house had a clothesline out back, the lawns were neat, the fences were painted, and everybody knew everybody. Highland Gardens, as the area is called, is located in Resurrection parish, which was considered the Irish parish in Klecko's youth. The Polish section lies to the south across the railroad tracks, and a predominantly black neighborhood is located in between. Klecko's father, Joe Sr., a first-generation American who was born in Chester, insisted on maintaining the family's ties to St. Hedwick's Catholic Church in what was considered the Polish parish. Klecko was the third of four children, including a younger brother, Jimmy, and two older sisters, Janet and Joanne, to attend St. Hedwick's grade school. His father belonged to the Polish-American club, and the family income was deposited in the Polish-American Eagles bank. Nearby was a good Polish bakery and John's barber shop, where it seemed all the neighborhood men and their sons went to get their hair cut. Just around the corner from the Polish-American club was the tavern where Klecko's father worked as a bartender some nights after he finished his regular job driving a truck for the city of Chester. Klecko's mother Josephine worked full-time at a local hospital as a dietician.

When he was eleven years old, Klecko went to work cleaning oil burners, and the next year, he took a job at his uncle's gas station, which had cornered the local auto-repair market. But Klecko still found time to play a lot of sandlot baseball, basketball, and football games. His twenty-five-year-old cousin, Frank Koren-kiewicz, who ran the gas station where Klecko worked, didn't always approve. "What are you going to do," he'd say to young Joe, who was twelve by then, "play games the rest of your life?"

By the time he finished high school, Klecko was working as many as a hundred hours a week for a dollar an hour in his uncle's garage. "This was a working town," Klecko recalls. "Cars were the common bond for me and my friends. I bought a new Pontiac Grand Prix. We used to race the quarter-mile on I-95 while the cops sat there and watched us. Guys would unload dragsters off trailers. Gino's hamburger stand is where I hung out, and guys would drive their cars back and forth in front of the windows. My parents didn't have to worry about me because I worked and always had money. I had the ins with a lot of cops, and I wasn't going to do some off-the-wall thing to make my family look bad.

"I don't know how many friends of mine thought about college. I didn't. I really enjoyed working. After high school, I learned to drive a tractor-trailer, and I was making good money. When I drove trucks, it was not unusual for me to go two days straight driving, just stone driving. I loved it. All I did was work and sleep. A lot of times, my runs would be to Maine or Connecticut. I'd come home and sleep, get up and go to Texas. The two years I was out of football after high school, that was my tempo."

No one was waiting to hand a college football scholarship to Klecko when he was graduated in 1971 from St. James High. His high school football career was brilliant but brief. It consisted of six games his senior year, which was enough to earn him all-county and second-team all-Catholic mention but not sufficient to catch the eye of college recruiters. That was fine with Klecko. Schoolwork didn't hold the same fascination for him as did the practical economics of daily life. For an athletic outlet, Klecko played in the local baseball and softball leagues after high school. Softball is a lifelong passion for many men in Chester, where the leagues progress from the open division to over-thirty, over-forty, and over-fifty years old. Klecko could hammer a softball as far as anyone around, and his throws from the deepest part of any park came in on a line and stung when they hit the catcher's glove. He was hard on opposing catchers, too, because it was his habit to run over them rather than slide to avoid a tag.

"There used to be this old bum who hung out at the gas station, and he would ask me if I was going to be as good an athlete as my old man," Klecko says. "My dad was a hell of a football, basketball, and baseball player in the neighborhood."

Klecko's father was expelled from school in the seventh grade for fighting with a teacher he felt was roughing up another student, and he never tried to go back to school. It was 1929, and the Depression had just begun. For three years, he foraged for junk to sell or swiped coal from railroad cars and sold it. At fifteen, he went to work in the Philadelphia shipyards and then took a job in a pipe mill before moving on to work in a Ford plant. After that closed down, he was hired by the city of Chester to drive a truck.

Joe Sr. worked to survive, but he lived to play sports. Football was his first love, though he also was a pretty good pitcher in the local sandlot baseball leagues and could score a little in basketball. At 6 feet, 190 pounds, he wasn't exceptionally big, but like all Klecko men, he was hard-nosed and bullishly strong. "Football was my bread and butter," says the elder Klecko. "Anything that hit my fingers, I caught, and I punted and could drop-kick forty-five yards. I played end and then halfback for the Second Ward. They had a winning streak of like fifty-two games, and I coached a team called the Highland Rams that won thirty-nine straight games. I would play with one team from noon to two P.M. on Sundays and then play with the other team from two P.M. to four P.M.

"I used to eat and sleep football. When I was working at the South Chester pipe mill from 1936 to 1938 in the Depression, I'd take off a half day just to practice football. I was like a leader around the corner where everybody hung out in the neighborhood. They called me 'Shea,' which was short for O'Shea because they thought I was born on St. Paddy's Day, but I really was born on March sixteenth."

The thought of playing NFL football was nothing more than a dream that "Shea" Klecko nurtured as an ardent Eagles fan. As soon as his sons were old enough to go, Joe Sr. bought season tickets for them. Their Franklin Field trips began at the Polish-American club, where a group of fans boarded a bus and usually drank a few beers on the way to the game and tried to smuggle more into the stadium. Once when the Dallas Cowboys were playing the Eagles, Joe Sr. decided to sneak onto the field, where he persuaded the mascot to let him put on the Eagle head and dance around a bit. Then, he went over to the Cowboys' bench and shook hands with all-pro defensive tackle Bob Lilly. As the first half ended, he grabbed a brand new football and brought it back to the stands to give to young Joe, which prompted his youngest son, Jimmy, to say, "What about me, Daddy?" In the fourth quarter, Joe Sr. sneaked back onto the field, but since there were no footballs lying around by the Cowboys' bench, he went around to the Eagles' side.

"I got near the ball bag, but the trainer says, 'Beat it. I saw what you did in the first half,' " the elder Klecko recalls. "But the Cowboys' quarterback throws an interception, and while everybody got excited, I pulled a ball out of the bag and ran back to the stands. Jimmy gave that one away to another kid on the bus home, so a couple weeks later when the Cardinals came to town, I went on the field and got another ball. I'm climbing into the stands, and the fans are trying to grab it. This black cop comes over and says, 'If that guy was good enough to get that football the way he did, leave him alone.' "

The cop's sense of fair play and his recognition of a hard-won victory conformed to the code by which people lived in Chester. They fought to earn all they had, and sometimes, they fought to prevent others from taking it. The man who wasn't afraid to hustle or to stand his ground when the time came gained respect. Fighting also served as a means of meting out justice in the sense that disputes often were settled man-to-man.

Once when young Joe and a friend "borrowed" another boy's wooden go-cart, the owner showed up to claim possession, and the friend blamed Klecko for stealing it. To settle the question of who was responsible for taking the go-cart, Klecko's father ordered him into the street to fight his friend to see who was right. "The kid was three years older than me," Klecko says. "I lost, and my old man told the kid and his father, 'Now don't bother us no more.' He stood up for me in front of them. I came in the house, and he kicked my ass for losing. My dad was hard on me, very hard."

The Klecko household was not a permissive one. Worried about keeping his kids out of trouble, Joe Sr. often was critical and demanding. His method of discipline frequently took the form of corporal punishment. In fourth grade, Joe and his whole class stayed after school on detention, which upset his father, who was waiting outside to pick him up.

"My dad walks in the door, pulls down my pants in front of the whole class and whips me," Klecko remembers.

"I was bad that time," Joe Sr. says. "I cried that night after giving him a licking. I told that nun, 'Now, are you satisfied?' Then, I brought him home."

During high school, Klecko came home after midnight once when he had been drinking beer. His father was waiting. "It was dark, and I didn't see him when I came in the door," Klecko says. "He hit me and knocked me down. Then, he took me out to the kitchen and ripped my sleeves up and was looking at my arms for track marks. He had watched a drug show on TV that night, but I never got into anything like that at all."

Out of respect, Klecko never challenged his father or swung back. His father's method of discipline was the way of many fathers in a tough neighborhood, and Klecko didn't see other kids getting off any easier than he did. Street life in Chester reflected the same hard attitudes. Scuffling was routine for boys trying to establish themselves as the toughest guy on the block. When he finished playing basketball or baseball after school at St. Hedwick's, Klecko sometimes got into fights with kids from the black neighborhood that he passed on the way home. It wasn't a matter of racial tensions; they all played together on the same sandlot teams. It was competition between kids whose closets weren't overflowing with material goods.

"If I was carrying a basketball or a baseball glove, I'd get in a fight trying to protect it," Klecko says. "That stuff was like gold. Nobody had any money where we came from. I got my ass kicked more times than you can shake a stick at. I remember coming home with bloody noses, and once, a kid chased me into my house."

Although he always was bigger than most kids his age, Klecko generally took a backseat and followed the lead of his friends. Seldom was he the aggressor in fights. He was quiet to the point that he became a target of abuse from others. "I was a big, slow, methodical kid," is Klecko's harsh self-appraisal. "I was good athletically, but I really was just a chicken. People would needle me and challenge me.

"One guy used to take apples from other kids and watch me pop them because of my hand strength. One time, a kid stole my pie at lunch, and I caught him and hung him over a rail in a stairwell. Another time, two kids jumped me in the hallway, and it turned serious. Every time I did something, I got caught. I was thrown out of high school three times."

School sports weren't important to Klecko because of his interest in working at the garage and his success in sandlot leagues. He quit the St. James football team as a freshman and didn't go out again until he was a senior. Occasionally, Klecko would fill in as an offensive and defensive lineman for a neighborhood team called West End. They played games on Sunday afternoons against other neighborhood teams and a few semipro teams, such as Ridley Township A.A. from Delaware. Running-back Billy "White Shoes" Johnson, who went on to star at Widener College in Chester and was drafted in 1974 by Houston, played for West End in those games. Some teams, such as Ridley Township, were fully equipped, but some of the players for West End had little protective equipment beyond a helmet.

As a sixteen-year-old playing in those games, Klecko was known for his prodigious natural strength. It was not unusual for him to pick up an engine block at the gas station and toss it in the back of a truck. Most people would have needed a winch to lift something that heavy. "My dad was a brute, and all his brothers were big, barrel-chested people," Klecko explains. "My uncle John was a pipefitter. At my high school graduation party, he did the only trick I can't do with my hands. He put four red bricks together and picked them up with one hand. I've bent quarters, but I never could do that."

If his strength was obvious, Klecko's speed came as a surprise. He could match strides with most of the running backs he faced, which made him a powerful force in those sandlot contests. The fact that he hadn't played football at St. James came as a bitter disappointment to his father, who was an enthusiastic but demanding coach. Baseball was Klecko's favorite sport when he was young, and his father worked constantly with both his sons on pitching and teaching them to be switch-hitters.

"My father taught me all about sports, but he didn't always give me the recognition I deserved," Klecko says. "When I was twelve, I won a baseball game with a home run. I usually batted left-handed, so my father always sat out in right field to catch my home runs. I walked out to meet him after the game, and you know what he said? 'How come you booted the ball at short?' "

When Joe was in high school, his father's emphasis shifted to football. Joe Sr. told his son he'd kick his butt if his grades didn't improve by the end of his junior year so that he could go out for football as a senior. Still a dedicated "motorhead," Klecko finally decided to cut back his work hours at the garage and join the football team because most of his friends were on it.

"I told the old man I had a chance to play in the first game," Klecko says. "It was a big deal to him. But I didn't play a down."

After the game, Joe Sr. jumped over the fence onto the field to confront the coach and tell him the other players couldn't carry his son's helmet. When he got home, Joe Sr. charged upstairs to give his son a scolding.

"I remember what he said like it just happened," Klecko says. "He said, 'You wouldn't make a pimple on my ass. I'm totally ashamed of you.' And he ran into his room to get away from me. My father was a real hard-nosed guy, and I never thought I'd see that type of feeling from him."

Klecko didn't play until the third game of the season when the boy playing ahead of him on the defensive line was injured. "The first game he played, he won the game for them," Joe Sr. says with pride. "They couldn't take him out after that."

High school kids simply were no match for Joe Klecko. In just six dominating games, he established a local reputation for toughness that assumed almost mythic proportions during the year he sat out of football after graduation. John DiGregorio, the Temple University athletic equipment manager and a veteran organizer in the area semipro football league, was equipment man for the Aston, Pennsylvania, Knights at the time. Describing the scouting reports he had on Klecko, DiGregorio says, "He was sort of a fable."

In 1972, one of the Knights' coaches found Klecko watching a softball game and asked him to come out for the team with a couple of his former teammates at St. James. Klecko had begun to miss football, but he was shy about taking the step to join the Knights. His girlfriend, Debbie, who later became his wife, persuaded Klecko to take a drive to the field where the Knights practiced.

"We were watching them practice from the car," Debbie recalls. "He said, 'I don't really want to do this. Let's go.' I took the keys out of the ignition and said, 'Just go out there and talk to them to see if you're interested. We're not leaving until you do.' "

While they were debating the issue, DiGregorio spotted Klecko and came over and talked him into joining the team. Except for a few young recruits, the Knights were composed primarily of seasoned veterans unable to let go of the game after their college playing days were over or they had failed at NFL training camps. On rare occasions, a player actually would make it to the NFL, but they almost never lasted more than a couple of seasons in minor roles.

Almost immediately, the nineteen-year-old Klecko proved he was better than any of them on the field and could hold his own at the postgame Oktoberfest, as well. He weighed 280 pounds with what looked like a few extra helpings of baby fat, but it didn't cost him any of his speed. Relying on brute strength, rather than technique, Klecko overpowered his opponents from defensive tackle and then chased down ballcarriers from behind. It wasn't long before the other players began kidding him about being able to lift the trucks he was driving.

Partly because so many players had nothing more to lose and were angry with the world for the breaks denied them, the brand of football the Knights played was extremely rugged. In a game against the Long Island Chiefs, two players set Klecko up and intentionally injured one of his ankles badly.

"That's not the way to play the game," Klecko says. "There was a lot of ignorance in that league."

By nature, Klecko gravitated toward the rough crew that occupied the back of the bus on road trips. "Our quarterback would be up in the front of the bus reading the Bible, and Klecko would be in the back with the thugs, telling stories about their sexual exploits," DiGregorio laughs. "They opened his eyes to the real world."

There was no doubt in DiGregorio's mind that Klecko had major-college ability, which is why he had Klecko play under the assumed name of Jim Jones in order to protect his college eligibility. But whenever DiGregorio talked to Klecko about going to Temple, where former Navy coach Wayne Hardin was attempting to upgrade the level of the football program, Klecko tuned him out.

"He was afraid of the thought of going to college, afraid of failing scholastically," DiGregorio says. "Joe Klecko could have been a truck driver playing semipro football for the Aston Knights for ten years, drinking beer and fucking around with a bunch of rowdies who played football because they liked to beat the shit out of somebody on Saturday nights. His main ambition in life was to own a Peterbilt tractor-trailer rig and drive it across the country."

Klecko would have been quite content with that life-style, and for that matter, Hardin would have spent a lot fewer sleepless nights worrying about the problems Klecko might cause for him with the NCAA. Convincing Hardin to take a chance on a semipro player was at least as difficult for DiGregorio as talking Klecko into going to college. Klecko's parents and Debbie were all for the idea, and they ganged up on him with DiGregorio.

"From the beginning, I told Joe he had the ability to make a lot of money playing pro football," DiGregorio says. "He thought I was blowing smoke up his rear end. But I said, 'All you've got to do is go to school and serve that apprenticeship.' There are some great semipro football players that had the ability but never could get the opportunity. They'd be the first people cut because the pro team had given Joe Schmuck from State University a hundred-thousand-dollar bonus. It's an unfair situation.

"I kept telling him, 'We have tutors; they'll get you easier classes. Things were easier back then as far as helping guys stay in school. But still, guys would flunk out all the time, and they carried that with them for a while."

Once or twice a week, DiGregorio would badger Hardin or one of his assistants about Klecko. Even though he once coached the semipro Philadelphia Bulldogs—or maybe because of that experience—Hardin was leery of the stigma associated with semi-pro players. But his curiosity had been piqued. When DiGregorio learned Dayton University planned to bring Klecko in for a recruiting visit, he went straight to Hardin with the news.

"I said to Wayne, 'What in the hell's wrong with you? Klecko's better than anybody you've got, and he's going to Dayton,'" DiGregorio recalls. "I told him Klecko had a letter from his high school principal saying he was a C-average student. You didn't need a transcript then. Wayne broke down and said, 'Bring him in.' I'll never forget the day I brought Joe into Wayne's office. He filled up the whole fucking doorway. Wayne said, 'Come in, Mr.

Klecko. Have a seat.' Then, Wayne went to Klecko's house and visited his parents, and he never visited parents because he didn't like going into people's homes to recruit."

Getting Klecko admitted to Temple was just the first hurdle. Keeping him there was another story. With just one season of high school experience behind him, Klecko wasn't prepared for the regimentation of his first preseason training camp at Temple. He bridled when forced to perform one drill after another and do the running necessary to get into condition. He was two years older and far more mature than the other freshmen, and he knew right away that nobody should be ahead of him on the depth chart. But Hardin had him playing third-string linebacker. It was dues-paying time, and the coaches seemed bent on making an example of Klecko.

After two days of training camp, Klecko went AWOL. "At four A.M. on the third day, Wayne was on the telephone to my room," DiGregorio says. "Klecko's roommate had told Hardin what happened. He was so pissed off at me that he wanted to strangle me. He said, 'Your boy jumped ship. You better find that son of a bitch!' "

Klecko's parents hadn't seen him, and when DiGregorio called Debbie, she lied and said she didn't know where he was. DiGregorio's wife told him to bring Debbie to see her, and they pressured her into telling them where to find Joe. When Hardin discovered Klecko had made contact with Dayton after leaving camp, he called the Dayton coaches and told them Klecko would have to redshirt for a year because he spent two days at Temple.

"He was screwing me," Klecko says of Hardin. "I hated him."

After DiGregorio found Klecko, he told him, "Joe, you've got to go through this like a carpenter and his apprenticeship. Just tolerate it for four years." When Klecko returned, Hardin moved him to defensive tackle, where he became a starter in his third game as a freshman.

Handling the football part of college was no problem, but Klecko never pretended that he was college material in the classroom. In fact, during his first semester, he never pretended that he was a student. Klecko didn't attend a single class, which was reflected in a 0.0 grade-point average. Only then did it become clear to Klecko that he couldn't make it through the college farm system on a free pass. He had to play by at least some of the major rules, such as going to class, even if his true course of study was NFL 101. Dropping out of school would have made it nearly impossible for him to have a pro career since he couldn't apply to join the NFL until his regular class was scheduled to graduate in 1975. One year of high school ball and four years in the semipro ranks wouldn't have provided him with enough of the basic training he needed to compete with the best players produced by the colleges. Temple was the only place for him to get the necessary experience.

"When I got in trouble, I had to go to class," Klecko says. "The big thing was learning what professors would help me and what classes to take."

In a way, that task allowed Klecko to make use of his street smarts and his rough-edged charm. It took him about two years to learn the ropes of how to get through school and cajole professors into giving him the grades he needed or allowing him the flexibility to work at an independent study program. Ultimately, he did open books and complete assignments. By the end of his college career, his grade-point average in history was 3.2 on a 4-point scale. Klecko finished nineteen hours short of a degree he knew he never would put to use.

There were some areas of the system to which he never conformed. The NCAA rulebook governing the conduct of scholarship athletes is as thick as a New York City telephone directory and as arcane as ancient Egyptian hieroglyphics. Klecko succeeded in ignoring the prohibition against holding a job while in school. The rule is intended to prevent schools or boosters from providing no-show jobs for good money as a way of covering up payments from a slush fund of some sort. Klecko figured the rule didn't take into consideration the circumstances of someone like him. First, he never received any inducements, financial or otherwise, to attend Temple beyond the chance to play football and receive an education. And second, he was used to working and having an income substantially more than the $15 per month laundry money permitted at the time by the NCAA. The need for money became all the more important when he and Debbie were married during his senior year at Temple. He continued to drive trucks locally, and he also worked nights as a bartender and bouncer, a job which required him on a few occasions to relieve some unruly patrons of their guns.

"When I was going to college, I'd jockey trucks after football practice for the company owned by Leonard Tose, the owner of the Eagles at that time," Klecko says. "I didn't have time to make a full run. I'd pull them into the bays and get them filled up. After that, I'd go tend bar at night. Debbie was working, too, so we didn't see much of each other. Sometimes, I'd get up real early in the mornings before school and take a truckload to downtown Philadelphia and then go to school in my tractor-trailer."

"Keeping Joe within the confines of the NCAA regulations was a problem," says DiGregorio. "He was a stick of dynamite waiting for someone to light the fuse. Hardin knew Joe was working, but he kept it quiet. Wayne was worried sick all the time about this guy putting him on the spot with the NCAA."

On the field, there were times when Hardin wished someone would light Klecko's fuse. He was a dominant player from the time he was a freshman, but in the minds of the coaches, Klecko never achieved the level of performance of which he was capable on a consistent basis. Whenever the coaches called DiGregorio in to ask him how to motivate Klecko, he told them, "That's your job; my job is keeping him here." But DiGregorio agreed that Klecko was letting much of his talent just sit in a personal savings account he only tapped on special occasions.

"Joe motivated himself for one game down at Delaware as a freshman because there were busloads of people coming from Chester that day to watch the game," DiGregorio says. "He played over the center on punts and placekick snaps and destroyed the guy. The center was just rolling the ball back in the second half. The rest of the time, he played defensive end, and the Delaware coach, Tubby Raymond, had some quotes in the paper the next day about a truck driver coming down and running over them. I don't think he ever had another great game at Temple. He had a lot of good games, but not another great game.

"He lacked intensity because he had the ability to handle the guys he was playing against without overexerting himself. Nobody here could motivate him. He hated Wayne Hardin; he hated the defensive line coach; he hated the whole set-up, except for me and a few friends on the team. He had a good game against Pittsburgh later on, but I don't think he ever played up to the same level he reached that day against Delaware."

"I disagree to a point," Klecko says. "I had a game against Penn State that was better because of the competition I was playing against. I remember catching some flak from the coaches after a game against the Akron Zips. What the hell did I care about the Akron Zips? Hardin came into a meeting and said, 'I asked a player here how he played, and he said he played well eighty percent of the game. No way. They were double-teaming him and moving him.' It was obvious he was talking about me, and I destroyed that team. When I played against Penn State, they doubled me, and I still used them up. That was because I had a reason to play. I agree my motivation was different in college because I never had any problems against anybody. In the pros, everybody's good; you respect your opponents, and you're getting paid to play hard all the time."

When he completed his four-year apprenticeship, Klecko still was something of a question mark in the minds of NFL scouts, who rated him as a middle-round draft choice. He had no chance to improve his stock in all-star games because Hardin never pushed for him to be included. When Klecko questioned him about it, Hardin replied with what seemed feigned ignorance, "Oh, I thought you were in about three of them."

When he was at Navy, Hardin had coached a whole team of players who fit his image of a role model for the youth of America. Klecko was from another category, and the fact that he couldn't maintain absolute control over Klecko's life was an annoyance. More than anything, Hardin acted relieved to see Klecko go without any repercussions from the NCAA.

"A head coach gets you into all-star games, and when Hardin said he thought I was in three, it was bogus," Klecko says. "I was never captain of the team because I wasn't an All-American guy. We never had any direct arguments, but he never really took a liking to me. In the pros, it's different. You can argue with a coach. In college, he's the boss, and you're the kid. I do think Hardin used a tender hand with me, though. He wouldn't jump on me as readily as someone else, and he never said a word to me about the fact I was working."

When it was time for the 1977 NFL draft, Klecko suspected he might wind up with the hometown Eagles, who had traded away their picks in the first four rounds and told him they planned to take him in the sixth round. But the Jets, picking one spot in front of the Eagles, chose Klecko first. DiGregorio still shakes his head over the way the Eagles used their fifth-round pick, which actually was their first selection of that draft.

"They drafted Skip Sharp, a defensive back from Kansas who weighed a hundred and seventy and never played one down anywhere in the pros," DiGregorio says. "But it was the best thing that ever happened to Joe because he got more notoriety and more money in New York."

5

Joe, Meet Joe

During lunch breaks at the annual May minicamp for rookies, the hopefuls who comprised the Jets' Class of 1977 lounged in the locker room wearing T-shirts and shorts, and tried to maintain poker-faced expressions while they checked out the competition like anxious adolescents at their first mixer. It wasn't hard to spot the headliners: number-one draft pick Marvin Powell, a tall, athletic-looking offensive tackle from Southern Cal, and number-two choice Wesley Walker, a wide receiver from California who had sprinter speed. The Jets had eighteen picks in twelve rounds of the draft, which made it an unusually large class, so the rest of the draftees blended together with the crowd of free agents sharing the locker room. A minicamp is sort of like the swimsuit competition in a beauty pageant. Since no live hitting is allowed, everyone runs through his paces and judges the body size and strength of his fellow contestants from arm's length.

But there was one pudgy, baby-faced kid who caught the eye of Dan Alexander, who was an eighth-round pick from Louisiana State that the Jets planned to convert from defensive to offensive line. "There was a guy wearing a T-shirt that said 'I'm a Polack' about seven times, and 'Polack' was spelled seven different ways," recalls Alexander. "I'd never heard of him before, but I thought he had a funny T-shirt."

It was Joe Klecko, the sixth-round defensive tackle from Temple. There was no reason for Alexander or anyone else to recognize Klecko. Compared to the Jets' other draft picks, most of whom were from established college football powers, a player from Temple was an unknown quantity. He wasn't even the first defensive lineman drafted by the Jets that year. Third-round pick Tank Marshall of Texas A&M held that distinction.

When regular training camp opened in July, there was one player who did know of Klecko and even had met him and watched him play. While still a junior at Widener College in Chester, Jets center Joe Fields was introduced to Klecko by Neil Taylor, Widener's offensive line coach. Taylor had been a coach with the semipro Aston Knights and was trying without success to recruit Klecko from that team. The next year, Taylor took Fields and some other Widener players, including tackle Bobby Hurchala, who served as the best man at Klecko's wedding, to watch Klecko play for Temple against Penn State at Veterans Stadium in Philadelphia.

Fields knew all about Klecko, but in 1977, veterans and rookies still observed a strict protocol, which held that rookies should be seen and not heard unless they were called upon to stand on their chairs in the training camp dining hall and belt out a few bars of their school fight song. It was part of the indoctrination-by-intimidation process all rookies had to go through in order to make the team. Klecko understood the code and played it by the book, but another friend who had played at Widener asked Klecko to say hello to Fields for him in camp.

"It took me a while to say anything to a veteran," Klecko says. "I was a good rookie who never got in anyone's way and did everything the veterans asked me to do. But I finally went up to Fields and said there was a guy from home who asked me to say, 'Hi.' Fields said, 'Okay,' and he walked away without another word. That was the first time I ever tried to talk to him."

If Fields's behavior seemed strange, he was just treating Klecko the way he had been treated as a rookie by veteran guard Randy Rasmussen, who played next to him but barely spoke to him throughout his rookie year. "Back then, veterans didn't talk to rookies," Fields explains. "An offensive veteran especially never talked to a defensive rookie. It's a head game, the pressure the vets put on rookies by not being their friend and the pressure of learning a new system."

When Klecko opened his mouth as a rookie, it usually was to sing the Temple fight song, which was number one on the training-camp charts, at least, in terms of frequency, if not quality. "I was always the last one to leave practice, and since I spent so much time lifting weights, I was always the last one in the cafeteria," Klecko says. "So, the vets always made me sing."

"The only guy you heard singing that year was Klecko," adds Fields.

As the number-one draft choice, Powell was expected to be the featured rookie act, but he performed a silent solo, refusing all attempts to force him to sing. Veteran defensive lineman Richard Neal tried to talk him into going along with the light-hearted tradition, but Powell raised such a stink that first-year head coach Walt Michaels put a stop to the singing after a couple of weeks rather than cause hard feelings.

Coming from Temple and the Aston Knights before that, Klecko was properly humble when he joined the Jets. Even though he had handled the Penn States and Pittsburghs in college, he assumed his opponents weren't good enough to make it in the NFL. Stepping into a dormitory elevator with three other rookies who towered over him, Klecko felt small by comparison at 6-3, 256 pounds.

"I never gave myself the credit for being good enough to be there," Klecko says. "Training camp was a chore because of the fear and insecurity I had. I was just hoping to be there long enough to make a little bit of money and get a start toward buying a house. My expectations changed from day to day. You'd see a guy next to you that you thought was pretty good go down the road, and you'd have to build that confidence back up. I never gave myself a chance to take a break mentally. I was always listening and studying. In college, I was never afraid of anybody physically. When I played against Pittsburgh for the first time in an exhibition game, I was in awe."

The Steelers were coming off their second straight Super Bowl championship when they met the Jets in the fourth game of the preseason. Their offensive line was not as big as some but was extremely strong and quick. The defensive line known as the "Steel Curtain" was huge and overpowering. Facing the Steelers also left quite an impression on Dan Alexander, who had the pleasure of lining up at right guard across from "Mean" Joe Greene, a future Hall of Famer who was the driving force that made their defense so strong.

"On one play, I was supposed to pull right, and Fields, who

was at center, was supposed to take Greene," Alexander says. "I was waiting for Joe to make the blocking call, but he didn't say anything. I said. 'Joe, what are we doing?' He still didn't say anything. We were just about to snap the ball, so finally, I said, 'Joe, I'm pulling.' Greene was laughing across from me. He must have thought I was talking to him because he came through the hole and crushed the running back."

Call it the textbook definition of a rookie mistake. But there was plenty of time to make up for it in that brutal training camp. Including the Hall of Fame game at Canton, Ohio, the Jets played seven exhibition games, which was half as many as they were scheduled to play in the regular season. Rookies always go live in camp, hoping to be noticed, but the young veterans were going just as hard that year, trying to impress the new coach.

Klecko was all business. At first, the coaches put him at defensive tackle, but they quickly moved him outside when his speed became apparent. "His body was not the body of an NFL player," says Dan Sekanovich, who was the Jets' defensive line coach from 1977–82. "He was a little soft and pudgy, but he knew what it was going to take and took it upon himself to start pumping those weights. Joe came in with a lot of determination, and he had super-strong hands, as strong as anybody I've ever seen."

Klecko's hands were those of a trained boxer whose skills were honed in the Cloverlay gym run by former heavyweight champion Joe Frazier in north Philadelphia near the Temple campus. "Smokin' Joe" Klecko won twenty-five matches for Temple's boxing team and lost one. Of course, it's the only fight anyone ever mentions to him around the Philadelphia area. The man who defeated Joe Klecko is named Bruce Blair, but he had behind-the-scenes help from a blonde Klecko met at a time when he and his future wife, Debbie, weren't dating. Klecko won a morning semifinal match and was scheduled to return for the tournament final at eleven P.M. that night. In between, he violated the boxing canon prohibiting sex before a fight because of its enervating effect on the legs. Klecko wasn't the first boxer who failed to observe that rule, but he wasn't the exception to it, either.

"I broke the guy's nose in the first round," Klecko says, sounding aggravated by the memory. "He was all blood. In the second round, all he did was run from me, and I made the mistake of chasing him. I had no legs in the third round, and I just held him. He was hitting me, but he wasn't hurting me. I beat the shit out of the son of a bitch, but the fight was in his hometown and they awarded him a split decision. When we were done, the kid kissed the mat.

"I've knocked guys through the ropes; I've knocked them cold. Once, I busted this kid's nose real bad, and I turned to the ref and said, 'Will you stop this?' I didn't want to hurt him any worse. The Temple boxing coach didn't like me because I trained on my own at Cloverlay. He brought in a black kid to try out for heavy-weight, and I knocked him down ten fucking times. He couldn't get rid of me because I'd win. Fighting was a sideline at Temple, but I loved it."

It's a cliché that nobody gets hurt in football fights because of all the protective equipment they wear. But Klecko *was* the exception to that rule in his rookie training camp. He established himself right away as the heavyweight champion of pass-rush drills. On dull, humid training-camp afternoons, there's nothing like pass-rush drills to put a charge in the atmosphere. The be-hemoths on the offensive and defensive lines take turns banging heads one-on-one like bull elephants. The ground shakes, hard plastic pads crack together sharply, tempers flare, heads turn to watch, and you know this is what football is all about.

"I just did what I had to do to make the football team," Klecko says. "It was a pain in the ass to go against me because I always went full-tilt in practice. I got in a lot of fights. The last week of cuts, there was a guy who had played for St. Louis who kept hitting after the play. I told him to quit it, and when he didn't, I busted his teeth out with an uppercut under his facemask. He was bleeding pretty good. I always thought that kind of thing brought good attention from the coaches."

About a month into training camp, veteran defensive tackle Carl Barzilauskas took Klecko under his wing for the ostensible purpose of instructing him in the ways of NFL life. At 6-6 and 280 pounds, Barzilauskas was a giant among Jets, but he only talked a good game. Fields took note of the association and steered clear. "Barzo" always was putting his hands in Fields's face and holding him during practice, and Fields didn't want to have anything to do with him or his rookie friend.

Barzo told Klecko he was in a numbers game with Marshall, the second-round draft pick, and said the Jets never let a second-rounder go. That thought weighed on Klecko's mind until the end of camp, when he made the team and Marshall went on injured reserve. Klecko excelled in passing situations as a rookie but didn't make his first start until the ninth game of the season in place of injured Abdul Salaam. Ironically, an injury to Barzo in that game gave Klecko the chance to start the remaining five games, and he wound up leading all NFL rookies with 8 sacks.

"I found out Barzo wasn't that good a football player, even though he was a mountain of a man," Klecko says. "He held himself in high esteem and that bugged me. One day in the weight room, Barzo said, 'Come on, let's go.' I said, 'I've got to lift,' He said, 'You don't need weightlifting. If you've got it, you've got it. Look at me. I don't lift.' He was gone the next year.

"Making the team was the greatest feeling of jubilation. The eight sacks put me more at ease, but they came on natural ability. I didn't know what I was doing. That's the truth. Guys then weren't as strong as they became in the eighties. I'd get on the corner and run people over real easy."

The Class of 1977 arguably is the best draft the Jets ever had. It produced six players who made major contributions that helped turn the franchise around after almost a decade of decline. The six included three future Pro Bowlers (Klecko, Powell, and Walker), two running backs who each led the team in rushing for a season (Kevin Long and Scott Dierking), and one ironman (Alexander, who put together a consecutive games streak of 171). The Jets also drafted one half of a future quarterback controversy (Matt Robinson) that year.

It marked a definite departure from the Namath years and the formation of a nucleus around which one of the most talented but unpredictable NFL teams of the eighties would continue to grow. At the end of that training camp, Fields let down the veteran facade long enough to invite Alexander out for a few beers, an act that meant the "rook" from Louisiana had passed muster.

"I was shocked but excited because I wasn't talking to the older guys," Alexander remembers. "He just took me to a little bar near camp and told me how things worked. It fired me up. That was the beginning of a long relationship. I started at right guard in the third game of my rookie season and played by Fields's side for eleven years.

"We knew each other like brothers. He wouldn't even have to make a blocking call. He'd just say, 'Caj' or grunt at me, and I'd know what he was going to do. The defense couldn't pick it up.

At first, my nickname was 'Bayou,' then 'Cajun,' then 'Caj.' But Joe called me 'Tijon,' which sounds like Dijon mustard with a 'T.' That was the name of a bayou boy that the cajun singer Justin Wilson sings about on one of his albums. One year, a rookie heard Fields say 'Tijon' on a blocking call, and he asked me, 'What is that 'Tijon' call? I can't find it in the playbook.' "

It wasn't until Klecko's second season that the lines of communication between him and Fields opened up. Barzo had departed for another team, and Klecko and Alexander were sharing a house with third-year linebacker Greg Buttle. On their days off, Klecko would drive home to Philadelphia and drop Fields off at his house in south Jersey on the way. But it really was through a friendship that developed between Debbie Klecko and Kay Fields that Joe and Joe came to know each other much better.

"The rarest thing two players could have is wives who are level-headed people," Klecko says. "Some wives take on this role of being married to a big-deal football player and become very impressed with themselves. Our wives never did that. Coming from the same background as us, they didn't try to be someone they weren't, which is why they got along so well. That made it a relaxed atmosphere for Fields and me."

Following Klecko's second season, Fields invited him to a New Year's Eve party at a friend's house on the Jersey shore, where they discovered they had several mutual friends. The high point of the evening came when Klecko decided to model a tuxedo jacket belonging to one of Fields's friends.

"The guy took about a forty long, and Klecko wore about a fifty-four long," Fields says, laughing at the memory. "Klecko put it on, and all he was wearing were the arms. It just ripped apart."

Later that year, Klecko and Fields took their wives to Las Vegas for an NFL arm-wrestling tournament that Klecko won, and they began to discover how much they had in common from their working-class backgrounds to their relationships with their fathers. It was a basis for trust and understanding between them that developed into a sense of common purpose in their roles with the Jets.

There were times when they would sit in a bar and talk about the similarities between their fathers and how it shaped them. "My father was very hard on me to the point of being both my worst enemy and my best friend," Klecko says. "There's many things he did that I thought were cruel, but when I look back, it made me that much stronger as a person."

"Our dads were simple," Fields adds. "They felt that, if you wanted something, you had to work for it. If you wanted more, you had to work more. My mom worked as a cashier and a bookkeeper, and when my dad was home from his job as a state trooper, he was working a second job at the pig farms and not making very much money."

Neither one imagined a career as a professional athlete was in his future. Klecko figured he would be getting up at five A.M. and going out to a cold truck he would drive until late at night. Fields saw himself grinding out a living as an accountant, the man in the gray flannel suit. For the first several years of their NFL careers, Klecko and Fields worked at second jobs, just as their fathers had, Klecko as a trucker and Fields as an ironworker.

They hoped football would be a stepping stone to better things outside of the NFL, and they worked to prepare themselves in case their careers suddenly ended. Even as their salaries climbed and they gained recognition, Klecko and Fields continued to think of themselves as they were before football.

"I go to a little bar in Gloucester, New Jersey, called O'Donnell's and listen to the construction workers talk about this job and that," Fields says. "It makes me feel good because I understand a little bit about what they're doing."

"Driving the biggest rigs was kind of a big-shot deal for me," Klecko says. "There's a lot of solitude when you're out there by yourself, and it's like you're your own boss. I get the greatest thrill when truck drivers come up to me and tell me about the rigs they drive. They can identify with me, and I think of them as a special breed."

In some sense, Fields and Klecko were the extension of a construction worker and a truck driver on the field. Both are physical occupations in which men value the capacity for hard labor and the ability to take a hands-on approach toward problem solving. Those jobs, by nature, seem to attract men who instinctively measure each other first by their physical prowess.

Nowhere are those attitudes more obvious than on a football team, which requires the largest roster of any major team sport and then breaks it down into compartmentalized units by position.

As a result, players usually develop closer relationships with those at the same position. Football demands physical courage from all who play the game, but on a broader scale, players may be divided into two groups—speed and power—those who handle the ball and those who spend most of the game beating on each other, two different mindsets.

Fields's concept of a bubble covering the portion of the field where the two lines are waging trench warfare while the ball is flying around somewhere beyond their control conjures up a vivid image of violence under glass. The outcome of that battle generally is what determines the final score of most games.

"The physicalness is the intriguing thing," says Klecko. "Whether it's clean or dirty, the challenge makes you come back for more. There's a lot of animal in everybody out there in the world. You find it in little people when they get drunk, the closet-case tough guys. Only we get the chance to display it on a football field. Once you've tasted it, it's hard to give up.

"I always wanted to be the enforcer on the team whenever something happened. It's very rare that I start a fight, but when one breaks out, everybody knows I'm always the third man in. I love to mix it up. You get in fights on the football field, and you can be a tough guy. You get in fights on the street, and you never know what's going to happen. As a bouncer, I saw many a brawl. I've taken guns away from guys a couple of times, and that's scary. But I have a lot of confidence in my hands. Nobody worries me. I don't care how big a guy is. I'll bet anybody in this world that I can knock him down, unless he's a prizefighter or really knows what he's doing."

After surviving enough collisions, punches, headslaps, and general beatings, many football players, especially linemen, come to believe they are invincible. It hurts on Monday, but hey, they lived. It's a mentality that enables the best players to perform uninhibited by any inbred fear of pain they may harbor. The ability to do that is what makes a player the type that gives those around him a sense of security and affords a certain level of comfort in the middle of the grappling tangle of large bodies. When reality intrudes in the form of pain or injury, they naturally lean on each other for help in restoring the belief they can block it all out and continue to function effectively.

"Fields was a tough cookie who played with a lot of nagging injuries," Alexander says. "He would get dinged in games to the point where his knees were killing him. He'd grab my arm and say, 'Caj, you've got to help me get through this.' We'd do that for each other, and it would help give you the lift you needed to keep going."

The physical respect gained on the field forms bonds that often carry over to the social setting away from the game. "I think bigger guys like to get physical," Fields says. "When a bunch of guys are out having beers, you see some wrestling and jousting around. It's kind of like a yearning for that contact. Good, physical football players gravitate to each other. That's why it's rare to see a defensive or offensive lineman hanging out with a wide receiver. They're in different worlds. Where we are on the line, it's force against force; out there beyond the bubble, it's all speed. You respect the people that can give it and take it, and you want to be around them.

"When I first came to the Jets, there was a receiver named David Knight. He wouldn't hit with his face; he didn't want his face to get hurt. Where I am, that's all you do every play is hit with your face. That's why you have a facemask."

When the fighting is over, the boys who know what it's like to slug it out with an opponent for sixty or seventy plays, the ones who understand why God made facemasks, those guys tend to go off someplace where they can tell war stories and apply a few cold drinks to their bruises. In Fields's early years with the Jets, that place was a clam and beer restaurant called Chicolino's, which is located in a beach community called Point Lookout on the southern shore of Long Island, a twenty-minute drive from the Jets' training complex. Every year when the summer rentals move out, young Jets move in for the duration of the football season.

The social atmosphere was nothing fancy. The salary boom was years away, and the Jets' parking lot looked more like a used-car lot than a luxury-car showroom. People had bills to pay. Fields once had trouble coming up with the money to pay his $179 per-month rent. Nobody much was rubbing elbows with the glamorous or the wealthy in Manhattan. When their husbands were in the team hotel the night before a game, the Jets' wives would meet at Chicolino's for dinner. On Fridays and days off, the parties usually included Fields and fellow offensive linemen Darrell Austin, Gary Puetz, and Randy Rasmussen (after he began talking to Fields in his second year, of course), defensive lineman Ed Galigher, and a couple of funny running backs, Louie Giammona and Ed Marinaro, who later became well-known as an actor on the *Hill Street Blues* television cop series.

"Marinaro was a nut," Fields recalls. "He was just with the Jets in 1976, but he was such a ham that he kept me going through training camp. The first game that Marinaro rushed for a hundred yards, he bought all the offensive linemen Dom Perignon champagne."

Marinaro, Giammona, and Galigher were released in 1977 and gradually were replaced over the next few years by Klecko, Alexander, Dierking, quarterbacks Richard Todd and Pat Ryan, defensive lineman Marty Lyons, and placekicker Pat Leahy, who had joined the Jets a year ahead of Fields and become close with him. Kay's sister, Cindy, married Puetz, but he was released in 1978. By that time, the Jets were the youngest team in the NFL and were just getting to know each other and build some camaraderie. After games at Shea Stadium, they ate at the stadium club and then moved the feast a few miles down the road to a bar called Patrick's Pub in Little Neck, Long Island.

"The guys weren't impressed with themselves," says Debbie Klecko. "They were fun-loving the way you picture a football player to be like. Gary Puetz was crazy. He and Randy Rasmussen would make the whole party. These guys liked to have a good time, and their wives were the same way. We'd all meet somewhere for dinner and then go out and dance. It's a good thing they left, or we'd all be dead by now."

Comparing the scene a decade later, as Klecko and Fields were approaching the end of their careers, to what it was like when they were young, Debbie says, "The guys now are getting a lot more money. They're more yuppieish, not wild and crazy at all. Their wives are more respectable. They have to be more sophisticated. After games, they all go into New York City or go their separate ways. We never went into the city. It seems like they all talk behind each other's backs. It's really strange."

As Kay Fields remembers it, the wives she knew when her husband was starting out were just as spirited as the guys when it was time to party. They all sat in the same section at Shea Stadium and cheered under the direction of Dottie Hampton, the wife of longtime equipment manager, Bill Hampton. "Somebody would bring a bottle of blackberry brandy, and we'd all yell and scream," Kay says. "Dottie Hampton was the greatest cheerleader. You could hear her mouth all over. The wives would look out for each other, and they really stuck together."

Once he established himself on the field, Klecko's natural leadership qualities took over off the field, as well. He and Fields created parties, and they usually were the last ones to leave the team parties in Point Lookout. On the nights Fields stayed home, Klecko would take Lyons or anybody who was game along for the ride. If it came down to it, Klecko would find a good time by himself.

"Klecko always had the attitude that he ran things," says Pat Ryan. "He just took charge in the locker room, and if you were out someplace, he was running the show. The funny thing was that he could do it without offending anybody. His attitude was, 'Hey, I'm the boss.' But he'd do it with a smile, and people would laugh. You could go to a restaurant, and in five minutes, he'd be in the kitchen checking on the food. He'd go in with a loaf of bread and a bottle of wine and sit down in the kitchen and start ordering people around. And they liked it."

"When we go to a restaurant, I always let Klecko order first," adds Fields. "He has a way of ordering that makes it sound so good that I'll just say, 'I'll take the same.' Every time."

For as long as he was with the Jets, Klecko owned Friday nights. A tame evening at home watching television was not part of his game plan. Friday was attitude-adjustment night for him; his game face could wait until Sunday when it mattered. In that respect, he saw himself in the mold of the hard-living players who came before him, and onetime Jets offensive line coach Jim Ringo, who played for the great Green Bay teams under Vince Lombardi, told Klecko he would have fit right in with those Packers.

"I got a little bit caught up in the idea that you had to drink to be a pro football player," Klecko says. "I never drink at home, but when I go out, it's like I'm unchained. I'm not an alcoholic, but I can put it away. No doubt, I have a reputation as a partier, but I'm not rowdy or abusive. Even big guys get beer muscles, but I'm a person who gets happy when he drinks. I enjoyed my life in pro football because New York was a party town. I never made the headlines Joe Namath did, but I was right in there."

Toward the end, Klecko and Fields realized their Friday night soirees had become an issue to coach Joe Walton and some of the younger players, the yuppies, as Debbie Klecko called them. But Klecko and Fields came from a hearty, back-slapping breed of football players, men who thought of a good bar as an extension of the locker room. The Jets team of their youth enjoyed a chemistry and camaraderie that was fostered by the roistering good times they had in places like Chicolino's and Patrick's Pub. They believed it was up to everyone to decide what he could handle, and they resented it when others tried to force their values on them. The bottom line, as far as they were concerned, was to do the job on Sunday.

One thing about Joe Klecko and Joe Fields," says Alexander, "is that, whatever they did or didn't do on Friday nights, they always were ready to let it all hang out on Sundays."

"You couldn't find two tougher guys than Klecko and Fields," adds Ryan. "They were the type of guys who, if it got to a fight, you had to kill them."

A Team Is Born

A little drinking and hell-raising never bothered Walt Michaels. In the first place, it would have been hypocritical for a shot-and-a-beer guy like him to impose some arbitrary code of behavior on his players' personal lives, and in the second place, Michaels concerned himself with how players performed on Sundays and didn't get all wrapped up in the petty stuff. Hell, if anything, he thought it was healthy for his players to blow off a little steam and come to work ready to kick some tail.

Michaels was a gnarled relic from the fifties when he played a mean linebacker for the Cleveland Browns, making the Pro Bowl four straight seasons from 1957–60. He had worked as an assistant coach for the Jets under Weeb Ewbank from 1963–72, and he rejoined them in 1976 as an assistant on Lou Holtz's staff, a match that produced a real culture clash. In private conversations late at night in hotel bars with reporters covering the Jets, Michaels would laugh and scoff at the college-style methods employed by Holtz. That was ironic in that Michaels had his own odd personality quirks, but when he succeeded Holtz in 1977 as head coach, it was clear the Jets were getting a man who understood the things that were important to pro football players and who also recognized talent. His values were the old-fashioned values, and toughness was first on his list of the character traits defining a Walt Michaels-type player.

In that respect, Klecko and Fields were made to play for Michaels, but at first, the coaching change worried Fields. "My first impression of Walt was one of anxiety," Fields says. "I had become the starter my second year, and Walt came in and drafted Gary Gregory, a big center from Baylor, in the fifth round. Walt said, 'Here's a guy who can start for us now.' I always was insecure anyway. I had seen twenty-five new guys come in under Lou Holtz, and I couldn't imagine Walt keeping the same players. I didn't know where I stood."

As it developed, Fields had nothing to worry about. Gregory never played a down for the Jets, and Michaels soon learned of Fields's ability to play hurt. But of all the Jets, it was Klecko for whom Michaels had a special affinity from the time he first saw him play as a senior for Temple against Penn State. He liked Klecko's powerful, brawling style of play and his hunger and was touting him as a future all-pro by the end of Klecko's rookie season. On a deeper level, Michaels felt a kinship with Klecko because both were Polish. Before going to Philadelphia for the final game of Klecko's rookie season, Michaels said, "I'm going to load him up with Philly kielbasa." Michaels and Klecko had their confrontations, but that was all right because Michaels wanted players who could stand on their own two feet, not brown-nosers.

"I was a hard-headed Polack just like Walt, and there's a very strong bond in that," Klecko says. "He was very ethnic. Walt loved my old man. He met him at games, and Walt always would say, 'I bet your old man wouldn't have done it like that when he was a kid.' Walt and I had some very tense little conversations. We used to yell at each other behind closed doors, but he respected that and could handle it. He didn't think you were trying to undermine him, and he never held a grudge against you. There was nothing hidden about Walt. He wasn't up one day and down the next; he was very even.

"Walt hated change. He liked the old work-ethic type people. Playing hurt was really commended by Walt because that's how he played. Walt didn't like pansies, and he couldn't understand a guy making excuses. He was like my father that way. He didn't pat you on the back for doing your job because that's what you were supposed to do. That was the problem he had with our wide receivers, Wesley Walker and Lam Jones. They wanted to be patted on the back a lot. Walt didn't understand wide receivers. He thought they were the sissies of the group, and he didn't have much time for it."

In his blunt manner, Michaels displayed his frustration with the muscle pulls that often sidelined the sprinters the Jets had at wide receiver, saying they had the delicate legs of "thoroughbreds." Communication never was one of Michaels's strong suits. There were times he made cryptic comments that seemed to have a subterranean logic only he could follow, and both players and reporters would be left puzzled. With his gruff countenance, he could be intimidating when he was angry, but the players singled out for criticism joked later about joining the "Cocksucker Club" because that was the expletive Michaels usually used to vent his rage.

Michaels's hands were as thick as bear paws, and his Popeye-like forearms were evidence of exceptional strength. He often kiddingly challenged Klecko to arm-wrestling matches, and Klecko always told him the kids coming up were stronger than in Michaels's day. Then, they'd get in each other's face, growling and roaring like grizzlies in the woods for a moment before Michaels would walk away. They never actually tested each other's strength, but it was one of the things that gave Michaels such a special feeling toward Klecko.

The Jets were in Philadelphia for the last game of Klecko's rookie year, and Klecko was headed to the team snack following a meeting in the Jets' hotel the night before the game when he saw Michaels walking toward him. "It was a real wide hallway, like an atrium with flowers," Klecko recalls with a smile. "Walt was mumbling to himself, and I was veering away from him. But he wouldn't let me get away. He kept walking right at me, and he knocked me into the potted flowers with his shoulder. Never said a word, just kept walking. I thought he was a strange motor-scooter, but you know what that was? That was a sign of affection from Walt."

If there was one area where Michaels showed some sensitivity, it was toward players who were struggling to play with injuries. Michaels was familiar with pain. He was troubled by arthritis, and he was required to take medication to alleviate sometimes severe neck, shoulder, and lower-back pains that served as a reminder of his playing days. It wasn't until after his days with the Jets ended that Michaels discovered he needed surgery for his neck problem.

"When you play as many years as I did, you're going to have physical problems," Michaels says. "People said I was a hothead, but many times, I was in excruciating pain. I learned how to play with pain, but I never learned I didn't have to live with pain until later when two specialists diagnosed problems with the nerves coming down my arms. It was like somebody shot a knife down my arms. I had bone chips in my neck that were pressing on my nerves, and I had arthritis. I had to take medication, but I tried to keep everyone from knowing."

So, Michaels understood the physical limits to which players could go, and he often could tell from film study the extent of an injury. In a 1980 game at Denver, Fields suffered a severely sprained right knee in the first half, had it taped at halftime and managed to finish the game on a bad leg. "I was stretching at practice the next Wednesday," Fields says, "and Walt walked over and looked down at me and said, 'I seen where the guy hurt your knee in the films.' Then, he walked away."

The previous year, Fields suffered a shoulder injury while tackling a defensive back who had made an interception, but he played the rest of the game because the Jets had no other long snappers. They signed one the next week, but Fields was planning to start the game in Green Bay. "We were in church the night before the game, and Walt was standing about one person away from me so he could shake my hand," Fields says. "I held my hand out, but I couldn't reach out because my shoulder was bothering me. He reached out and shook my hand and looked at me. I came in to get taped, and our trainer, Bob Reese, tells me Walt knows my shoulder really hurts, and he's starting someone else. I said, 'How the hell does he know that?' Reese said, 'From church last night.' "

When Fields tore a tendon in a finger on his snapping hand during training camp in 1982, doctors said the finger had to be operated on immediately or frozen in a hooked position forever. Not wanting to miss any games, Fields was uncertain of his decision, but Michaels ordered him to have the surgery.

His assistant coaches also appreciated the way Michaels operated. Practices usually lasted less than two hours, and the coaches had a strict time limit in which to complete their drills because Michaels wanted to save his players' legs for game day.

"Walt wasn't walking the halls to see if you were in your office working," says Bob Fry, who was Michaels's offensive line coach with the Jets. "He didn't believe in having a lot of coaches' meetings. It's unbelievable what some coaches think makes you win.

Walt was rough-talking, but he was very fair. You knew where he stood."

If he was satisfied with a player's performance, Michaels generally would pass him by in the hall at the Jets' complex without saying a word. On the day in 1980 when the Jets drafted linebacker Lance Mehl, Michaels mentioned Mehl's background working with his uncles in the coal mines of southern Ohio. "You're a coal miner; you're a good guy," Michaels said to Mehl. That was the extent of their conversation for the year.

"His bottom line was that you played," Mehl said. "It didn't matter what you did any other time. He realized you were an adult. He figured his responsibility was what you did on the field. I thought he was great that way. You respected the guy."

In his first season, Michaels made Richard Todd his starting quarterback, and the Jets went 3–11 for the third straight year. But Michaels was continuing the rebuilding process begun by Holtz. He focused first on the offensive line, drafting tackle Marvin Powell number one in 1977 and tackle Chris Ward number one in 1978. Michaels called the pair his "bookends." In 1979, Michaels shifted the emphasis to the defensive line, taking tackle Marty Lyons and end Mark Gastineau with the first two choices. Michaels believed in controlling the line of scrimmage with the kind of big men who commanded respect from opponents.

During games, Michaels stood at the 50-yard line and watched the play without the distraction of wearing a headset connecting him to the coaches in the press box. He often dropped into his old linebacker's stance, hands on knees, as if he were ready to run out and start making tackles. It appeared that Michaels had very little involvement in the coaching because he delegated so much authority to his offensive and defensive coordinators and let them run the show. But he determined the general guidelines and expected his assistants to carry out his directives. If he wasn't happy, he let them know. The area in which Michaels had the most direct involvement was the defense. The coordinator was Joe Gardi, who had been a special teams coach, but it was not Gardi's defense by any stretch of the imagination.

"Walt put the defense in," Klecko says. "I asked Gardi a couple of questions one time on the practice field, and he couldn't answer me without looking in the playbook. If it's your defense, you understand every aspect of it."

In 1978, the Jets went 8–8, and Michaels was named NFL coach of the year for his work with the youngest team in the league. They were a .500 team again in 1979 and beginning to attract some notice for the depth of their talent. The Jets also were gaining a reputation for toughness and physical play, which gave credence to the bromide that says a team takes on the personality of its coach. It seemed only natural for Michaels to appoint both Fields and Klecko as team captains year after year because they represented the work ethic he admired, and they didn't back down on the field. They were the type of players Michaels felt could help the Jets win a Super Bowl.

"Klecko was a little different style of guy," Michaels says. "He was a little stockier, not the picture-perfect build. He was very strong and would just take you and push you back. Some guys just pump iron; Joe Klecko lifted weights and was a player. Certainly, he was one of the best who ever did it. I firmly believe he was a sixth-round Hall of Fame choice.

"Fields had leadership qualities, and he was very much a student of the game. He knew his blocks and made very few mental errors. Fred Smerlas, the Buffalo nose tackle, gave him some of the hardest times. We devised the blocking to make sure Joe got his share of help, but he never looked for it. Going into a game, Joe would say, 'Don't worry. I'll get it.' But you don't want to hang up an all-pro without help."

Michaels never wasted time telling his captains how to lead; he chose them as captains because they already had shown they could lead. "To me, Klecko and Fields were both natural leaders," says guard Dan Alexander. "Fields was more of a 'rah-rah' leader, always whooping it up in practice. They were the heart and soul of the defense and offense."

Klecko's physical presence in a physical sport had much to do with his leadership role. He not only studied and understood the game, but he could back it up with authority on the field. Mehl remembers a time during his rookie year when he was talking in the huddle and Klecko turned to veteran linebacker Greg Buttle and, indicating Mehl, said, "If you don't shut him up, I'll shut him up."

"I was a rookie; I had a place, and he wanted to put me back in it," Mehl says. "You knew who was in charge. In my second year, I said in a newspaper interview that I was more laid-back in practice because I was just trying to get my keys down and learn the other team's offense. The headline said: MEHL HATES PRAC-TICE. Klecko jumped down my throat and told me to keep my mouth shut if I didn't like something. I was more intimidated than anything else. I certainly wasn't going to question him. He was setting the tone, telling me the things you should say and shouldn't say. That's being a leader."

Klecko had a sense of humor, too. He and Alexander appointed themselves in charge of rookie hazing during training camp. "We were on the fire extinguisher crew," Alexander says. "We'd roust the rookies with a wet dream. We had some bottle rockets we used to light and shoot under the rookies' doors and then run down the hall. Normally, they would run out in the hall to see who did it. One time, we decided to mess with the old man, our tight end, Jerome Barkum. We could see the smoke from the bottle rocket coming out from under his door, but Barkum didn't open the door or make a sound. After five minutes, Klecko says, 'You don't think he had a heart attack, do you?' The next thing we heard was Jerome laughing. He got us."

Fields never dominated physically, as Klecko did, because he was slightly undersized, but he was a fighter with the take-charge attitude demanded at center. "Fields is the best center I had in the nineteen years I coached," says Fry. "For the first two years, we were trying to replace him, but when we had to play him, he always played well. By the time we realized he was good enough, he was in the Pro Bowl. He was smart, and he had his input into the game plan. I'd ask him what we should do in different situations."

When his teammates nicknamed Fields "The General" and started drawing stars on his helmet, it was meant to be a joke about his gung-ho approach to the game. But the tag stuck because it was a perfect fit.

"Like a good center, Joe was always the hub," quarterback Pat Ryan says. "He never had any problem about running things on offense. He was really intelligent, and he never missed an assignment. That's how you get to be a leader."

By 1979, the Jets' offensive and defensive lines were solid, and they appeared ready to make a run at their first playoff berth since the 1969 season. But Todd still was struggling to establish himself as the quarterback who could take the Jets to the playoffs. He missed much of the 1978 season because of a broken collarbone that he reinjured when he came back, and backup quarterback

Matt Robinson performed well enough in his place to create a quarterback controversy when training camp opened in 1979. As an Alabama quarterback succeeding Namath in New York, Todd started out facing unusual pressure, and his development was slowed by a changing roster of offensive coordinators. In his first few years, he was a 50 percent passer who tended to throw more interceptions than touchdown passes.

On a personal level, the soft-spoken Todd was well liked. As a player, he had a strong arm, but his reserved nature transmitted a disturbing lack of self-confidence to some of his teammates. Although Todd clearly was more talented than Robinson physically, Robinson had a more forceful personality and had shown he could do a respectable job.

"Matt didn't give a damn about anything," Ryan says. "He let the chips fall where they may. Guys admire that because most of them can't do it. And he never backed away from a good time."

"Matt never rattled; he was 'Cool Hand Luke,' " Klecko adds. "Richard was an emotional basket case. But I didn't have much of an opinion about the whole thing. Defense leaves the offense alone. It's like there are two different teams."

The Jets drafted Robinson in the ninth round in 1977 for the purpose of making him Todd's backup, so, the expectations for Robinson were minimal when Todd's injuries forced him into the lineup in 1978. When the Jets reported for camp the next year, Todd still was considered the starter by most, but Robinson played exceptionally well to win the starting job.

"I still felt Richard should be the starter, and if we got in trouble, we could bring Matt in and expect him to do a decent job," Fields says. "Matt was a great relief pitcher. He'd come in and do what he could do, and if that wasn't enough, he was going home. You couldn't bring Richard off the bench like that because he'd get shaken. He wasn't the kind of guy you could jerk in and out. He had to be in there all the time to get in the flow."

The training-camp battle between Robinson and Todd fed the four New York daily newspapers, as well as the suburban papers, with lively stories throughout what otherwise might have been a dull preseason period. But the announcement that Robinson had won the job hardly signaled an end to the controversy. Quite the opposite.

On Friday night before the regular-season opener against Cleveland, Robinson sprained the thumb on his throwing hand under somewhat mysterious circumstances. Michaels was furious, and he grew angrier when Robinson gave him the old "I-ran-into-a-doorknob" ploy. Trainer Bob Reese and Robinson worked all day and night Saturday to control the swelling by game time. Robinson was able to start even though the thumb had to be taped. The Jets scored late in the game to take a 22–19 lead, and Robinson came to the sidelines and had Reese cut off the tape. But Browns quarterback Brian Sipe guided a last-minute drive for a field goal that sent the game into overtime. Reese re-taped Robinson's thumb for the extra period, but it was too late. The thumb puffed up badly, and Robinson threw a flutterball that fell far short of an open receiver and was intercepted to set up the winning field goal by the Browns.

Now, Michaels was really mad, and he came looking for Klecko, who had been seen with Robinson and three other players Friday night at a bar across the street from the Jets' complex. "Matt was three sheets to the wind that night," Klecko says. "I still was arm-wrestling all the time, and Matt came over to where I was sitting at the bar and said, 'Come on, Joe, you want to arm-wrestle?' I put my arm up on the bar, and I'm still talking to another guy on the other side of me. I let Matt win without much resistance. Somebody told Walt they saw me arm-wrestling with Matt in a bar. On Monday after we lost the game, I was riding a stationary bike in the weight room. Walt comes up and puts his arm on the bike and says, 'Hey, you want to arm-wrestle me?' I looked at him and said, 'What the fuck are you talking about?' He said, 'Somebody's lying to me!' and he walked away. I had no idea what he was talking about or what was going on. He never told me he thought I hurt Matt. We were on the road the next week, and our groundskeeper, Bobby Hansen, came into my hotel room like he couldn't hold back this guilt complex. He says, 'I was the one who told Walt you were arm-wrestling.' That explained why Walt was mad, but Matt didn't get hurt arm-wrestling with me."

In fact, Robinson injured his thumb later that Friday night while wrestling with his roommate, wide receiver Bobby Jones. Fueled by a night of revelry, Robinson kept pestering Jones until he got fed up, grabbed the quarterback and pounced on him in a way that was meant to be playful but ultimately had serious repercussions. The interception Robinson threw against Cleveland was his last pass for the Jets. Todd started the next week at New England, where the Jets suffered a 56–3 loss that was the worst in franchise history. Michaels stuck with Todd the rest of the way in an erratic season in which the Jets salvaged an 8–8 record by winning their last three games.

While Michaels placed his confidence in Todd, the controversy grew more divisive as players chose sides and the team stumbled through a season they remember as the Year of Deep Jet. That was the name *New York Post* beat writer Steve Serby gave to an anonymous source who was critical of Todd's leadership and seemed to be speaking for a large pro-Robinson contingent.

"Guys wanted to know who the hell Deep Jet was," Fields says. "He was saying some things that really were happening, and then he was coming up with things that were being manufactured. The fact he had some things right made Deep Jet credible. It got to Richard and bothered him more and more. You wonder why somebody would continue to say these things and create turmoil in the quarterback's head. It wasn't helping the team win. It seemed like Serby was riding Richard almost every day in the papers. A player can only handle so much when there's pressure to win and play well."

Strong undercurrents of suspicion, animosity, and not a little bitterness roiled the waters in the Jets' locker room day after day that season. Always sensitive to criticism, Todd withdrew from all but his closest friends on the team.

"Matt probably did have a little bigger following because of his personality," Ryan says. "Richard felt threatened by the whole situation, and he kept up his guard toward his teammates. He didn't know where he stood with them, and he felt a lot of them weren't behind him."

"It shook Richard up, and I can see why," says Alexander, who was among Todd's best friends. "All of a sudden, they were going to give the job to Matt. It divided the team. You'd hear little comments when players were out in the bars. You knew which side people were on. It was an uneasy situation."

Even though the Jets traded Robinson to Denver before the 1980 draft, the memory of Deep Jet had a lingering effect on Todd's relationship with his teammates in subsequent seasons. It was like a scar that remained to remind him of a painful time.

Because Fields and Todd had the most responsibility for how the offense performed, they occasionally bickered on the field. "Richard always thought I liked Matt Robinson better than him, which wasn't true," Fields says. "If I yelled at him, he'd say, 'You always liked Matt better than me, anyway.' He said it jokingly, but I knew that's how he felt.

"If he did something wrong or called something I didn't like during games, I'd give him a dirty look. He'd never say anything. In one game, he checked off to the wrong play against a certain defense. He called for us to run it one way when we were supposed to run it the other way. I turned my head and was saying, 'No, Richard, no!' He kept calling the signals, and we blocked down and gained seven yards. I jumped off the ground and scowled at him, and he yelled at me, 'I'm the quarterback! I'm the quarterback! I'll call what I want to call!' We went down and kicked a field goal, and he came off the field and asked the line coach, Bob Fry, 'Which way was I supposed to run that play?' Richard and I had our ins and outs, but he was a good guy."

With the quarterback controversy behind them and the memory of a strong finish as evidence they were ready to win, the Jets went into the 1980 season thinking they had a chance to reach the Super Bowl. Under the category of famous last words, Fields predicted they would win the division. But the Jets started the season with five straight losses on their way to a 4–12 record, and Todd led the NFL with 30 interceptions. It was a total team breakdown. In the fifteenth week of the season, the Jets even contrived to lose at home to the New Orleans Saints, who were 0–14 to that point.

"I think it was a maturity thing," Klecko says. "We didn't know what it was like to be winners or to fight back from adversity. We were a bunch of young kids, and losing didn't really bother us that much. Why, I don't know. Losing is a contagious thing, and so is winning. There were times the next year when we'd be down in the fourth quarter and know we were going to win. Not knowing how, but believing we were going to win."

Despite the disappointment of the 1980 season, the core of the team Walt Michaels had assembled was on the verge of reaching NFL maturity, but the quarterback situation still needed to be stabilized. Michaels made it a policy never to bother his quarterbacks, some said, because he was afraid of the problems they could create. But it was clear he needed to find someone to help Todd begin to realize his talent. In Washington, a new administration was coming in for the 1981 season, and outgoing Redskins offensive coordinator Joe Walton was available. Michaels hired Walton to be Todd's personal counselor and quarterbacking guru.

It took a few games for Todd to get the hang of Walton's high-percentage passing game, but when he did, the change was profound. Suddenly, the Jets had a dangerous offense to go with a monster pass rush. At last, they were ready to replace potential with performance. The post-Namath Jets were on their way to the playoffs for the first time in twelve years.

The New York Sack Exchange

In the middle of the afternoon on Tuesday, November 24, 1981, trading on the floor of the New York Stock Exchange stopped; the engine driving the wheels of commerce slipped into neutral, and the price of everything from AT&T to Xerox froze for two minutes in time. What, short of the death of a sitting President, could bring about such a momentary glitch in the graph charting the progress of the Dow Jones average? This rare occurrence was caused by the presence of four visiting dignitaries, Joe Klecko, Mark Gastineau, Marty Lyons, and Abdul Salaam, who formed a defensive line known as the "New York Sack Exchange."

It's mind-boggling to think that four football players from the Jets could make traders at the world's most important financial center take their minds off business for even two minutes, but it was the first taste of pro football success for New Yorkers after more than a decade of failure by the Jets and even longer by the Giants. If there's one thing stockbrokers love, it's a winner, and the New York Sack Exchange was made up of four bulls who were running roughshod over the Oilers, Patriots, Giants, and Dolphins and would have trampled the Bears, too, if they had been on the schedule.

The phenomenon of the Sack Exchange captured the imagination of New Yorkers in the same way the name of "Broadway Joe" Namath once had. It was the perfect marriage of PR and performance, hitting on a nerve running from the Jets' Madison

Avenue offices to the defensive line's Wall Street namesake. It had that ethnocentric "I Love New York" ring to it. Oh God, how the hotshot copy writers at Young & Rubicam would have loved to have come up with that one! But this most clever of sports nicknames did not spring from one of the big ad agencies or the back-page imagination of some tabloid headline writer.

The "New York Sack Exchange" name became the logo identified with the Jets through the efforts of a quiet, earnest, twenty-seven-year-old man named Pepper Burruss, who worked as an assistant trainer for the Jets and also led Bible study sessions for a small group of players. During a game in which the Jets bounced New England quarterback Steve Grogan off the Shea Stadium turf eight times, Burruss happened to notice a cloth banner in the stands that read: N.Y. SACK EXCHANGE. On his way into work the next morning, Burruss was listening to the stock report on his car radio when the idea came to him to write a weekly tongue-in-cheek report detailing the achievements of the defense. He distributed it in-house for the amusement of the team and office personnel.

"I wrote it as a stock report and put the Business Day logo from *The New York Times* financial section at the top," Burruss recalls. "We had nicknames for guys that I used as the name of a stock. Abdul Salaam was known for his hats, so his company was Salaam Hats. There was Klecko International (as in International Harvester trucks and heavy equipment), Lyons' Loonies, and Gastineau Theatrics. I'd start by saying, 'Gold is up, the dollar is down, and the New York Sack Exchange gained four.' If we had eight sacks and the other team had four, I'd write, 'Gainers outpaced losers, two to one.' Instead of the Amex, we had the Enemex opponent board to keep track of enemy sacks compared to the New York Exchange."

After the Jets enjoyed a second eight-sack game against New England on November 15 to set a club season record with 46 sacks, while the offensive line allowed no sacks by the Patriots, Burruss wrote: "This week's index peaked at a 21-year high, opening Monday morning fixed at 46. The previous New York summit was 43 reached in 1968. Analysts were left all wet when they discovered winners shut out losers on the big board for the first time in recent history in what was termed 'Bull Utopia.' With the shutout looming inevitable, losers tried to average down but could not get the sale past the brokerage house of Alexander, Rasmussen, Ward, Powell and Fields. The subsidiary house of Roman and Waldemore protected early gains with some impressive shelter offers. The bell tolled for the big board onslaught 1 point below the year's record volume of 9 reached during the November 1 Meadowlands exchange. Big board actives were led by Klecko International up 3 to 15½, followed by Gastineau Theatrics up 3 to fix at 14."

A story giving Burruss credit for the idea appeared in *The Sporting News*, and Jim Kensil, the president of the team, got an irate phone call from the fan who made the banner. "He wasn't really mad; he was just a true Jet fan who wanted credit for thinking it up," Burruss says, "I told the guy, 'This thing's a joke. I dreamt up the stock report. What you did, and what I did are two different things.' It was not my idea, but I made it fly. It became an intriguing thing for insiders. They were dying to see this thing."

By midseason, Jets publicity director Frank Ramos had picked up on the "Sack Exchange" name and was publicizing it as part of the Jets' weekly news release. After the name hit the newspapers, a broker contacted the Jets and arranged for Klecko, Gastineau, Lyons, and Salaam to visit the trading floor and have lunch on their day off as guests of his brokerage and the New York Stock Exchange.

The brokerage sent a limo to pick the players up at the Jets' Long Island complex. The first thing Klecko and Lyons did was order the driver to stop at a delicatessen to pick up a ration of beer for the forty-five-minute ride into lower Manhattan.

"We were drinking the whole time on the way to Wall Street," Klecko says, laughing at the thought of how they played the celebrity scene to the hilt. "We turned the corner onto Wall Street and saw the whole block was packed with people. Every TV station had its cameras there. We all put our sunglasses on when we got out of the limo. We were kicking ass. Empty beer cans fell out of the car, and we were laughing. This is what it was all about. We walked across the floor of the exchange to go upstairs to the club, and everybody was going crazy and yelling, 'Jets! Jets! Jets!' "

After lunch with the brokers and Stock Exchange officials, the four players were paraded onto a balcony overlooking the trading floor. Spontaneously, trading stopped and the traders began cheering the players, who led them in chants of "Jets! Jets! Jets!" and "Defense! Defense! Defense!"

"It was unbelievable," Klecko says, "We actually stopped trading on Wall Street."

Oh, there may have been a few diligent traders trying to work the phones amid the commotion, which was remarkable even by Wall Street standards. "You want how many shares of IBM? Did you say five hundred or nine hundred?" Stock Exchange officials were touchy on that point. They instructed the Jets' public relations people not to use the term "stopped trading." But that, in fact, is exactly what happened.

It was a heady time for everyone involved. Win in New York, and the world is a blank check. NBC ran footage of the Sack Exchange's Wall Street appearance as the lead-in to the Jets' next game, and within three weeks, Pro-Keds offered $50,000 to pose for a poster to Klecko and Gastineau, who were dueling for the NFL lead in quarterback sacks. The "New York Sack Exchange" was fast-becoming a show biz commodity, but there were growing behind-the-scenes problems between Gastineau and his teammates. Having readily grasped the power of publicity, Gastineau was intent on breaking off from the group to do a solo. His vehicle was the sack dance, a foot-stomping, fist-pumping gyration he performed after each sack that upstaged his teammates, humiliated his opponents, worked the crowd into a frenzy, and, most importantly, drew the television lenses in for close-up shots.

The negotiations for the poster were typical of Gastineau's concern only for himself. "A lot of people wanted just me and Mark to do appearances, and I refused unless they took all four of us," Klecko says. "The New York Sack Exchange was four guys. When Pro-Keds made the offer for the poster, Mark was all for the two of us doing it. He said, 'Gee, we could have a lot of money.' I said no. That wasn't important to me. I told him I wouldn't do it unless Abdul and Marty were in it, but Mark didn't want to split the money four ways. The poster never would have happened if I hadn't decided to give up part of my share so Ab and Marty could do it and get paid. Mark made twenty-five thousand dollars, and I only got fifteen thousand. Ab and Marty split the rest. I knew what it meant to them. They knew I would not do the poster without them, but they never knew the money came from my share. I think it kept us together as a defense."

The Year of the Sack Exchange began with the Jets in a three-game depression. They started with a 31–0 loss at Buffalo, fol-

lowed by a last-minute 31–30 home loss to Cincinnati in which
the pass rush showed signs of developing into a weapon, and
then, they nosedived again in a 38–10 loss at Pittsburgh. The
brunt of fan and media criticism fell heavily on quarterback Richard Todd and coach Walt Michaels.

"It got a little tight, but Walt never really condemned any single
person," Klecko says. "It was a team thing. He didn't lose his cool.
Walt never beat us into the ground. We did what we had to do
in practice, and he got us off the field. He saved our legs, and that
helped get us to the playoffs."

The turnaround began in a 33–17 victory over Houston in
which quarterback Ken Stabler, who was sacked eight times, was
battered so badly it was hard not to feel sorry for the old gray-
beard. "We were feared," Klecko says. "People were worried about
lining up against us; you could see it in their eyes. It was third-
and-ten, and you knew we were coming. The way we got after
quarterbacks was unbelievable. I don't think you'll ever see that
kind of dominance again in the NFL by a four-man line because
offensive linemen have gotten so much bigger and better and the
game is geared toward offense."

The offense caught fire in that game against the Oilers when
Todd took a pitchback from a running back and hit a surprise
touchdown pass. "As an offense, we knew that if we could get
seven or ten points ahead, nobody was coming back against us,"
says Joe Fields, who was on his way to being voted the AFC's Pro
Bowl center for the first time. "No one could pass consistently
against us without getting sacked."

"And the thing of it was that we not only got so many sacks,
but we beat quarterbacks up," Klecko adds. "If we weren't sacking
them, we were hitting them. I could sense they were looking
around. They were going down before we even got there. Abdul
was such a good stop guy at tackle against the run, which was
good because he was on Mark's side, and Mark didn't play the
run. Marty was the same way, very tough up the middle. Then,
we had me and Gastineau on the ends. It was a scary thing to go
against us because you couldn't double-team everybody."

In his first four seasons, Klecko totaled 33½ sacks and had
begun to establish a reputation throughout the league, but the
Pittsburgh Steelers' defensive line, known as the "Steel Curtain,"
made it difficult for other defensive linemen to gain public rec-

ognition. The fact that the Jets were not a playoff team worked against Klecko in the Pro Bowl vote, though he was an alternate behind Pittsburgh's L. C. Greenwood in 1979 and 1980.

From the year Klecko led NFL rookies in sacks, he was a force, but the Jets didn't have much of a supporting cast until they drafted Lyons and Gastineau 1–2 in 1979. "I carried a lot of the load on the line," Klecko says of his early NFL years. "I never had that other player who could break things open for me. I had Richard Neal next to me, and the other end was Lawrence Pillers, who wasn't bad but didn't do anything exceptional. When Gastineau came along, you could see he was a great pass-rusher. The defensive line jelled because other teams had to worry about both of us, and it made the other two guys in the middle play a little bit harder and better. And I had Lance Mehl playing behind me at outside linebacker in 1981. He was a hell of a ballplayer. Everywhere I went, he went, and that helped a lot.

"I liked Marty right off the bat when he and Gastineau were rookies because Marty was a little bit of a rowdy guy. Mark never hung out with us even back then. He tried to be friends, but you could see where he was coming from. He met his wife that year, a flashy blonde, and he started with his act. But I had to play with him, and I was always happy to get guys who could help us."

The Sack Exchange had one totally unpublicized ingredient that contributed to its success. Defensive line coach Dan Sekanovich, who joined the Jets when Klecko was a rookie, was an outstanding teacher and a good friend to his players.

"Dan meant a lot to me," says Klecko. "If you made an appearance around his town, he'd come listen to you talk. He was sincere, not a phony. Dan taught me everything I know about pass-rushing techniques. That's important because sometimes you have to rely on your skills when natural ability isn't enough. You have to get the feel of a situation. I concentrated on the small things Dan taught me—shoulder technique, countering moves, and how to use my hands. In a game, it came naturally. When you're getting beat, you revert to the basic things you learned. I wouldn't lose my cool. I'd talk to myself and tell myself what to do."

Klecko assumed control of the defensive line for Sekanovich on the field, and his self-confidence had a positive effect on everyone around him. "Whenever he had to do something, he did it with authority," Sekanovich says. "He was a leader by action. I don't ever remember Joe Klecko having a bad football game. He was technically sound against the run and the pass, plus he was a bull rusher and had a change of pace. Once, I saw Joe pick up a two-hundred-eighty-pound offensive tackle two feet off the ground without breaking stride to get a sack. On the next play, Joe came with an arm-over move and got another sack. I couldn't wait until third downs that year."

Still, the Jets' 1–3 start hardly seemed promising, especially since they were headed to Miami to face Don Shula and the Dolphins. A back-and-forth game full of big plays on both sides resulted in a 28–28 tie, and another fifteen minutes of overtime failed to produce a winner. They still were just 1–3–1, but the Jets knew now they could play a little.

"That game proved a lot as far as us being a team of fighters," Fields says. "We ran ninety plays. The temperature was ninety degrees with eighty-seven percent humidity. Five quarters. The guys beside you were just dead, dead. But everybody kept doing it, and we felt like we'd won because we all were exhausted but nobody came out. It was such a brutal game, and the way we faced hardship brought the team together."

Through the first five games, the Jets had allowed 145 points. In the next eleven games, they gave up just 142 points and held eight opponents to 15 points or less. Four weeks after the tie at Miami, the Sack Exchange had a 9-sack game, including 3 by Klecko, in a 26–7 victory over the Giants in front of the Giants' crowd. The win evened the Jets' record at 4–4–1, and it also was the start of a five-game winning streak.

During the eleven-game stretch in which the Jets mounted their run at the playoffs and the Sack Exchange went after the NFL team record for most sacks in a season, Joe Klecko essentially was playing on one foot. He had injured his left foot at Miami when Lyons stepped on it, causing some torn tendons and a deep bruise on the top of the foot.

"I played on it and played on it and made it worse," Klecko says. "It didn't cause problems; I was leading the league in sacks. It just hurt, and I couldn't walk on it. There was a lot of soft tissue and ligament damage. I took painkilling shots to numb it, but that was just something I thought you did. I could drive off it because adrenaline overcomes the pain."

Including the playoffs, Klecko spent the last twelve weeks of the greatest season of his life on crutches. After each game, his injured foot was placed in a cast to immobilize it. He never practiced. But on Sundays, the cast came off, Klecko took a shot once before each game and once again at halftime, and he played. He didn't give much consideration to questions about the risk of further injury or the long-term effects on his foot. Klecko was in the middle of a season so amazing that it seemed like a work of fiction. If injections of Marcaine and cortisone were what it took for him to continue playing, that was just a fact of NFL life.

"The needle was four inches long, but it never bothered me," Klecko says. "Fields held my foot down because it would jerk when they put the needle in. It hurts, but it goes away very quickly. They don't just stick it in a vein. They move it all around and shoot you in different areas. They'd stick it in the top of my foot, and then, they'd go through the bottom of my foot."

"Sometimes, you can see the needle bend," Fields says. "I'd look at Joe and go, 'Ooooh, Joey.' He'd be watching my face, and he'd say, 'Shut up.' The only time it bothered me was when they went through the bottom of his foot; it's such a sensitive area. But you really get hardened to needles. I had to get my foot shot for the second half of a game against New Orleans one season. It was like having a stump instead of a foot."

Painkilling shots are fairly commonplace, but what Klecko did in 1981 went far above and beyond the call of duty in the eyes of coach Walt Michaels and his teammates. It took an act of will to keep going as he did while still maintaining an extraordinary level of play.

"A lot of it was mental," Klecko explains. "The films show I limped during games, but it never really affected me. My foot never bothered me the rest of my career, but I don't know what it will be like down the road as I get older. I did anything to play. I was stupid in that way, I guess. Playing hurt is something that hurt me toward the end of my career, but it helped me to be the hard-nosed guy I was throughout my career. I've played with a lot of bad things. More than anything, I think it meant something to my teammates, knowing I would do that and play so well. It gave them a lot less to complain about."

If Klecko was a source of inspiration to his teammates, Mark Gastineau, for all his wondrous physical gifts and his ability as a pass rusher, was a source of exasperation. It's hard for a player having as good a season as Gastineau was having, a Pro Bowl season, to do so much to become a pariah among his teammates.

He stood 6-5 and weighed 270 pounds, and he could run the 40-yard dash in 4.55 seconds. His speed on the outside was a major factor in the success of the New York Sack Exchange, but it was clear Gastineau was more concerned with self-promotion than he was with winning. Gastineau grew up in the mountain country of northern Arizona and later moved with his family to a rural community in Oklahoma. After quitting the football team at Arizona State University, he finished college at East Central Oklahoma. He was a small-town kid with big-time dreams that were whispered in his ear by his father, known to one and all as Big Ernie.

Part of the thrill of playing pro football is hearing the applause when you play well and the team wins. But Gastineau apparently was trying to generate applause and attention for himself through something that had nothing to do with playing the game of football—the sack dance. It was an extraneous event, irrelevant, nonessential. It served one purpose, and that was the glorification, not of the Jets, but of Mark Gastineau. Most of the time, his sacks came at times when the Jets' defense was taking control of the game, so some show of enthusiasm was appropriate. But the sack dance was more like a "floor show" of enthusiasm. And on those occasions when he recorded a sack at a time when the Jets were losing, Gastineau performed his routine anyway.

Gastineau's first sack dance, by his own account, was a spontaneous response to one of the 2 sacks he had as a rookie. He became a starter in 1980 and led the Jets with 11½ sacks, one more than Klecko, and he began to do the sack dance on a regular basis. By 1981, Gastineau's act was a fixture anticipated by the fans and dreaded by his teammates. Big Ernie made it clear in interviews with reporters that he had big ideas in the field of commercial endorsements for his son, and he even hoped to include other members of the family. Gastineau's agent, Gary Wichard, got him a national television commercial in which Gastineau and his mother appeared to promote an electric shaver. But after Wichard and Gastineau ended their relationship, the agent said the sack dance, far from being spontaneous, was as choreographed and as phony as professional wrestling.

"There was a camaraderie among the defense, but Gastineau alienated himself with the dancing," Klecko says. "When it started, I think he was really sincere. He was that excited. He was a young, dumb kid. When he found out it could bring him some notoriety, boy, did he start playing to the crowd. After one game that we won in 1981, Lenny Dawson came down on the field to do a television interview with me and Mark. I'm standing there, and Dawson is waiting. But Mark was running around the stadium jumping up and down and waving and putting on a big show for the fans. I finally walked off and said, 'I'll see you later. I ain't waiting for that fucking idiot.' That's when it really started irking me. I used to talk to Mark about it. I'd say things like, 'How would you like to be the offensive tackle?' He used to pacify me, saying, 'Yeah, I know, Joe.' He lied to me more than anyone about the things he was doing on the field to attract attention. He lied about the sack dance all the time.

"One time, I took him into Rob Reese's office in the training room and locked the door and wouldn't let anybody in. I threatened him and told him to cut out the bullshit. I pounded my finger through his chest. He said, 'Yeah, okay, all right,' and he went out and did the same thing."

The Jets were on a roll, and the Sack Exchange was piling it on opponents when Lyons went public with the feud in an interview with the New York *Daily News*. The headline read: KLECKO, LYONS DESPISE GASTINEAU. Michaels called the three of them into his office and angrily told them to put an end to their argument and concentrate on football. Then, Sekanovich took them aside for a discussion.

"Sek asked Mark a question, and Mark lied through his teeth," Klecko says. "I don't remember the question, but I told Mark, 'You're a no-good, fucking liar. Why don't you just try to be one of the guys?' He sat there like a puppy and didn't say a word. Sek told us to handle it, and I said, 'No problem, Dan. Forget it.' Marty continued to say things to Gastineau, but from that day on, I stopped bugging the kid.

"Our disagreements didn't interfere with anything on the field, or I would have taken care of it. It put a strain on public appearances by the Sack Exchange. Mark always wanted to be on a pedestal. He'd come late all the time or stand by himself or not show up, always something to set him apart. Mark did the same thing on the field. He'd stand apart from the huddle, sometimes with his helmet off, to attract attention from the TV cameras. In later years, I did get on him about getting in the huddle during games."

Neither Michaels nor Sekanovich ever told Gastineau to stop dancing. The team needed Gastineau's sacks, and it was easier to ask others to live with it and let him do his thing. "I know the sack dance disturbed a lot of people, but it didn't disturb me," Sekanovich says. "I told Mark, 'If that's how you truly feel, I don't see anything wrong with it.' People on other teams frowned on it, and it upset our players. But it was hard for me to control."

It wasn't long before Gastineau's teammates began coming up with derisive nicknames for him, such as "Gasti-Don't-Know" and "Manchild," meaning he had the body of a man and the mind of a child. But the nickname of choice was "Scarecrow" after the character in *The Wizard of Oz*, who often lamented, "If I only had a brain." Gastineau complained that many of his teammates shunned him, and it was true. There were times when he sat down to eat during training camp that other players would get up and walk away. If they had to live with his self-promotion, he was going to have to live with their disapproval.

Klecko and Gastineau had no other major confrontations after the one in Reese's office, though Klecko did tell Gastineau on a couple of occasions to stay away from him. Gastineau said he was ostracized because of jealousy over the recognition and endorsements he received, but Klecko denies that was the case.

"I did not give a damn about endorsements," Klecko says. "I got my share and was happy. As God is my judge, nothing he received ever bothered me. I got a lot of respect from other players. They would say, 'If it wasn't for you...' I even took that with a grain of salt. A lot of it was because of hatred of him, and I knew that. Nobody that I know in the league liked him, nobody."

But nobody could deny the impact Gastineau could have on a game with his big plays. Sacks and consistent pressure disrupt the flow of an offense, put teams in obvious passing situations that allow the defense to step up the pressure and lead to penalties on linemen trying to get into their pass-sets too quickly and interceptions thrown by quarterbacks who don't have time to pick out their target.

Gastineau always said sacks were like home runs in baseball. The problem was that Gastineau also committed a lot of errors on defense that were overshadowed by his sacks. Other players often had to cover up for his mistakes. Once offenses realized he didn't play the run very well, they would run draw plays to his side or pull a tackle to trap-block him to the outside while the back ran behind a tight end who was trying to seal off pursuit from the inside. At other times, offenses would take advantage of

Gastineau's hard upfield charge by floating swing passes or screen passes over his head. The outside linebacker was partly responsible for those passes, but he got no help from Gastineau, whose self-centered play sometimes hurt as much as his sacks helped.

In all his years with the Jets, Gastineau seemed never to realize how dependent he was on those around him to make it possible for him to get free, and he either never understood the defense or ignored basic rules for how to play his position. As a rookie, Klecko also relied on natural ability much of the time, but over the years, he learned proper techniques and understood the defensive concept.

"When I was a rookie, I had a strength advantage, but I didn't know how to channel it until my third year," Klecko says. "I guess I know how Gastineau felt all his life. He never knew what the hell he was doing.

"At his peak, Gastineau was an awesome pass-rusher. There was no doubt. He played the run badly, but he was such a good athlete that he could make up for his mistakes by catching up to a runner or getting back into a hole he had just opened up. It didn't bother him that he was doing things wrong. I think the coaches felt it was better to leave him alone rather than try to discipline him. I tried to impress on Mark what everybody around him did for him.

"Greg Buttle, who was the outside linebacker on Mark's side, used to bitch all the time because Mark would get Buttle killed on certain plays. Buttle would get hollered at, and Mark would go scot-free. That kind of thing really bothered me. I always told the coaches it was horseshit. It showed all the rest of the guys Mark could get away with it, and they felt slighted. The defensive backs were bothered by Mark's antics more than anyone. They didn't always realize how much the pass rush meant to them. They thought they were doing a good job when the pass rush was knocking the shit out of the quarterback. They would blame Mark when he didn't get a pass rush.

"Mark was so vulnerable to the run that Abdul, who played the tackle next to him, was told not to rush the passer so he could stay home and cover up for Mark. Abdul saved his ass a lot. More than Mark will ever realize. Mark would say, 'Yeah, I know,' but then, he'd tell someone else he didn't need the SOB beside him.

"Mark never knew defense. The defenses we played together for nine years, he never knew what the fuck they were. The linebackers would line him up, or I would tell him where to line up. A lot of times, he would ignore the call because he knew he'd be blocked down and taken out of something. So, he'd line up wide. He never seemed willing to sacrifice his chances for making a sack so that someone else could make the tackle."

Despite their differences regarding the sack dance, Klecko still tried to work with Gastineau on various technical aspects of playing defensive line. Gastineau watched and listened politely, even solicitously, but the lessons never took. Once the game started, he was back to the old Gastineau, taking one wide rush after another with the occasional spin move thrown in. He didn't much like to run stunts with the tackle next to him because it meant looping inside and getting caught in traffic, and even though Gastineau had tremendous leg strength and a well-developed upper body, he never learned how to bull-rush or overpower his opponents. When Gastineau lost just a fraction of the speed on which he relied for his explosive first step off the ball and his recovery steps, it ruined him as an effective player because he never developed the technical skills to compensate.

Linebacker Lance Mehl spent most of his career playing behind Klecko when he was an end and moved to inside linebacker when Klecko moved to nose tackle. But he also played behind Gastineau at times. "The difference was like night and day," Mehl says. "Mark just played the pass. I told Buttle, 'I know what you're going through.' I started and played behind Mark in the 1981 opener at Buffalo. We were down 31–0 in the fourth quarter, and it was obvious Buffalo was going to run out the clock. I told Mark, 'Close it down because they're going to run the ball.' Mark kept rushing upfield, and Buffalo ran a power play at me three or four times in a row. Finally, Walt Michaels pulls me out of the game and says, 'You've had enough of that.' He could see what Mark was doing.

"When I played outside linebacker behind Klecko, I just looked to see which way Joe was going, and I went the other way. Without question, it freed me up to make tackles. Once against Baltimore, the lead back was blocking down against Joe, and the off guard was pulling to block me. I mentioned it to Klecko, and he said, 'Don't worry about it; it won't happen again.' The next time they tried it, Joe threw the lead back into the guard, and I was there waiting to tackle the ballcarrier. Joe got smarter as he got older."

Tales of Klecko picking up opponents and tossing them aside

abound among those who played with him. He could bench press 535 pounds, military press 405 pounds, squat 800 pounds, and leg press 1,400 pounds. The combination of his steel-clamp grip and his knack for using leverage enabled him to lift opponents while he was in motion toward the ballcarrier or the quarterback.

"We played the Oilers at Shea Stadium in 1980," recalls right guard Dan Alexander. "They had a tackle named Angelo Fields who weighed about three hundred pounds. Klecko bull-rushed the guy, grabbed him under the armpits, picked him up in the air, threw him on the ground, and made the sack. It was like the guy wasn't even there. Everybody talked about that one for years. At my wedding reception, all these little kids were hanging around Klecko and asking how strong he was. I said, 'Pick me up and show them.' I'm wearing a tuxedo, and he grabs me by the legs and shoulders and presses me over his head. I'm two hundred seventy-five pounds of dead weight."

In the second game of the 1981 season, Klecko picked up 6-6, 280-pound Cincinnati offensive tackle Anthony Munoz, who became a perennial Pro Bowl selection. Bob Fry, who was the Jets' offensive line coach at the time, says, "Klecko spun Munoz like he was a revolving door and carried him back to the quarterback. Munoz talked to me about it when I was coaching at the Pro Bowl after the 1982 season. It was amazing to him."

The play that stands out in Klecko's mind involved a slightly smaller player that he hefted with a more spectacular effect. "I kind of caught a Miami running back off balance, and I had all the momentum," Klecko says. "I picked him up over the top of my head with one hand and slammed him. It was an awesome-looking thing on film. The coaches would run back films of me running somebody over like a lady and them barely touching me. That's where confidence comes in."

With Klecko's strength on one side of the defense and Gastineau's speed on the other, it seemed as if the Jets' opponents were caught between Scylla and Charybdis, the rock and the whirlpool, the twin terrors of mythology. No matter which course an offense chose, it risked destruction. Only two baffling losses to a poor Seattle team marred the Jets' record in the eleven games that followed the tie at Miami as the Year of the Sack Exchange progressed. The Jets' offense had its finest moment in the rematch against the Dolphins in late November at Shea Stadium. Todd took a painkilling injection for a rib injury and played on a sprained ankle but managed to lead the Jets on a drive in the final minutes of the game that ended with a touchdown pass to tight end Jerome Barkum for a 16–15 victory. But it was the Jets' defense that overwhelmed opponents game after game. In the Jets' last eight victories, the point totals for their opponents were: 14, 7, 14, 6, 15, 0, 13, and 3.

The Jets clinched their first playoff berth in twelve seasons with a 14–13 victory in the fifteenth week at bitter-cold Cleveland. All that remained to be decided in the final game against Green Bay at Shea Stadium was the outcome of the sack race between Gastineau and Klecko and whether or not the New York Sack Exchange could get the 10 sacks needed to tie the league record of 67 sacks in a season set by the 1967 Oakland Raiders.

For the first time since injuring his foot eleven weeks earlier at Miami, Klecko tried to get by without taking a painkiller before the game. "I sacked Lynn Dickey on the Packers' third play, and I couldn't take the pain in my foot," Klecko says. "I just looked at the bench and ran into the tunnel leading to the locker room. The doctor knew what I wanted. The reporters asked me after the game why I went in, and I just said, 'My tape job was killing me, and I had to retape it.' The truth was I couldn't exist without the shot that day."

Dickey took a fearful pounding in a 28–3 loss as the Jets sacked him nine times to finish the season with 66 sacks, one short of the NFL record. The four members of the Sack Exchange accounted for 53½ of those sacks. Going into the game, Klecko and Gastineau were tied for the league lead in sacks, but Klecko added 2½ sacks to Gastineau's 2 that day to finish with 20½ sacks and win the NFL sack title by exactly half a sack. Klecko also averaged 8.5 quarterback pressures per game, while Gastineau was credited with a 7.2 average.

John DiGregorio, the equipment manager who convinced Klecko to attend Temple so that he would have a chance to make it to the NFL, has a theory that Klecko's rivalry with Gastineau was the motivating factor that drove him to overcome his foot injury and win the sack title in 1981. But Klecko doesn't see it in quite the same light.

"When it got down to the end of the year with me nipping-and-tucking with Mark, it meant something to be the one to lead the league," Klecko says. "Being the best in the league meant a lot, but the fact I beat Mark out to do it did not mean a lot. I'm sure a lot of people won't believe that, but I never wanted to show Mark up in particular. I just wanted to be the best."

Klecko was the consensus choice as NFL defensive player of the year. "I could not believe I was being compared to great players like Dick Butkus and Randy White and all the great pass-rushers," Klecko says. "The adulation I received for that one year is enough for a lifetime. Paul Zimmerman of *Sports Illustrated* made me his most valuable player of the league; Kenny Anderson was chosen by everybody else because he took Cincinnati to the Super Bowl. I don't care if it's just one man's opinion, but somebody had the consciousness to put me on that level. I was there, and it was a hell of an honor."

Two years before there ever was a Sack Exchange, Dan Sekanovich told Klecko he was good enough to make the Hall of Fame if he continued to work at it, and that really was all the motivation Klecko ever needed. "Sek knew what to say to turn me on," Klecko says. "From the day he said I had a chance to make the Hall of Fame, I always dreamed about it."

"I told Joe, 'Reach for the stars; you're looking at being enshrined,'" Sekanovich says. "I felt he was destined for greatness. In his time, he was the most feared and most respected football player in the NFL."

While Klecko and Gastineau are linked as members of the Sack Exchange, the rivalry is such that Klecko doesn't feel the player who was at the opposite end of the line and the spectrum from him merits election to the Hall of Fame. "I'd feel that it was a very big injustice if he got in," Klecko says. "It would be a product of media hype more than of him being a complete player. Mark was a good ballplayer, but he was one-dimensional. I don't think he was dominant, except for one or two years. He wasn't as good as he could have been."

But in 1981, Klecko, Gastineau, Lyons, and Salaam were as dominant as any four-man defensive line before them in NFL history. Sekanovich has a tape of all 66 sacks by which to remember the New York Sack Exchange, which is a good thing because injuries and changes in coaches and defenses altered it forever the next season.

Even the 1981 season seemed to end prematurely for the Sack Exchange and the Jets, who lost a 31–27 decision to Buffalo in the wild-card playoff game, which was played two days after Christmas at Shea Stadium. The Jets got off to a disastrous start when the Bills recovered a fumble on the opening kickoff to score a touchdown and added two long touchdown passes for a 24–0 lead in the second quarter. The Jets rallied, but Todd threw an interception after reaching the Bills' 11-yard line with fourteen seconds left to play.

Only then did Klecko yield to the pain he had endured for twelve weeks since his foot injury. "There was a great picture of me coming off the field after the Buffalo playoff game," Klecko recalls. "I had to turn my foot sideways and drag it because it hurt so fucking bad."

When they were on a roll, the young Jets began to believe for the first time that they were good enough to reach the Super Bowl, but the miserable fashion in which they lost left them with a sick feeling about the opportunity they had wasted. Walt Michaels kept his final speech to the team the next day short and to the point.

Still seething over the loss, Michaels walked into the team meeting and yelled, "I hope you enjoy your fucking New Year's!" Then he walked out. And on that note, the Year of the Sack Exchange ended.

The Ring That Got Away

Keep the pedal to the metal. The truck driver's creed was a way of life for Joe Klecko. Playing with a foot injury for twelve weeks of the 1981 season conditioned Klecko to push himself to his physical limits. He had learned to trust in three things—doctors, painkillers, and his own ability to ignore pain. When questions of how to treat injuries arose, Klecko never considered applying the brakes. He looked for ways to jury-rig his body to keep it rolling from one game to the next, and he tried not to think about that oil slick over the next hill. With the help of the painkillers that made it possible for him to play in 1981, he had been NFL defensive player of the year. Nothing could stop him. Driven by a vision of himself as the role model of physical and mental toughness required to excel in pro football, Klecko was determined to play as long as he could limp onto the field as an example to his teammates.

During the 1982 preseason, Klecko developed tendinitis in his right knee after injuring the patella tendon early in training camp. At first, he nursed the knee, skipping an exhibition at Green Bay and playing just two series of downs at Houston. But then, he played three painful quarters against the Giants, and because they felt he needed the work to prepare for the regular season, coach Walt Michaels, team physician James Nicholas, and trainer Bob Reese encouraged Klecko to play in the final exhibition game against Denver.

"My knee was sore, sore, sore, but I tried to play anyway," Klecko says. "I was a young, dumb kid. In the second half, I was just standing out there. There were times I couldn't get in my stance and just plant on it because it hurt so damn bad."

Klecko later said in a newspaper interview that he asked Nicholas and Reese to inject the knee after the Denver game so that he could play on it and they refused. In fact, he agreed to an injection, and he was trying to shield the Jets' medical team from potential media criticism for the way his injury was handled.

"Dr. Nicholas shot it with cortisone after the Denver game," Klecko admits. "Everybody told me later I shouldn't have done that. It never really got better. I don't know if I could've said no. I don't know how it would've been looked upon."

Klecko's right leg was placed in a splint to immobilize it, and he was unable to practice the week before the regular-season opener against Miami at Shea Stadium. Nicholas, Reese, and Klecko then met to consider the options concerning treatment of his patella tendon.

"They talked extremes, the low extremes and the high extremes," Klecko says. "The doctor has to make you aware of the worst possibility. We talked rupture a lot, but I don't believe they thought there was that much of a risk."

Nicholas and Reese said at the time they had no way of knowing exactly how severe the damage was to Klecko's patella tendon, the strongest tendon in the body. In eleven previous seasons in pro football, Reese never had seen a patella tendon rupture. He told Klecko the injury would take longer to heal if he played on it but that it would improve gradually. Nicholas said he advised Klecko he could spend six to eight weeks wearing a cast and undergoing rehabilitation, or he could play hurt.

Klecko recalls a slightly different version of events. "They never really offered the six-to-eight-week deal to sit out," he says. "It was just a thing where they said, 'Either we take you out, or you're going to play with pain.' I said, 'What the hell, pain ain't nothing I haven't suffered before.' "

There was no resemblance between the Joe Klecko who couldn't move in a 45–28 loss to Miami in the 1982 season opener and the Joe Klecko who overpowered opponents the previous season. The Dolphins twice ran reverses for long gains around Klecko's end while he flailed helplessly, and they ran power plays in his direction at other times. Klecko's knee was sending warnings that he was in danger of a serious injury, but the fact he was able to practice for the next week's game was taken as a hopeful sign.

On a golden New England afternoon, the Jets played the Patriots in what was expected to be the last weekend of games before the NFL Players Association called a strike that had been anticipated for months. The Sack Exchange had been shut out for the first time in twenty-eight games by Miami, but Klecko recorded the first two of six Jets sacks on a day when they set a club defensive record by holding the Patriots to 57 yards total offense. The Jets were leading 10–0 in the second half, and Klecko told the coaches he was coming out if they scored again. The Jets increased their lead to 17–0, but when the Patriots returned the kickoff for a touchdown, Klecko decided to stay in the game. After the Jets extended their lead to 24–7, defensive line coach Dan Sekanovich told Klecko to let him know if he wanted out.

"Like a fool, I went in again," Klecko says. "It's just me, I guess. The second play of that series, it happened."

As he was preparing to fight off a block by 6-7, 288-pound tackle Brian Holloway, the patella tendon in Klecko's right knee snapped so loudly it could be heard all across the field, and he let out an agonizing cry as he jacknifed in a spasm of pain. Holloway blocked Klecko as he was on the way down, and tight end Don Hasselbeck dove at his legs in what Klecko always has regarded as a cheap shot.

The pain was the worst Klecko ever had experienced, enough to make him cry as he was wheeled off the field on a stretcher. "I felt the knee give, and when Holloway hit me, it felt like it was torn apart," Klecko says. "It's amazing the things that go through your head sitting on the field. Honest to God, I was thinking about where I could get a trucking job the next year."

Two days later, the players went on strike for fifty-six days, which would have been time enough for Klecko's knee to mend if he had chosen to sit out a few games or been ordered to rest the knee by Nicholas and Reese. But NFL players, doctors, and trainers all operate in an environment that is geared toward returning the player to the field as soon as possible. The pressure is especially great in football because the injuries often are severe, and time is short in a sixteen-game season. Decisions on when a player should return from an injury or play hurt are based, in part, on how much the team needs that particular player at that particular time. It always was Klecko's inclination to play if at all possible.

In retrospect, Klecko shouldn't have taken the cortisone shot following the Denver exhibition game for the purpose of trying to play hurt. "It was part of my makeup not to challenge them," Klecko says. "If I had it to do over, I wouldn't do it without a doubt. I was just on the brink of stardom then. Thank God, my will to come back was so strong. A lot of guys have played hurt, but I don't think there have been many who played at the level I did with the kind of injuries I had."

He should not have risked his career, especially not for one game against a poor New England team. But he was a willing participant with Nicholas and Reese in the decision to keep playing, and it was a point of great pride with Klecko that he never ever let the Jets down.

The surgery, performed by Dr. Bart Nisonson, was a success, but Klecko was experiencing intense pain when he returned home. "They gave me thirty Percodan I was supposed to take for the pain my first week home," Klecko says. "But I was in such pain the first weekend that I took that thirty and got more from my own doctors. So, I took about forty-five Percodan pills in a weekend. I was like a zombie. No one could fathom why I was in so much pain. Finally, they X-rayed my knee and found the wire tying my kneecap to my shinbone was crimped. They cut a window in the cast and straightened the wire, and it was like the world was lifted off my shoulders."

The doctors assured Klecko he would play again and gave him an outside chance of returning for the playoffs if the season resumed and the Jets qualified. In a way, he was happy for the strike because it meant he wasn't missing any action. But he also was worried that he might not be the same player.

"I don't want to just line up," Klecko said. "I want to play the way I know how."

Klecko spent most of the first four weeks after surgery confined to bed with his injured leg suspended from a pulley. Many of the Jets had remained on Long Island to work out together during the strike, and it was through Joe Fields that Klecko maintained contact with the team. By now, Klecko and Fields were well-established as the team leaders, and they were thinking of going into business together. But this was the first time one of them literally needed to lean on the other.

"My first knee injury was the lowest point in my life without a doubt," Klecko says. "Until then, I thought I was invincible. It was hard for Joe and me because we're not the kind of guys who are sympathetic people. He'd bring Debbie to the hospital, and later on, he'd come over and get on me about working my leg in the cast. Even though it was a little thing, it was the first time I needed something."

"We had a strike meeting, and I went to pick up Klecko," Fields recalls. "He's in pain, and I'm saying, 'Klecko, you've got to get out and blow the stink off you. You can't be lying around all the time.' I had my dog in the car the day before, and the backseat was covered with white hair, but Klecko had to sit there because of the cast."

"I was in real, live pain because the wire was digging into my kneecap," Klecko says. "The pain took over my whole body."

"At the meeting, some of the guys asked how Klecko was doing, and I told them he was in the car," Fields says. "They came out to see him, and he's covered with dog hair. They're laughing, and he's sitting there dying in pain. A week later, I asked him out for drinks. Lying down with his leg was one thing, but when he had to stand up, the pain really got to him. I made him stay out for an hour before I'd take him home."

"I had the reputation as a tough guy," Klecko says. "Everybody at the bar would come up and slap me or throw ice at me, and I couldn't do nothing. I told them, 'You wait, you SOBs.' When I got that wire out, I started going to the gym. If it weren't for Fields doing that with me, I wouldn't have done it by myself. I would have stayed home and made my wife wait on me like a big pig."

The strike ended just before Thanksgiving, and the schedule was cut to nine games. The Jets finished 6–3 and qualified for the expanded sixteen-team Super Bowl tournament. Their first-round playoff game was January 9 at Cincinnati against the defending AFC champion Bengals, and Klecko was in uniform for the first time just sixteen weeks after his patella tendon snapped like a worn rubber band.

It was amazing, and then again, it wasn't because it was Joe Klecko. "I remember calling him in the hospital and saying, 'If anybody can come back, you can,'" says Sekanovich. "He said,

'You said the right words.' Joe Klecko had something inside him. I knew he could come back."

When the cast came off his right leg, Klecko's thigh had withered like a rotten vegetable so that it didn't fit with the rest of his body, and his strength in the leg was about one-tenth of normal. "I could easily have walked away and said, 'This is it for the year,'" Klecko says. "There were times I couldn't do the weights because it just killed me. Pain is something that makes you weak, makes you something you don't want to be. Pain makes you weak even if you think you're a tough person.

"Everybody said it would take me two weeks to bend my leg ninety degrees, and I was well beyond that in nine days. The more pain I could take, the more I could bend it. There were a lot of skeptics among the orthopedics at the hospital. Some people told me they were saying I'd never come back. But once I recovered, I never had a problem with it again."

Klecko played less than a quarter in the second half against the Bengals and knew right away that he couldn't get close to quarterback Ken Anderson, but it was a start. His presence wasn't critical because Freeman McNeil rushed for 202 yards, and the Jets came back from a 14–3 deficit to dominate the Bengals, 44–17. The Jets put more offensive weapons on display than a May Day parade in Moscow, and it seemed they were ready to live up to the label of "the most talented team in football."

But to reach Super Bowl XVII at the Rose Bowl, the Jets first would have to play the Raiders in the Los Angeles Coliseum and the Dolphins in the Orange Bowl. The thought of Raiders owner Al Davis and Dolphins coach Don Shula, the two opponents he hated the most, was enough to put Jets coach Walt Michaels on edge.

"Everybody was paranoid of Al Davis and Don Shula back then," Fields says. "We had guards watching our practice the week we played the Raiders. We put up a stuffed dummy next to the bushes at one end of the practice field to fool Harry Fisher, our regular security guard. It looked like a person standing there. I started yelling, 'Yo, Harry, somebody's down there spying! I think he's got a camera!' Harry starts sprinting and yelling. He got close before he realized it was a scarecrow. Even Walt was pissing his pants laughing. But they really thought Davis and Shula had spies."

A crowd of more than ninety thousand filled the Coliseum to watch the first playoff match between the Jets and Raiders since

the 1968 AFL championship game. The Jets took a 10–0 halftime
lead. Just before the break ended, Michaels received a strange
telephone call from a man criticizing the play-calling in the first
half. "Walt went off on a tirade," Fields says. "He swore it was Al
Davis, and he flipped out. But it turned out to be a bartender from
Queens, New York who got the Coliseum switchboard to put the
call through."

Most of the Jets were unaware of what happened and unaf-
fected. They had their hands full with the Raiders, who scored
two third-quarter touchdowns for a 14–10 lead. Although he still
was weak against sweeps, Klecko played most of the second half
and once drove two linemen back into Raiders quarterback Jim
Plunkett and pressured him on a few other plays. The battle was
more like a gang war than a football game, the Jets against the
Sharks instead of the Raiders. At one point, Jets tackle Chris Ward
grabbed a handful of Raiders defensive end Lyle Alzado's crotch,
and Alzado ripped off Ward's helmet and flung it at the retreating
Jets tackle like Goliath with a slingshot. The NFL Films crew
caught Jets linebacker Greg Buttle coming off the field and yelling
from the sheer thrill of the contact, "What a great game!"

It was such a rugged and brutal contest that it seemed as if
it were in the Colosseum in Rome rather than the Coliseum in
Los Angeles. But the toughness of Klecko and the Sack Exchange
was a match for Alzado and Howie Long and the Raiders' defense.
In the fourth quarter, Richard Todd and the Jets' offense showed
their mettle. Todd hit a 45-yard pass to Wesley Walker at the
Raiders' 1-yard line to set up a touchdown that gave the Jets a
17–14 lead, and linebacker Lance Mehl made two interceptions
in the final three minutes to preserve the most significant victory
for the Jets since Super Bowl III.

At the end of the game, the last fight of the day was between
Raiders linebacker Ted Hendricks, who had been Klecko's drinking buddy at the previous Pro Bowl, and Fields. "It was the last
play of the game," Fields says. "He was pushing on the previous
play while we were running out the clock, and I got off-balance
and squeezed his tit. We went back to the huddle, and I said, 'If
he starts up again, we're going to go.' I tried to pick him up, but
I couldn't do it. The SOB ends up throwing me on the ground. A
lot of guys were walking off the field. Klecko came running on the
field, and I remember Bobby Jones, one of our wide receivers,
came running and drop-kicked Hendricks right in the head."

These Jets had never known such excitement as they experienced in the next week before the AFC championship game with the arrival in the locker room of the national media in addition to New York's media corps. By popular demand of his teammates, running back Bruce Harper performed his Stevie Wonder imitation for them and later climbed up on a table in the middle of the dressing room during the interview period and did a striptease that rocked the house with laughter.

"That week was media hype like I never experienced," says guard Dan Alexander. "It was an awesome week. Each game of the playoffs, Walt Michaels would hold up a wad of hundred-dollar bills equal to the playoff share for that game and say, 'This is what you get if you win!' It was great."

The Jets spent the week in New York practicing in windy conditions that dropped the wind-chill factor to minus-18 degrees one day. The weather was warmer when they arrived in Florida and had to wade through a mob of fans to reach the elevators at the team hotel. But it had been raining most of the week in Miami, and that evening, it began raining some more. And it kept raining. All night. Puddles in the hotel parking lot turned into pools that became lakes that emptied into rivers flowing to the Atlantic shore.

And all the time, Don Shula was smiling because there was no tarpaulin covering the field at the Orange Bowl while Miami was turning into Mudville. It still was raining the next morning, and Michaels was furious about the situation during the pregame meal.

"I had never seen Walt so mad," says placekicker Pat Leahy, whose job had been threatened by Michaels earlier in the season and in previous years. "I mean, he used to chew us out individually and collectively, and he would rant and rave. But this time, he was really hot. Luckily for everyone, he never got near Shula that day."

Most of Shula's enemies in the AFC East division dislike him because he wins so much and because he's a powerful voice on the NFL rules committee. But with Michaels, it was more personal than that. Shula had characterized Michaels's attitude toward him as "his Swoyersville mentality," an apparent knock at Michaels's hometown in Pennsylvania.

"Walt said, 'If he talks about my hometown again, I'll kill him,' "

Alexander says. "It was Shula this and Shula that. Everything was Shula's fault."

Michaels based his suspicions about Shula's role in the un-coverup on the fact the Dolphins had reached the title game with defense and a ball-control offense that was restricted by the limited talents of quarterback David Woodley. Poor footing would help them because the Jets had the speed advantage at wide receiver with Walker and Lam Jones and in the backfield with the shifty running style of McNeil.

"I found out on the Wednesday before the game that the field wasn't covered," Michaels says. "But I felt the water pumps they had to drain the field were going to be on. I was sure it wasn't going to be one hundred percent, but I never expected what I saw. The night before the game, I got more information they weren't doing anything about it. There's no question I was mad the morning of the game because I heard the field still was brutal.

"When I got to the stadium, there was a maintenance worker laughing and pounding on the pumps. He said they weren't working. He got them running when I hollered. It was easy to get mad. We didn't have a two hundred and fifty-pound fullback. We had Freeman McNeil, and we planned things in relation to the speed we had and then playing defense. With that field, we were off base. I always felt the Dolphins didn't care to take care of the field."

Michaels wasn't alone in blaming Shula for neglecting to cover the field. "I'm sure it was on purpose," says quarterback Pat Ryan. "It had to be. We were lighting it up with Wesley and Freeman. All the Dolphins had to do was put their cornerbacks tight on our wide receivers and double-cover them deep."

"The league rules say you have to have a tarp for the field," adds offensive line coach Bob Fry. "The Dolphins said it was the city's responsibility. Only two of the four water pumps that were supposed to drain the field were working. They threw wood chips on the field and spray-painted them green."

Fields, Ryan, and Leahy, the placekicking unit, were the first Jets on the field for pregame warmups. "I was standing in four inches of water on the two-yard line," Fields says. "I snapped the ball, Leahy kicked it, and he drenched my whole back. After twenty kicks, my back was caked with mud. I was thinking, 'Holy shit, this field's a mess.' It was still pouring, and the pumps hadn't been turned on fifty-five minutes before the game. When we came out for introductions, the lake was gone, but it was muddy like quick-sand."

Klecko had come out of the Raiders game in good condition and was making rapid progress with each game. He didn't start against the Dolphins, but when Abdul Salaam was injured early, Klecko replaced him at tackle and played well for more than three quarters.

"I was effective at tackle because I was able to power rush and didn't have to worry about my mobility on the outside," Klecko says. "If we were going to the Super Bowl, I wanted to start. That was my concern."

After getting drilled by the Dolphins in the season opener, the Jets lost the regular-season rematch, 20–19, on a last-minute field goal at the Orange Bowl. But in the previous four seasons, the Jets were 7–0–1 against the Dolphins, and they were confident they were the better team. Prior to 1982, Todd seemed to have the Dolphins' number, culminating with the fourth-quarter touchdown pass that beat them, 16–15, near the end of the 1981 season.

"Richard was playing on a bum ankle that day," Fields recalls. "On the drive for the winning touchdown, somebody stepped on him and he was having a hard time getting up. Shula was on the sidelines, yelling, 'Todd, get up! Get up, you hero son of a bitch!' Richard got upset and jumped up and started yelling back at him and walking toward him. I had to grab Richard and pull him back. That's the first time I ever remember Richard losing it on the field."

Actually, Todd kept it together that day to lead the Jets to an important victory. But in the AFC Championship Game a year later, it looked as though Todd lost all feel for how to throw a pass. The conditions had a lot to do with it because they threw off the rhythm of the Jets' passing game. Todd and his swift receivers resembled dinosaurs struggling to free themselves from the tar pits. McNeil was held to 46 yards rushing on 17 carries in the muck. Neither team could sustain anything in a first half that ended 0–0.

"It was a tough day to make anything happen," Klecko says. "It was an impossible day for the pass rush. The only thing you could do was bull-rush because no one could get any footing."

"I remember saying at halftime, 'We'll win this game if we just get a field goal,'" Fields adds.

"We would have, too, if Richard didn't throw those fucking

interceptions," Klecko says. "Goddamn Richard made a star out of fucking A. J. Duhe. It was unbelievable."

Starting with the tie at Miami in the fourth game of the 1981 season, Todd had played two seasons of outstanding football in which the Jets had gone 18–5–1, but his football fortunes changed forever in that mud-caked AFC title game at the Orange Bowl. He threw five interceptions, including three to Dolphins roving linebacker A. J. Duhe. The second interception by Duhe on the first series of the third quarter gave the Dolphins the ball at the Jets' 48. A 15-yard penalty on Jets cornerback Bobby Jackson, and an apparent fumble that the referees ruled wasn't a fumble helped the Dolphins sustain a drive that ended with ex-Jet Woody Bennett scoring a touchdown on a 7-yard run. The Jets' offense, which gained only 139 yards, continued to struggle until Todd tried to loft a feeble pass over the onrushing Duhe early in the fourth quarter. Duhe leaped high in the air to make interception number five, and he returned it 35 yards for the touchdown that made the final score 14–0.

"If we couldn't score seven points before then, there was no way we could score fourteen," Fields says. "It was futility."

"It came down to the end, and I got in a fight," Klecko says. "Marty Lyons grabbed me, and I almost tore his fucking head off. I said, 'Don't ever grab me in a fight.' I was getting hot, and I wanted to do anything to win. I was frustrated."

"After the game, I walked off the field, threw my helmet in the locker and sat in the shower with all my gear on, shoes and everything, for ten or fifteen minutes," Fields recalls. "I was sand head to toe, all down inside. I was depressed. I thought that would help me. I felt we should have won the game and there was more football to come."

But there wasn't. On a fast track, the Jets looked like a better football team than Miami, but the Dolphins were the better mudders. They made the trip to Pasadena to play Washington in the Super Bowl, while the Jets went home to think about the championship ring that was within the grasp of their talent but had washed down one of the drains at the Orange Bowl.

"Klecko and I sat together on the plane home," Fields says. "I said, 'The worst thing is we may never get this chance again.' It's worse to get that close and not get there."

"The sad part is we know we would have matched up so much better against Washington than Miami did," Klecko adds. "I'm not saying we would have kicked their ass, but we would have matched up so well defensively and offensively."

The Jets' feelings toward Todd were not very charitable that day, and the fact Todd stayed behind in Fort Lauderdale with his wife and went into seclusion rather than fly home with the team didn't improve the situation.

"I hated Richard at that point, but it went away," Klecko says. "That was part of the game. Richard got us there. He did the most to lose the game; a fact's a fact. But Richard didn't do it on purpose. I felt bad for him after the game. I know what he was going through. It didn't bother me that he stayed behind. If I had a bad game, I wouldn't want to be on a plane with a bunch of fucking guys getting drunk and complaining about the game."

Compared to what was going on up in the first-class section of the airplane, the players' ride home was relatively calm. Michaels was mad at Shula, mad at the NFL, mad at Todd, mad at Jets president Jim Kensil, mad at the world. It was understandable. He was coach of a team he thought was good enough to go to the Super Bowl, and he had just lost a game under what he considered unfair conditions.

"Walt had a knack of hating his opponents," explains Fry. "It was the way he played and the way he coached. Walt went to Miami mad, and all the things that happened down there were fuel for the fire. It wasn't make believe. There was no tarp on the field, and he was angry at Shula and the NFL."

Almost as soon as he boarded the Jets' charter flight, Michaels's anger boiled over in a screaming rage he directed at Kensil. He wanted to make a protest to NFL commissioner Pete Rozelle to take action against Shula. "I'm going to get these guys!" Michaels vowed. "We got screwed! The league has to do something about it!"

Kensil grew angry and told him the game was over and the Jets would do nothing of the kind. Then, Michaels berated Kensil for bringing his wife and the wives of other front-office personnel on the team flight and forcing the coaches' wives to fly commercial the next day.

"I was very upset," Michaels admits. "I had just been involved in one of the things I'll remember the rest of my life. I definitely was not trying to create a lifelong problem with anyone, but I was so mad we couldn't perform to our capabilities because the situation was out of our control."

Michaels persisted complaining throughout the flight about the game, Shula, and the league, and while he may have had some drinks during the course of the flight, they hardly could have been considered the source of his anger and frustration, which had been building all day because of the condition of the field. The players didn't hear Michaels, but word filtered back to Klecko, who went forward to see what was going on.

"Walt was sitting with our equipment manager, Bill Hampton, and Hamp calmed him down after his major tirade with Kensil," Klecko recalls. "But later, Walt was throwing hangers at people and going off. He was very mad at Richard for not coming back on the flight. He kept saying, 'Joe [Namath] wouldn't have abandoned us.' I think he felt a little betrayed by Richard. Walt was just mad, and he was getting everything off his chest. He didn't like losing, and after a couple of hours on the plane, he was lit up."

After witnessing Michaels's outburst, Dr. Nicholas cornered a reporter who knew Michaels well, Newsday's George Usher, and began asking a lot of questions. "Nicholas wanted to know if Walt had been drinking and what kind of mood he was in," Usher recalls. "He was very interested in Walt's behavior."

Most of the players were aware Michaels sometimes drank during his late-night, film-watching sessions at the office, and it was common for Michaels to sleep in his office, as many head coaches do. But he never drank in front of the players during regular business hours.

"Everybody knew he drank," says Klecko, "but I don't think it hurt us as a team. Walt's drinking never bothered anybody."

Not everybody was aware that Michaels also took medication for his neck injury. "The Jets accused Walt of having a drinking problem, but he was taking pain pills," Fry says. "Take one drink with the pills, and you're drunk."

After the Jets returned from Miami, Michaels acted angry and drunk, arguing with the driver of the team bus he boarded at the airport. Apparently, he drank more later that night, and the effect of the drinking may have been compounded by the effect of the pain medication Michaels took regularly.

When the Jets showed up the next morning at the training complex to clean out their lockers and have the season-ending team meeting, Michaels was not in shape to show up at the meeting. Offensive coordinator Joe Walton addressed the squad in his place and also met with reporters while Michaels remained out of sight.

"In seventeen years with the Jets, I missed two days," Michaels says. "That was one, and the other was for my mother's funeral. I was still upset and mad. I stayed up and watched the game films from one end to the other all night. I didn't go to bed until six A.M. I could have missed that meeting as a very strong psychological point. There was a method to my madness. I wanted an indelible mark on their minds.

"If I had wanted to meet with the team that bad, I could have. I had walked around the complex and seen some of the players. Everybody there is over twenty-one, and the players weren't exactly teetotalers. I'm not about to say I never had a drink in my life. But the season was over. I was so depressed. It was painful to lose it that way, to know I couldn't control anything. The hurt of it all creates a lot of strong feelings."

Dr. Nicholas was at the training complex to administer year-end physical exams. When he heard Michaels failed to meet with the team, he went to trainer Reese, a confidant of Michaels, who told Nicholas of the coach's condition and drinking habits.

The players' understanding of what happened next is that Nicholas then went to owner Leon Hess, with whom he had a close friendship of long-standing, and persuaded him to fire Michaels. "I do not know what Jim Nicholas did," Michaels says. "But I knew him for nineteen years, and when I left the Jets, I never got a call from him. Maybe he had a guilty conscience. I sure hope Jim didn't try to play God with me."

From a public relations standpoint, it didn't look good for the head coach not to meet with his team or the media at the end of the season. But Michaels hadn't thanked the Jets for their effort at the end of the previous season, either. "That wasn't his way," says Klecko, "and it didn't bother me one bit."

The Jets had to wait until after the Pro Bowl to announce their decision to fire Michaels. As AFC runner-up, Michaels and his coaching staff were obligated to coach the AFC team in the postseason all-star game in Honolulu. But Michaels suspected he was a goner.

"At the first staff meeting at the Pro Bowl, Walt told us to look for a job," says Fry.

Fields was voted to the AFC team for the second straight season, and he took his wife, Kay, to Hawaii for the game. "One night, Walt was sitting in the hotel lobby reading the paper, and my wife was next to him," Fields says. "He talked to her for forty-five minutes about everything. He talked longer to my wife that one night than he talked to me in the six years I played for him, and I was one of his captains."

Three days after the Pro Bowl, the Jets announced Michaels had "retired." The next day, they introduced Walton as the new head coach and defensive coordinator Joe Gardi as the assistant head coach. Michaels wasn't present, but the Jets released a "retirement statement" attributed to him.

"I didn't lose the use of my writing hand, and I don't have any copies of me writing a retirement letter," Michaels says with a laugh. "I still don't know who wrote that retirement release. I didn't. But I never said anything because it wasn't my nature to say anything."

Under terms of a settlement with the Jets, Hess paid off the remaining two years of Michaels's contract and provided him with an additional amount of severance pay. "I got some money, but I don't know what it was for," Michaels says. "It could be construed as a bonus or as money so I wouldn't say anything. It was written up as a 'termination contract,' entitling me to X amount for services rendered. The contract forbids me from talking about it for a lifetime, but they can't hold me to that."

Michaels surfaced less than two years later when he was hired to replace Chuck Fairbanks as head coach of the USFL New Jersey Generals for the 1984 and 1985 seasons. The Generals, losers under Fairbanks, won 25 of 36 games and made the playoffs in both years under Michaels.

"If it was so wrong with the Jets, why did it come out twenty-five wins somewhere else with no problems?" Michaels asks.

There was some suspicion on the coaching staff that Kensil hired Walton as offensive coordinator in 1981 with the intention of making him head coach. As soon as Walton arrived, Gardi attached himself to the heir apparent in ingratiating fashion, and they soon became best buddies, sharing a ride to work every day.

The spectacle was too much for Sekanovich and Fry to handle. They quit out of loyalty to Michaels rather than accept Walton's offer to remain. Their action was interpreted by the players as an indication that Walton and Gardi had conspired to stab Michaels in the back.

"I respected Walt Michaels," Sekanovich says. "The New York

Jets didn't belong in the NFL when he became head coach. They were noncompetitive. Walt built them through the draft. He wanted people who could give him ten years and sixteen games a year. The Jets didn't know what they had."

From 3–11, Michaels had built a team that fell one step short of the Super Bowl, in part, because it slipped in muddy conditions that would not have been so severe if the Orange Bowl field had been covered. If excessive drinking was the charge against Michaels, then, some of those at the highest levels of the Jets' organization were hypocrites of the first rank.

"I decided not to stay because I didn't think Walt got a fair deal," Fry says. "Dr. Cal Nicholas, the brother of James, told us he'd be glad to say he didn't think Walt was a drunk."

Klecko and Fields were as sorry to lose Sekanovich and Fry as they were to see Michaels fired. "Sek and Fry were a couple of guys you could respect," Klecko says. "They never came down on you or told you that you were in trouble because you were playing bad. Sek would talk to the defensive line and say, 'You guys are tough, and you have to show it. This is the NFL, and it's a hard life. That guy [Michaels] up there is standing behind you.' Walt did stand behind us, but we didn't really know it then."

In his two years as offensive coordinator, Walton made a definite contribution to the Jets. He made the offense more complex and diverse, and he nurtured Todd to the point where he not only committed far fewer mistakes but won games by making clutch plays. At least, he did until the confidence-shattering Mud Bowl. Walton's arrival coincided with the Jets' return to the playoffs, so, his progression to the head coaching chair was viewed as a natural step. Because Michaels had an uneasy relationship with the media and sometimes communicated in indecipherable ways, his removal at the height of his success did little more than raise a few eyebrows. Reports of his demise hinted at a drinking problem and portrayed Walton's promotion as the last piece in the Jets' Super Bowl puzzle.

"I liked Joe Walton and thought maybe he could help us win," Klecko says. "I knew Joe Gardi was a hoax. When Walt made Gardi defensive coordinator, I said, 'Oh, shit.' We had a lot of troubles defensively because Gardi didn't think very well on his feet and change defenses. But it didn't take too much to play our basic 4–3 defense, and we knew what we were doing."

Somebody should have warned the Jets to watch out for that last step to the Super Bowl. It was a big one. Todd's confidence got another jolt when the Jets took unknown California-Davis quarterback Ken O'Brien with their number-one pick in the 1983 draft. Ten games into Walton's first season as head coach, he and Todd were arguing in private and maintaining a cool distance in public. The Jets finished 7–9, and Todd was traded after the season along with several other players. When the Jets again went 7–9 in 1984, Walton got rid of "ol' pal" Gardi and brought in Bud Carson to install the 3–4 defense.

That move was welcomed by the players, but they also sensed that a cycle of blame had begun. It seemed Walton always found an excuse for things that went wrong without ever accepting the responsibility himself. Unlike Michaels, Walton made his players meet to death, and his practices were longer and more physical, which may have accounted for the rash of injuries they suffered and their tendency for late-season collapses. Michaels confined his criticism to football matters, while Walton's anger often expressed itself in the form of personal insults.

"Walt never said one word to me during a game," Klecko says. "He'd yell at the coaches if he was mad. Contrary to what people believe, Walt was a very smart guy. He wasn't a politician. I'm sure he didn't tell off Mr. Hess, but when Dr. Nicholas or someone would come around, he'd tell them where to get off if he got fed up. Walt knew what he was doing, and he never second-guessed himself.

"One time, Joe Walton told us we had turned into a bunch of fighters instead of football players. Well, I'll tell you what, I sure know a lot of football coaches who would love a bunch of fighters. If you're a fighter, you're a good football player. Our defensive line got in a lot of fights, but we played well because that was our style. When we beat the Raiders in the playoffs, we weren't afraid of them.

"Walton talks about how team leaders aren't the type who take people out to bars. Who cares what you do off the field as long as you play on Sunday? That's how Walt was. He didn't nitpick, but he was disciplined. He'd fine you in a minute if you broke curfew in training camp.

"We knew Walt was missing a couple of bricks, but when it came to football, he knew how to handle it. He was a legitimate tough guy, and you knew it. He wasn't trying to psychoanalyze everybody. Just shoot from the hip. You could relate to that. See, the difference between Walt Michaels and Joe Walton is that Walt remembered what it was like to be a player, and he treated you like you wanted to be treated. If you didn't know Joe Walton played, you'd never guess it."

Big Money

The formation in the spring of 1983 of the United States Football League accomplished for NFL players what their strike the previous season couldn't. It raised their standard of living to a level more comparable to those of major league baseball players and professional basketball players. On no NFL team was the change more profound than the Jets. Their fortunes on the field went down in the first two seasons under head coach Joe Walton, but their payroll went from the middle of the pack to number one in the NFL, according to published salary surveys.

Two things combined to make the Jets the leaders in salary inflation. In 1983, they lost four draft picks and veteran defensive back Jerry Holmes to the USFL, which created more pressure for them to spend enough to sign all their 1984 picks. The second major factor was the influence of Walton in convincing management to pay top dollar to the Jets' best players and leaders. While he was sweeping out quarterback Richard Todd and several other fringe players with one hand, Walton was cushioning the blow with the other hand by rewarding his top producers, many of whom were underpaid by comparison to the rest of the league. Walton was supported by Leon Hess, who gained 100 percent ownership of the club in early 1984.

The windfall began when defensive end Mark Gastineau received a five-year deal worth $3.71 million. Then, running back Freeman McNeil received a six-year package worth $4.67 million.

By the time training camp began, five more veteran leaders signed major deals, including Joe Klecko, who got three years for a total of $2.1 million (in 1986, Klecko signed a three-year extension for 1987–89 worth another $2.5 million), Joe Fields (four years, $1.7 million), guard Dan Alexander (five years, $2.17 million), defensive tackle Marty Lyons (five years, $1.89 million), and linebacker Lance Mehl (five years, $3.12 million). Wide receiver Wesley Walker had to hold out for his share, but he wound up with a five-year deal worth $3.52 million.

Fields was shocked by the sudden change in the payscale. He always had received a blue-collar paycheck by NFL standards for his hard labor at center. In nine previous seasons with the Jets, Fields had negotiated his own contracts because it was important to him to save the commission he otherwise would have paid to an agent, most of whom he didn't trust to do a good job. But Klecko had done very well in negotiations with Marty Blackman, a Manhattan-based attorney specializing in endorsement deals for athletes. Fields took Klecko's advice to let Blackman handle his contract talks before the 1984 season.

"One day, Marty called me up and said, 'Here are the numbers.' " Fields says. "I was flabbergasted. I was speechless on the phone. I said, 'Marty, how long would it take to get this in print? Get it!' I've never been so excited about something. Talk about Cloud Nine. I was crazed. I had no idea I'd ever make that much money in my life. Here I was getting paid for doing the thing I love. I was beyond excited."

The contract Fields signed called for him to receive a $100,000 signing bonus and base salaries of $325,000 in 1984, $375,000 in 1985, and $425,000 in 1986 with an option year of $467,500 in 1987. The 1986 salary tied him with Alexander as the highest-paid offensive lineman in the NFL that season.

"I think they wanted to bring everybody up and make up for the inequities of previous years," Fields says. "I think Joe Walton definitely was involved in my contract. Maybe he told them, 'I want Fields to be paid.' "

It was an unbelievable deal for the fourteenth-round draft pick from Widener College who wasn't expected to last more than a few years as a snapper. All Fields had to do to earn it was last until his tenth year in the league, make the Pro Bowl twice and try not to let it bother him that the Jets paid him less than the average salary at his position as long as they could get away with it.

The pro football boom began in the sixties, but most players didn't share in the general prosperity for another twenty years. As late as Fields's rookie season in 1975, the idea of an offensive lineman making several hundred thousand dollars in one season bordered on lunatic.

"When I showed up at my rookie camp," Fields recalls, "I was driving a beat-up 1966 Mustang. It had a white body, one red door, no back window, no muffler, no heat, and a hole in the floorboard on the passenger side.

"I cleared a hundred forty-two dollars in my first check for a week of training camp, and I busted my ass for that hundred forty-two dollars. During summers in college, I had been working for the boilermakers and was clearing two hundred twenty-five a week. I remember writing to my mom and telling her, 'There's got to be an easier way to make a living than this—a hundred forty-two dollars for seven days a week.' Now, I say there's no better way to make a living. Playing football is the greatest thing I've ever done."

Coming out of college, Fields consulted with running back Billy "White Shoes" Johnson, who became the first player ever drafted out of Widener the previous year when Houston chose him in the fifteenth round. Johnson told Fields he received a $5,000 signing bonus and a $20,000 first-year salary and a $5,000 roster bonus for making the team his second year with a base salary of $25,000.

That sounded great to Fields, and he told Jets general manager Weeb Ewbank he wanted the same deal as Johnson. Obviously, Fields never had met Ewbank and had no way of knowing that he had a reputation as the Ebenezer Scrooge of GMs. "Weeb said he would think about it and send me a contract," Fields says. "When I got my contract in the mail, it was for seventeen thousand dollars my first year with a three-thousand-dollar signing bonus and twenty thousand my second year with a three-thousand-dollar roster bonus. I remember thinking, 'Geez, I thought I was going to do so much better.' "

Fields's father, Joe Sr., got on the telephone and discussed the contract for an hour with Ewbank. "Weeb said, 'Joe can hang around ten or fifteen years. He'll get his money when he gets experience, but right now, a three-thousand-dollar bonus is the best we can do,'" Joe Sr. says. "We couldn't move him, so, I told Joe he better sign it before they took it away."

The Jets had themselves a hungry football player—and they made sure he stayed that way. Fields always was willing to sign away more years of his career in exchange for a few more immediate dollars in base salary. Even he didn't have much faith in his staying power.

"I wasn't secure enough to make any kind of demands," Fields says. "I was excited to be there. I always thought I'd be replaced if I had a bad play. The Jets drafted a center four of the first five years after I got there."

Jets pro personnel director Jim Royer, who handled negotiations with Fields, certainly didn't mind feeding those insecurities and using them to his advantage. Fields became the starting center in 1976, but the three-year deal he signed before the 1977 season called for token raises to $33,000, $37,000, and $41,000. After two seasons in that contract, Fields was allowed to renegotiate a deal that paid him $52,000 for his fifth season and then $58,000 and $65,000.

"The first time I renegotiated, Royer gave me a list of about twenty centers and said, 'Where do you put yourself on this list?' I put myself fifth, and he said okay and let it go at that. There were no salaries on the list. Nobody told each other what they were making. That was unheard of. I think it's good for the players to know what everybody is making, and I think your salary should be based on what you do for the team."

That contract lasted one year before Fields renegotiated again. Clearly, he had not received the fifth-best salary among NFL centers. The NFL Players Association released a study that year, listing the average salary for players at each position, and Fields found that $52,000 wasn't close to the league average for the 1979 season.

"I was pissed off," Fields says. "I thought I was an above-average player. But the only way I could get what I wanted from the Jets was to sign for more years. Say, I wanted fifty thousand dollars for one year. They would say, 'Sign a three-year contract, and we can give you fifty thousand, sixty thousand, and seventy thousand. If you only sign for one year, we can give you forty thousand.' As I got deeper into my contracts, the money changed drastically in the NFL. By the time I finished a contract, it was really outdated. The union started sending out average salary information, just the averages, not even individual salaries. I was always below the average."

Between his fifth and sixth seasons, Fields jumped from $52,000 to $90,000 in the first year of a contract that escalated to $100,000 in his seventh season, and then $115,000 and $125,000. But after his second trip to the Pro Bowl in 1982, the Jets dropped the last year of that contract and gave him a new one that paid $180,000 and $225,000. It was after the season at $180,000 that Fields went to Blackman when he heard the Jets had opened the vault.

"I was fortunate the Jets did renegotiate all those contracts," Fields says. "After a year or two in them, I would realize I had made a bad deal. Most of the time, the Jets agreed with me."

And then, the Jets would talk Fields into another bad deal, which wasn't surprising considering his eagerness to play and his persistent lack of self-confidence. Because he saw himself as a player of average physical talent who had to outwork everyone to get to the NFL and stay ahead of the competition, Fields found it difficult to give himself credit for being good enough to fight off the challenges from his would-be replacements and to make himself an important part of the Jets' offense. Unlike baseball and basketball, the majority of NFL contracts are not guaranteed, which means the club has little or no obligation to the player beyond his last game. The Turk's sword always is poised to fall, and in a sport where players are more interchangeable and quickly become damaged goods, the strongest temptation is to grab the cash on the table.

Klecko had a slightly different experience from Fields because he excelled as a rookie and developed a strong belief in his ability once he had tested the competition. As a sixth-round rookie, he didn't do much better, signing for salaries of $21,000, $27,000, and $31,000 and receiving a signing bonus of $12,000 that he used to pay off the debts he ran up because he was too busy training to hold a job before his first training camp.

The coach of the semipro Pottstown, Pennsylvania, Firebirds, Dave DeFillippo, represented Klecko as a rookie. "Dave was the kind of guy who promised you the world, and I didn't know any better," Klecko says. "He was a good friend of mine, and I trusted him. He said he'd get me a lot of extra money if I just played a little bit with the Jets, but it didn't turn out that way. After my first year, when Dave wanted to get paid, I said, 'I've been starting, and I led the league in sacks for rookies. You promised me a lot of things you couldn't deliver.' Dave sent a sheriff with a subpoena because he said I owed him thirty-five hundred dollars, but nothing ever came of it. I didn't pay him because he didn't do what he said he would do.

"A lot of guys come into the league and get screwed by their agents. Marty Lyons is one. He signed for seven years because his agent wanted to get paid upfront. A lot of agents get players by offering them perks—cars and money. You get a new Corvette, but the only thing they're doing is delaying the payments until the player gets paid. The player signs the contract and still has to make the payments. It's almost impossible to avoid getting screwed unless you're a first-rounder who can go to an agent like Howard Slusher, who's a real ball-buster in negotiations."

In his second season, Klecko took on Blackman, who had contacted him in college and was working with him on personal appearances and minor endorsement deals to generate outside income. During his third season, the Jets came to Klecko and offered three years for a total of $270,000.

"Marty said, 'It's a great offer, but tell them no. We'll wait.' I ended up getting two hundred fifty thousand dollars for the next two years. Marty has steered me in the right direction over and over, and we've had a great rapport in negotiating."

Some players stay completely out of negotiations to avoid becoming involved in bitter disputes with the club, but Klecko always felt it was important to hear what the Jets had to say. "They try to bring up how you graded out by the coaches," Klecko says. "As a defensive lineman, that's very shaky. If you don't do the correct thing, you get marked down, but if I take out three damn offensive linemen by doing the wrong thing, is that a detriment or is it good? When they brought that up, I always felt I could argue that better than Marty. He thought it was good for me to be there because I was never intimidated in negotiations. I never let them hold grades over my head because I knew I could play anywhere in the league.

"I'd lose it a little bit at times. After my big year in 1981, Jim Kensil, the team president, said, 'Joe graded out this and that way.' I said, 'What are you doing? I never knew they had a grading system. I never received a grade since year one. Explain to me what I didn't do. You can say that to people who don't know football, but you can't say that to me because I know what the fuck I'm doing out there!' I'd get upset. They'd talk about a mistake some coach said I made, and I'd say, 'Bring the SOB in here!' I thought it was bad because I lost it, but when we walked out, Marty looked at me and said, 'That was a pretty good show you put on.' "

In 1982, Klecko signed a three-year contract for $375,000, $405,000, and $435,000 in 1984. But after the Gastineau deal that opened the pipeline to the Jets' cash reserves, the Jets went to Klecko to begin the renegotiation process. Klecko received bonuses that brought his 1984 salary up to $655,000 with an increase to $695,000 the following year and $745,000 in 1986, which tied him with Gastineau as the highest-paid defensive lineman in the league. Klecko passed Gastineau in 1987 when his salary went up to $812,000.

With big money came big expectations from both the coaching staff and management. Because the stakes were so much higher, the pressure was turned up several notches on players with the most expensive contracts. Klecko and Fields noticed a shift in emphasis from assistant coaches, whose criticism was expressed in terms of a player proving he was worth all the money in his contract. During the bad times in 1984 in particular, it seemed as though the coaches started at the top of the salary list and worked their way down, suggesting to players they had relaxed after signing big contracts. If anything, players in the top salary brackets assume their contracts make them targets for removal at the first sign of slippage, even if they still are capable of making valuable contributions.

"If you don't live up to their demands, the coaches almost castrate you," Klecko says. "You're constantly reminded of how much you make. I think the coaches who were players resent the amount of money we make now. But when they started criticizing us and bringing up the money we were making, I told them I throw money out on Sunday. I don't play hard because I get paid a lot of money; I play hard because I want to beat the man in front of me.

"They take that away from you. That's one of the main reasons people get unnerved in pro football and feel pressure, big pressure. If coaches were smart, I think they'd never bring up money. They think it's a motivator to down you for making big money, but it stinks. I don't mind a coach coming up to me before a big game and telling me they need me to be a leader or do some things over and above; I feel proud of that. But if a coach makes the comment, 'You make so much money, you ought to do it,' that stinks."

The emergence of a rival league in 1983 ultimately created two different classes of players in the NFL, those with experience in pre-USFL days, when some found it necessary to hold a second job in the offseason, and those post-USFL players who seemed to assume the large sums of money teams were investing in them guaranteed their future. High draft picks always had an advantage because they started out fairly well up the salary scale, but after the USFL came into existence, they shot right to the top. That forced teams to upgrade veteran salaries, as the Jets did, but it also skewed payrolls so that top draft picks are rewarded for potential before they ever produce on the field.

"Jeff Van Note, who was Atlanta's center for a long time, said, 'Potential is a French word meaning you ain't worth a shit yet,'" Fields says. "It doesn't seem right to get all that money before you do anything. But it's not the players that are wrong. I say, get all you can get. It's the system that needs to be changed. They should give everybody minimum salaries and bonuses and then pay on merit. That's the way Klecko and I made it."

"You're going to have some guys be hungry no matter what, and you're going to have other guys who think they can't be cut because they were handed megadollars," Klecko says. "I'm not one to complain because I've been paid well. But they didn't give it to me; I worked for it."

When Klecko and Fields began their NFL careers, they hoped the money would give them a headstart toward purchase of a house, and the notoriety might be a stepping-stone to another career. But the main reason they played was for the thrill of the sport. So, when their salaries suddenly had an extra zero, it made a difference in their lives, but it didn't change their personalities or their habits recognizably.

"It made life come awake," Klecko says. "I can actually go out and talk about investments. But it didn't turn me into a spend-thrift."

Because of his interest in engines, Klecko does have some expensive toys, including a powerboat and several snowmobiles and four-wheel-drive vehicles. They're the extravagances he dreamed about as a kid, and if there's one area in which he spares no expense, it's in having fun with his two sons.

"I remember one Christmas I wanted a race car set that was

worth about eighteen dollars." Klecko recalls. "I remember everything about that set and the cars that were in it. My mom said,
'Joe, we just don't have that kind of money.' I never thought I'd
get it. I woke up Christmas morning, and it was there. I felt like
I'd received a Mercedes-Benz. It was exhilarating. I walk in with
a three-thousand-dollar snowmobile for one of my sons today,
and he says, 'Thanks, Dad.' It's different."

Fields grew up in more of a rural setting in south Jersey, and
while he never wanted for anything, all the members of his family
worked for what they needed. He learned at an early age to count
his change and check his pockets for holes. As placekicker Pat
Leahy says, "To say Joe is thrifty is an understatement. He wore
the same cut-off jeans and flip-flops to training camp for about
eight years straight, and I wouldn't be surprised if he still wears
the same tan leisure suit he had back in 1976."

In 1983, Fields bought a five-bedroom house, but for the first
five years he lived in it, he left the living room bare, except for a
baby grand piano he bought for his wife, Kay, in 1986. "We don't
use the living room, so, why have furniture in there," Fields says.
"My friends call it 'The Museum.' They say I should tell people I
had a party and moved all the furniture downstairs. Kay tells me
I always worried too much about what would happen when I had
to stop playing, and there's a lot of truth in that.

"My poor wife. Klecko has changed me a lot with her. We used
to have black-and-white TV. I ordered a microwave and dish-
washer for Kay back in 1980, and Klecko picked it up because he
knew the dealer. He drops this stuff off at my house, and there's
a color TV in there."

"I forced him to buy the microwave, too," Klecko adds, "and
the only reason he did that is because he got it for cost."

Both Klecko and Fields worked to prepare themselves for careers after football. Klecko took the streetwise route, learning
about auto wholesaling from a friend who was in the auto repair
business, and he also was part-owner of a Long Island night club
bearing his name for a few years. Fields went by the books, studying to obtain licenses as a financial planner and stockbroker and
as a real estate and insurance salesman. In later years, he also
began a food brokerage business. Following the 1982 season, when
both their salaries were beginning to accelerate dramatically,
Klecko and Fields decided they wanted to form a business partnership that would last long after their playing days ended. The

problem was in deciding what business to pursue and finding the right person to guide them without cheating them.

Because professional athletes have relatively high salaries and generally are perceived to be lacking in business acumen, they are targets for fast-buck operators. That was especially true for Klecko because he developed a high profile as a member of the New York Sack Exchange. "Klecko attracts people out of the woodwork like you would not believe," Fields says. "We were in Atlantic City playing cards at one of the casinos one night, and one guy he never met before told Klecko he was going to make him heavyweight champion of the world."

But promises of overnight millions held no appeal for Klecko and Fields. They were looking for someone with a solid reputation who was willing to make a long-term commitment to them. In 1983, a business contact of Klecko's introduced them to Tony Bariglio, who impressed them with his sincerity, knowledge, and cautious approach to business. Bariglio was in the process of recovering from the loss of a major investment in a restaurant in downstate Maryland, which wasn't the best recommendation, but he still had a good reputation in commercial real estate. Bariglio talked to them in terms of developing a ten-year plan to build a business, and he made it clear he would work with them every step of the way and keep them involved and aware of all the details of the business.

"I was on the rebound when I met Klecko and Fields," Bariglio says. "I had done well in business as a younger person, but a business venture that blew up in my face cost me virtually everything I owned. I can remember in December of 1982, I didn't have five cents. I mean it. My wife sold her jewelry to buy Christmas presents for the kids. I rented an office, but the phone wasn't ringing. Nobody knew I was there. I made up my mind I was going to work very hard, and I had just put together a couple of transactions and was starting to get back on my feet when I met them. My whole life changed. They know my salary is basically nothing, but my equity in the partnership is substantial. I have nobody to thank but them. It was just being honest with them that brought us together. I've never lied to Klecko or Fields, and I never would."

The original business included five partners. They began by buying two restaurants and eventually added two more restaurants, a pizza parlor and a liquor store, which they sold later. Then, they built a 40,000-square-foot shopping plaza. Along the way, two of the original partners dropped out, leaving Klecko, Fields, and Bariglio as the only partners of Jetgroup Inc. In 1986, the three of them had to come up with half a million dollars to buy out a fourth remaining partner to keep from losing their $5-million investment in the shopping center. The financial crisis came at a time when both Klecko and Fields were experiencing injury problems that threatened their football careers, but they survived the problems, which seemed to bring all three partners closer together.

"Tony has been a godsend for us," Klecko says. "He runs himself ragged managing the business. We get calls all the time from people, including ex-football players, who want to make deals. You might see something that looks great on paper, but Tony always says, 'Don't worry about it. If we miss it, there will be another one along behind it.' That's true. For everything we've passed up, we've found something as good, if not better. You don't have to stretch for any deal."

Jetgroup was able to establish itself as a solid enterprise, in part, because Klecko and Fields never took salaries as long as they were playing. They set it up in a way that would allow them to receive salaries and benefits after they retired. That approach helped them when it was time to obtain the bank loans necessary to acquire more properties. As a result, Jetgroup did not have to limit its investments to a level below its resources. Approaching the end of their football careers, the playing contracts of Klecko and Fields carried less weight with the banks, but by then, Jetgroup had built a solid track record.

Their name value as athletes has helped Klecko and Fields in promotions at their restaurants and because businessmen often enjoy the association with sports figures. But they still must be wary of the constant stream of con artists trying to separate them from their money.

"I get six or seven calls a week looking for investments, but I shield them from that," Bariglio says. "We do only real estate and restaurants. I find that people generally do not respect athletes as business-oriented. They feel they can put something over on them. You see quite a few ballplayers get in financial difficulty. I think the price has been the weird part of some of the transactions we've encountered. There's an asking price in real estate, but sometimes, they throw out a real high number, figuring the athletes don't know any better. The wording in contracts also has been very tricky, but we have good accountants and lawyers to guard against loopholes."

Friendships sometimes break up when money is involved, but Klecko and Fields have complemented each other well as business partners. "Fields is the more conservative of the two," Bariglio observes. "He always wants more explanation in a situation. Klecko does things based on the people involved, their reputation, and his gut feeling. He's more of a gambler or a guy on a game show who came with nothing and is willing to leave with nothing but is determined to take a shot at winning the jackpot. Fields is more detailed and technical. I'm a little bit of each. I have some street smarts because I was born in south Philly, but I'm also detail-oriented."

Before they formed their partnership, Fields had managed to provide a comfortable living for himself and Kay and still save some money, and Klecko had his Long Island night club. Together with Bariglio in Jetgroup, Klecko and Fields built a business with assets worth more than $8 million as they approached retirement. In an era when television dollars have poured into professional sports and the most difficult challenge faced by many athletes is not the games, but how best to manage their money, that's no small achievement.

Joe Klecko as a defensive tackle at Temple University

Temple Sports Information Department

Joe Fields (No. 51) as a seventeen-year-old freshman at Pennsylvania Military College (now Widener), coached by Bill Manlove (top left)

Placekicker Pat Leahy (left), the only player on the Jets when Fields joined them in 1975 who outlasted Fields, celebrates Thanksgiving 1979 with quarterback Pat Ryan (center) and Fields.

Rookies Joe Fields (left) and Darrell Austin (right) flank veteran guard Randy Rasmussen at the Jets' 1975 Thanksgiving party.

Joe Fields, who was in his second-year season with the Jets, snaps to quarterback Joe Namath, who was beginning his final year with the Jets, in a 1976 preseason game against the Giants.

Joe Klecko shakes hands with quarterback Richard Todd after finishing second to Todd in the voting for Jets MVP in 1981. Coach Walt Michaels looks on.

Opposite: Joe Klecko sacks Green Bay quarterback Lynn Dickey in the season-ending 28–3 victory in 1981 that gave the Jets their first playoff berth in twelve seasons.
Newsday/ Thomas R. Koeniges

Following pages: Joe Klecko grimaces in pain and grabs his right knee after his patella tendon snapped in the second game of the 1982 season at New England.
Associated Press

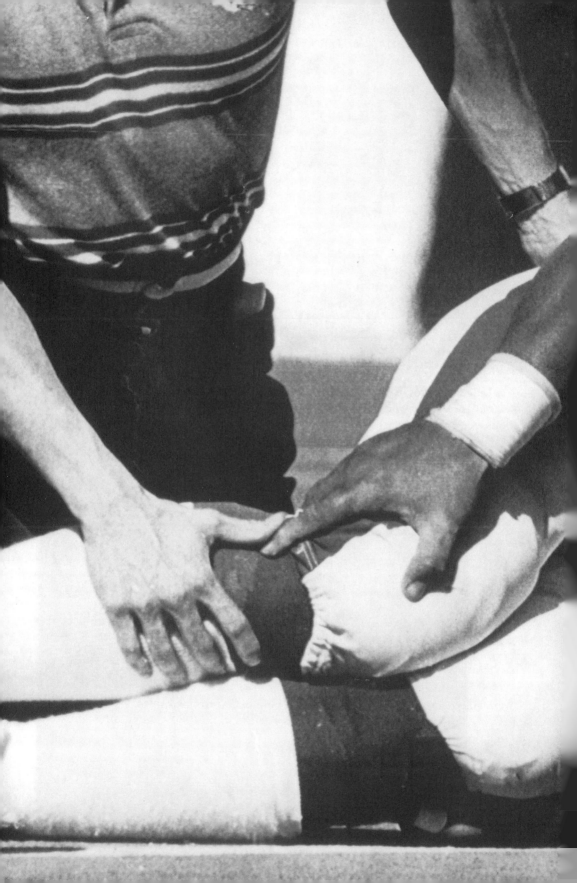

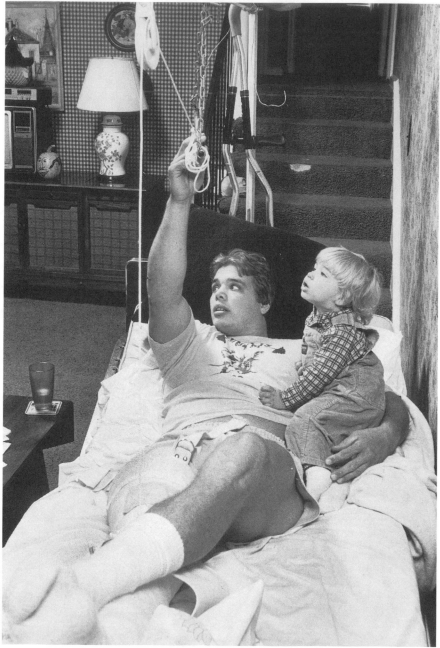

Newsday/ Thomas R. Koeniges

Joe Klecko rests at home and plays with his twenty-month-old son, Danny, after surgery to repair the patella tendon in his right knee in October 1982. He returned to the Jets in time to play in three playoff games.

Newsday/ Paul Bereswill

Nose tackle Joe Klecko sacks New England quarterback Tony Eason on the decisive defensive play at the end of the Jets' 16–13 overtime victory in 1985.

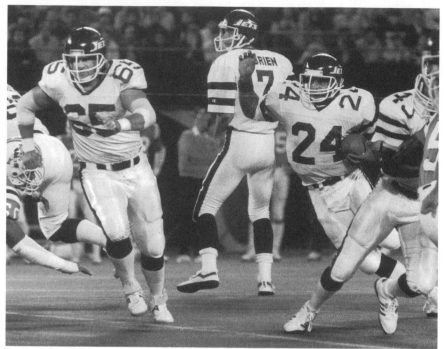

Joe Fields (No. 65), playing right guard, leads the blocking for Freeman McNeil (No. 24) in a 43–24 Monday-night victory over New England in the last game before the 1987 NFL players' strike.

Joe Fields takes a water break during practice in the strike-torn 1987 season.

Joe Fields (left) rests on the bench with Dan Alexander during the Jets' 19–14 loss to Indianapolis in 1987 in the second game after the strike ended.

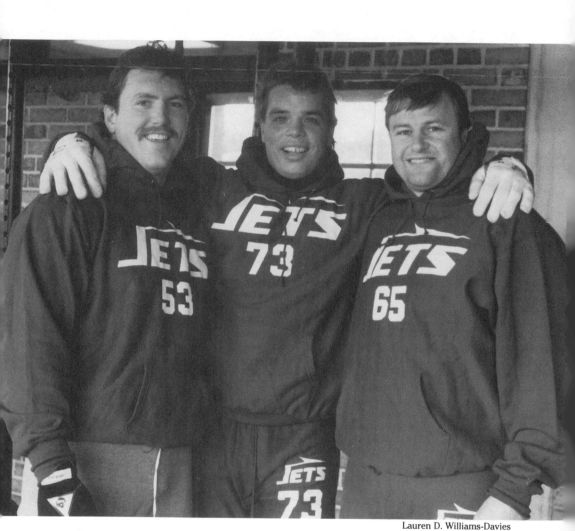

Roommates during the 1987 season are Jim Sweeney (left), Joe Klecko, and Joe Fields.

Joe Fields as a Giant during his final season in 1988.

Joe Klecko leaves the field for the last time. A neck injury forced him out of the Indianapolis Colts' 34–16 loss to the Jets at Giants Stadium in the fifteenth week of the 1988 season. It was Klecko's return to play in front of Jets fans as a member of the Colts.

Kay and Joe Fields enjoy dinner with Debbie and Joe Klecko at an Atlantic City, New Jersey, hotel and casino during the summer of 1987.

Joe Klecko and Joe Fields strike a prayerful pose while miscast as nuns for a Halloween party in 1982.

Joe Fields gets set to snap the ball in practice during the 1987 season.

Fame and Anonymity

There was only one "Broadway Joe" in Jets history. Although they succeeded Joe Namath as leaders of the Jets, neither Joe Klecko nor Joe Fields ever had much interest in making the celebrity scene in Manhattan. For starters, they were at the opposite end of the glamour scale from Namath. He was a quarterback; they were linemen. He was single; they were married. He did fancy things with the ball; they did the dirty work. He was a bit of a social rebel; they were company men. Klecko and Fields never thought of themselves as anything but "regular Joes," even though they did the hard, unglamorous fighting in the trenches that helped make the Jets winners again in 1981 after eleven straight seasons without a winning record.

Yet, a measure of fame did find Klecko because he led the league in sacks and was one of the featured players on the New York Sack Exchange defensive line that earned much of the glory when the Jets became a playoff team that season. New York, after all, is the city that learned to celebrate with chants of "Defense! Defense!" for the Giants football team of the late fifties that featured middle linebacker Sam Huff and the 1969 and 1973 NBA champion Knicks with Willis Reed and Walt Frazier. Jets defensive end Mark Gastineau often grabbed the spotlight with his sack dance sideshow, but it was Klecko who received the cheers of the crowd as a true gladiator, the symbol of the might of the Jets' defense.

Fields was at the center of it all literally but not in the figurative sense necessary to capture the public imagination. The most famous center in NFL history probably is Raiders Hall of Famer Jim Otto, who was best known for the double-zero number on his back and the number of operations on his knees—two dubious distinctions. Fields earned the respect of his fellow AFC players, who voted him to the Pro Bowl in 1981 and 1982, and he achieved a degree of recognition among Jets fans. But like most offensive linemen, he remained largely anonymous to the general public.

Broadway may be the street of dreams for those who migrate to New York in search of fame, but Klecko and Fields never really hoped to make it their address. Despite the opportunities for media exposure and business and social relationships in New York, they tried to maintain a sense of perspective and stay within their limits. Their attitude was: if Gastineau wants it so bad, let *him* take Manhattan.

"I see guys walk into this league and all of a sudden become somebody else," Klecko says. "New York high society never has impressed me. I like it, and there's no place like this town. But I can't see people who are not from here suddenly becoming a New Yorker. It happens to a lot of players, including the Giants, because of the glitter and the glamour. I see them taking on new lives. It's not a real life, though; it's plastic. You can see right through it."

"Where else do you go where there's ten or twelve reporters in the locker room almost every day of the week?" Fields adds. "A guy who hasn't done anything can become a star by shining up to the reporters. That wasn't important to me."

"I tried to cultivate some connections in trucking, and it wasn't a perfect marriage," Klecko says. "I was invited to a lot of different cocktail parties and public relations functions in Manhattan and didn't go because it wasn't my style like it was for Joe Namath. Joe was a single guy who enjoyed New York for what it was worth. I was married with two kids, and it was a little different for me. But there are certain advantages to playing in New York, and it's easy to let it take you."

Through his endorsement and public relations work with the U.S. Tobacco Company, which sponsors the Skoal Bandit stock car and Indy car racing teams, Klecko developed friendships with the top executives of the company. The relationship has been a comfortable one for Klecko, but it wasn't his goal to pile up as many endorsements as possible. He did only what felt right.

"Fields and I meet a lot of important people, but we never really wind up associating with them because it just seems we don't fit with them," Klecko says. "We don't travel in the same circles. It's not that we can't be like that; we don't want to be. We don't want to act phony. The truck drivers and mechanics that I know and the guys that I worked with back in college at the Anvil Inn are the guys who are my friends today.

"The people at the U.S. Tobacco Company have been so nice to me it's unbelievable. I can associate with them any way I want, from the guys who drive the trucks to the mechanics to the president and chairman of the board. I have a friend I go hunting and snowmobiling with who's a real mountain man from Potter County, Pennsylvania. He's a crusty old guy with a heart of gold, but he doesn't look like he's something. I took him up to the VIP section at a stock-car race and did not feel out of place. If they had asked me to leave, I would have because I like being with that guy. For him to go to the race the way I do—first class all the way—he was in heaven."

Success on the football field also enabled Klecko to take a backstage peek at the Hollywood scene. Following the 1980 season, he was chosen to play a bit part as a truck driver in the Burt Reynolds movie *Smokey and the Bandit II*. Klecko later played parts in two other Reynolds movies, *Cannonball Run* and *Heat*.

"I liked doing movies," Klecko says. "They were a cakewalk. It takes work to be a method actor, but there ain't nothing to playing a stereotyped part. I went to one Hollywood party in my life after *Cannonball Run* and hated it. I sat in a corner with Jack Elam, the character actor, and we played liar's poker all night. Jack was a real down-to-earth guy.

"I got along real well with all the stunt men on the set, and I got to know the director, Hal Needham. He used to own the Skoal Bandit stock car team, and I saw him at all the races. We were at a banquet together the week before I tore up my knee in 1986, and we had a few drinks. When I was in the hospital, Hal sent me a half-gallon of Stolichnaya vodka, and the guy who delivered it comes in the room with a big smile and says, 'This is from Hal, and he hopes you die.'"

His movie appearances gave a boost to Klecko's popularity and reinforced his image as a rough-and-tumble truck drivin' man. "One day in training camp after Klecko made *Smokey and the Bandit II*," recalls teammate Dan Alexander, "this eighteen-wheeler pulls up when practice is ending, and the driver started honking the horn and yelling for Klecko to come over. He wanted Joe to sign the cab of his truck. So, Joe signed it and got in and drove the truck around the parking lot for a while."

With fans like that, Klecko never made enemies. He wasn't seeking "People Page" notoriety in the newspapers, but he did enjoy his celebrity status in the company of real people. In a way, answering their questions made him appreciate his life as a football player even more. "People always wanted to know about Gastineau," Klecko says. "I gave him credit as a ballplayer, but I talked about the things he did that I felt were unprofessional. When things went bad, they'd ask about Joe Walton. The fans in New York were great. They were very honest."

Two New York City police officers who were partners in the 24th Precinct, Don Schaeffer and Hugh Gunder, organized a Joe Klecko fan club in 1980. They wore No. 73 Jets jerseys to games and identified their rooting section with a banner that read: KLECKO COUNTRY. Schaeffer is 6-2 and weighs 230 pounds, and Gunder goes 6-5, 300, which helps explain why they chose the 6-3, 265-pound Klecko as their role model. Over the years, they went from fans to friends because of the time Klecko, usually accompanied by Fields, spent with them in the stadium parking lot after games.

"Win, lose, or draw, Klecko came by and signed autographs for the young kids in the group," Schaeffer says. "There were times that the Jets lost that we knew he didn't want to be there, but he always took time for everybody. That's why a lot of people liked him. He would stay in the rain. One time, he had a dislocated thumb, and he came. I remember after one game there was a member of the band that played at halftime who knew someone in our group and wanted to meet Klecko. So, the whole band waited in their bus. When Klecko pulled up, the band got out of the bus and played for half an hour. Klecko grabbed a baton and conducted."

Then there was the time New York morning radio personality Don Imus and his young producer showed up at a postgame parking-lot party. The producer, beer can in hand, proceeded to tell a Polish joke to Klecko, apparently not realizing that Klecko is as Polish as it gets. Klecko gently wrapped his hand around the one the producer was using to hold the almost-full can of beer and squeezed until the can was flat.

"We were having a barbecue before one game, and a guy comes over and sees the KLECKO COUNTRY banner," Schaeffer remembers. "He says, 'That's my son.' I said, 'Yeah, right.' He went in his wallet and pulled out baby pictures of Joe. Baby Joe looked like something you would see climbing the Empire State Building. I said, 'You must be proud.' He said, 'I am, but I can still kick his butt.' "

Offensive linemen are used to seeing the running back or the quarterback get all the credit after they make the key block. Nobody knows how offensive linemen perform until after the game films are developed, and by then, it's usually too late for a headline. So, Fields was accustomed to handling situations in which he was overshadowed by Klecko, whose personality and demeanor tend to be more dominating. But offensive linemen have egos, too.

R. J. (Mickey) McBride, a friend of Fields's who works out at the same men's health club, has witnessed the difference in the attention Klecko and Fields receive in public places. "Because of his name and the powerful way he's built, Klecko is almost like a comic-book hero," McBride says. "I'm sure it's harder for him to maintain himself as a regular guy. People naturally gravitate toward Klecko. I've seen Fields put himself through some grueling workouts, hitting the heavy bag and the speed bag in a room where the temperature was a hundred and thirty degrees, but he doesn't look as much like a football player as Klecko. He doesn't have that mutant strength a Joe Klecko has. At first, I think it bothered Fields that Klecko was recognized right away and he wasn't, but he's grown more comfortable with that role. We've gone out to eat together, and you hear people whisper, 'There's Joe Klecko.' We used to kid Fields about what he'd do if somebody actually did recognize him."

If Klecko had gone chasing after celebrity, things might have been different between him and Fields, but that didn't happen. He didn't become Joe Klecko, product spokesman, or Joe Klecko, friend of the rich and famous. He was a football player, and he wasn't about to lose sight of that.

Klecko and Fields shared similar backgrounds and experiences and outlooks, but their love and understanding of football at its highest and most brutal level was the bonding agent in their friendship. They played different roles off the field, but once the ball was in the air, they were two bodies of one mind in their determination to play the game with the passion it demands. The main difference between their personalities parallels the difference between the offensive line and the defensive line.

Offense requires precision timing and concentration; everything must be under control. Defense also requires coordination, but since their purpose is to create mayhem in the offense, defensive linemen rely on more of an emotional release to get the job done. "When I first came up, we stayed at home instead of going to a hotel the night before a home game," Fields says. "My wife would come up from our home in Jersey to go to the game. She had better not talk to me, not even breathe because I would get so aggravated and upset before a game. I would get tight going into a game. Very tight. Klecko is the opposite. He's very loose. After we started rooming together, he helped me loosen up a little more, but I still had a lot of anxieties going into a game."

"I've never been like that in my life," Klecko says. "Until the time they play the National Anthem, I'm as giddy as can be. That bothers a lot of people, especially coaches. Over the years, they realized I was going to play on Sunday, but they think you should be sitting in your locker sweating bullets. Fields constantly questions himself about his ability, but I have the philosophy that I play as hard as I can and as well as I can. If that ain't good enough, I can't do anything about it. I'm sure my strength and the confidence my coaches always had in me allowed me to feel that way."

"When I was a rookie," says Fields, "my offensive line coach, Bob Fry, said, 'If you realize they're always going to try to replace you, then, you'll play ten or twelve years. If you forget, you're not going to last long.'"

"As a defensive player, I can make a mistake, and nobody in the stadium knows it," Klecko explains. "If Fields gets beat for a sack by a guy who's been getting crushed all day, everybody knows it. That's a big difference in temperaments between offensive and defensive players."

Klecko and Fields always studied each other's play and worked together to refine their knowledge, but Klecko's move in 1985 from tackle in the four man line to nose tackle in the three-man line had the effect of pitting them across the ball from each other like two grand masters of the trenches. They never tried to bury each other physically in practice, but they did try to get the best of each other. If Fields blocked down on Klecko when he wasn't expecting it or Klecko beat Fields with a quick move, the loser often would wind up cursing his best friend and really mean it at the moment. On some nights, practice continued in the living room of the house they shared. Furniture was moved up against the wall to make room for pass-rush drills, and by the time the issue was settled, they had a nice pile of kindling in place of the dinner table.

"Fields would tell me a certain blocking scheme will work against a certain defense," Klecko says. "I'd say, 'There's no way you're going to do that to me in a million years. You can't pull the center against me because I'm going to grab hold of you and I know what the guard is doing before he does it. We didn't move the furniture a lot, but we would do it to prove a point."

"We both have a stubborn streak," Fields adds. "Even if I know I'm wrong, I ain't going to let him know. It's amazing how hard some of the young guys make the game. There's a difference between being highly intelligent and being football smart. The other guy can only do certain things out of a certain set. You have to know that and react to it. Being around Klecko, I tried to learn from him everything about the job of the nose tackle I'd be playing against. I'd ask what he was trying to do in certain situations, muscle me or get off the ball quicker, and I'd figure out what to do to counter it."

"I understand the other side of the ball so well that I can tell Fields about blocking," Klecko says. "I'm inside the offensive lineman's head all the time. Before the quarterback is under the center, I'm standing up looking at every single guy on the offensive line, and I'm waiting for the backfield and receivers to set up because everybody does something out of certain setups. On the Jets, Bob Crable and Lance Mehl, who played linebacker, and Harry Hamilton, who played safety, picked up on things like that, but other guys didn't seem to learn as much as they should."

During games, Klecko and Fields always spent time watching to see how the other guy was doing and whether he could suggest anything to help. It was a matter of looking out for each other. On successful teams in any sport, players often talk about the "love" they feel for one another. It usually sounds artificial, and cynics are happy to note how quickly the "love" disappears when a winning team begins to lose and grow frustrated. But when things are going well, there really is a communal feeling of goodwill that supersedes whatever personal differences there are between teammates. "Love" on a team is a shorthand way of saying there is mutual trust and respect and confidence in the other guy to do his job or to make a sacrifice to help the team. It's caring and knowing they can count on each other, and it's the beauty of seeing a team come together and work in unison.

For Klecko and Fields, the feeling was strong enough to develop into a friendship that endured no matter what the circumstances. And because football requires players to subject their bodies to so much physical abuse, the shared understanding of pain and the support they gave each other to overcome it brought them closer together. As other friends fell victim to football's natural attrition, Klecko and Fields came to see themselves more as survivors, and it almost seemed as if the survival of one depended upon the survival of the other.

Fields even wove their friendship into his rituals of preparation for a game. For years, he made Klecko walk the field with him before a game until it snowed one time in Denver and Klecko refused to leave the locker room until it was absolutely necessary. "It was cold, and I told Fields, 'Go out and enjoy yourself, honey. Get away from me,' " Klecko recalls, laughing at the memory. "Joe had all the little quirks you could have. He had to use his old pads, and he didn't want anyone to touch his shoes. If I was there, I had to put his jersey on; nobody else could do it. Whenever I got hurt and couldn't be there, he'd say, 'Who's going to do this for me now?' I'd tell him, 'You're on your own, pal.' I used to hate doing it because it hurt my hands so much to stretch a skin-tight jersey over all the tape on his shoulder pads."

Sharing their home-away-from-home on Long Island during the season, they often joked about their status as a couple. "He's my wife," Fields says of his old roommate. "I call him 'Darling.' When I tore a tendon and had to have a finger operation in training camp in 1982, Klecko would cut my meat for me in the dining hall because I had a big cast on my right hand. The Associated Press came out and took a picture."

"We like to think of it as a manly relationship," Klecko says. "It's not like we run around holding each other's hand, but the true inner feeling is there."

Debbie Klecko says the two Joes complemented each other in the sense that Klecko brought Fields out of his shell socially, while Fields helped Klecko mature in terms of business and laying the groundwork for the future. To their teammates on the Jets, it seemed as though Klecko and Fields were like brothers, but they saw themselves as brothers-in-arms. To say more would be to deny their real brothers, and neither would think of doing that. Klecko is four years older than his brother, Jimmy, who is an engineer, and they didn't become especially close until they were adults. Fields's brother, Robert, is ten years younger and has Down's syndrome. Despite the love Fields felt for his brother, it was impossible for them to share the same kind of athletic experiences.

Living together for as long as they did under the same roof at the Jets' training quarters was almost like growing up in the same family. "Fields and I understand the same things," Klecko says. "I'd say our relationship is unusual in that you don't find two people who travel in the same circle who are so alike and can tolerate each other so well. We care a lot about what each other does. But he has his life and I have mine, and we really don't interfere with what the other one does. We just listen to each other's problems. When you get in confrontations like I've had with Joe Walton, you're looking at it with anger or a scared point of view. It helps to talk to someone who sees it with a clear head."

"I didn't 'need' a brother," Fields says. "But I can talk to Klecko and know I'm going to get a fresh view from someone I respect. Because we come from the same background, I know Klecko will be very realistic."

On a few occasions, Klecko has pulled Fields away from bar disputes before his temper got the better of him. "I could see he was about to hit somebody," says Klecko, "and I'd say, 'Do you see who you're arguing with and what you're doing?' "

"I don't know why I do that," Fields says. "I love an argument, but it will escalate to a bad point. Klecko is much more mellow than I am."

At times, they argue like an old married couple, but mostly, they helped each other get over the bumps and bruises of life in the NFL, kidding each other relentlessly to make the journey more enjoyable. Discussing their relationship one night toward the end of the 1987 season, their eleventh together on the Jets, Klecko and Fields seemed to capture it in this exchange:

Fields: Someone once asked Klecko what the difference was between he and I in training camp, and he said, "It's the difference between a normal person and a caveman." I come to training camp every year the same way. I have a bag of clothes and a bag of shoes. I have a sport coat and a pair of slacks. He comes, and he's got the TV, the radio, and enough clothes for eight months if he didn't wash any of them. I've got nothing.

Klecko: Ask him if he ever uses any of my clothes.

Fields: I didn't even have a coat in my closet up here until the season was about ten weeks old. Klecko has a coat fetish. He's thirty-four years old, and he has a coat fetish. This season, he only has a quarter of the coats he owns up here. He's got eight in the closet, and he took half of them home already. He's got some nice coats. I just pick one out.

Klecko: I picked up our clothes from the cleaners, and I grabbed a striped blue shirt, figuring it was mine, and took it to the complex to get ready to go on a road trip. I have all my shirts tailored. When I put it on and it didn't fit, I looked at it, and the collar was frayed. It was his. I told Fields, "I feel like a fucking bag man, like a slob. I've got a hundred dollar pair of pants, three-hundred-dollar boots, and I've got this shirt on."

Fields: One of my best shirts and he complains about it. I get 18½ × 36 shirts and have them taken in at the waist.

Klecko: He just says that to make himself feel good.

Fields: You asshole, they take them in a lot. I have blue button-down and white button-down and white without a button-down collar.

Klecko: Some day they're going to come back in.

Fields: He's a fashion plate.

Klecko: Did you ever go to a store and try to get something for this body? I have my clothes made. I found a tailor who is almost as cheap as going to the store. I like clothes, and my wife likes clothes and buys them for me.

Fields: I've got jeans and khakis and flannel shirts. I have six suits and six sport coats, and I haven't bought a suit or sport coat in six years.

Klecko: I'm always breaking his balls about how he has an old man's haircut.

Fields: I like to wear my hair high and tight, and Klecko has to get his cut by a stylist. I get my hair cut by an old lady.

Klecko: Fields actually thinks he's good-looking.

Fields: I ain't a bad-looking guy.

Klecko: See?

Fields: Just because you wear all the younger-man's clothes and stuff, you think you're better looking. We've said that, when we hit forty, we're going to buy two Porsches and get gold chains to wear around our necks. The other day, Klecko said he thought we should make it thirty-five because he wants to buy a Porsche. I'm thirty-four, but everybody always tells me I look more like twenty-eight to thirty now.

Klecko: I love this. He has a problem with reality.

Fields: Just because I have a few more wrinkles around my eyes? Isn't this whole thing, playing football, pushing back reality? Isn't it stepping away from reality? Well ... How'd we get off on that?

Nose to Nose

Joe Klecko was just an injured bystander watching from the sidelines one Monday night in the Orange Bowl as the Dolphins beat the stuffing out of the Jets. He knew he wasn't going to play because he still was recovering from arthroscopic knee surgery. From his vantage point at the battle's edge, Klecko was amazed at the level of violence he was witnessing. Detached from his involvement as a player, he could see it unfiltered by his mental conditioning to the hitting. It made him wince.

"I was talking to one of the doctors," Klecko remembers, "and I said, 'My god, I get involved in that stuff every weekend?' The hitting was tremendously fierce. Down in the actual trenches, it's mind-boggling how brutal the hitting is. When you get a high-intensity game, you look back and wonder how you did it and recovered from it."

On television, it's the open-field hitting that stands out. From the stands, fans may hear the impact of bodies covered with high-tech plastic weaponry. But down on the sidelines, where everything is lifesize, the power and the energy of the hitting are both frightening and thrilling. At close range, the brawling between the linemen is so utterly visceral that the path of the ball almost seems incidental. Living life at the point of attack, as linemen do, requires an absence of fear and an enjoyment of contact and tolerance for pain that isn't altogether rational.

"Even though you have a lot of intelligent guys on the line, it's a caveman attitude—kill or be killed," Klecko explains. "You have to be very aggressive, and you have to be able to take a lot of abuse and give it out. It's the gladiator spirit in every man. You prepare yourself for a planned collision, an ass-whipping every week, and it's a hell of a feeling to be able to accomplish something like that in a controlled manner. It's a very macho thing to be a lineman in the NFL. When people hear that, it automatically rings a bell that says you're a tough SOB. It's a very intriguing quality to people.

"A lineman understands you do anything you can get away with to win, except for putting a guy out for his career. If it takes gouging and kicking, you do it if you're a real gutsy football player. It's not really dirty, but it's so fierce. If a guy is holding me to death, I'll come off the floor with a right hand and hit him. That's where I get my point across. You can't let them get away with anything. If anybody cuts me at the knees in an illegal way, I don't care if the quarterback throws a touchdown pass, I'm going to get the guy that cut me. Some hotshots know about the problems I've had with my knees, but they don't give a damn. If I get cut in a flagrant way, I'm going to kick the guy that did it right in the face."

After snapping the patella tendon in his right knee at the start of the 1982 season, Klecko naturally became more sensitive to cut-blocking, which is the act of blocking down on the outside of a defensive player's knee, thus forcing his legs to collapse or risk injury. It's illegal if the defensive player is engaged in contact with another offensive player. Knowing Klecko had suffered a serious knee injury, it became standard practice for offensive linemen desperate to gain an advantage to cut-block Klecko as a way of trying to slow him down.

"I remember the exhibition game we played at Cincinnati in 1983 when a guy cut Klecko, and he chased the guy down the field," linebacker Lance Mehl says. "I grabbed Joe's arm, and he jerked it away. It was like grabbing a tree trunk. He picked up the tackle who cut him and threw him."

When the 1983 season began, Klecko at first appeared to have lost some quickness as a result of his knee injury, and he was shifted from right defensive end to left tackle, where he lined up beside Gastineau to improve the run defense. By midseason, he once again had become a dominating force, and he was chosen for the Pro Bowl at defensive tackle in the four-man line after making it at end in 1981. Despite a hamstring injury that caused him to miss most of five games in 1984, Klecko again made the Pro Bowl as a defensive tackle. Klecko had regained the quickness that made him so devastating at defensive end and could have returned to his old position, but after two 7–9 seasons, coach Joe Walton decided to fire defensive coordinator Joe Gardi and modernize the defense.

Bud Carson, who once had served as defensive coordinator for Pittsburgh's famous "Steel Curtain" defense when the Steelers won their first two Super Bowl championships, was brought in to install a 3–4 defense with an endless variety of blitzing schemes and different looks to confuse the offense. "Bud threw more different things at us than we'd ever seen, and it was the kind of stuff defensive players like because you could attack the offense," Klecko says. "Bud was an exciting coach, and the way he handled himself was great, too. Bud's a rough-and-tumble guy, very emotional. He would be changing coverages in a Friday meeting. He knew what he wanted; the only question was whether you could grasp it. If you did something good, he'd bring it to everybody's attention, but if you fucked up, man, he drilled you. He drilled me a couple of times. Bud would yell and scream, but the minute he walked away, it was forgotten. The big thing was that he wouldn't say a thing if you got beat physically, but if he thought you dogged it or made a mental mistake, he'd go crazy."

As part of the conversion, Carson planned to put Klecko at nose tackle in the three-man line, a move that seemed ill-conceived to some. Traditional nose tackles are considered garbage collectors for the way they try to hold their ground in the middle, tie up one or two offensive linemen, and absorb uncommon punishment so others can make the tackles. Putting Klecko inside appeared to be a waste of his pass-rushing talent, but Carson used his nose tackle in an unorthodox way. Instead of lining him up directly over the center's head, Carson had Klecko line up in a "cocked" position at a 45-degree angle to one side or the other of the center, and he gave Klecko the freedom to jump from side to side to confuse the offensive blocking scheme. Carson had no intention of using Joe Klecko as a mere punching bag.

"Bud Carson gave me a new life," Klecko says. "I could have been stuck playing the center head-up and getting the shit beat out of me, but Bud made it fun. He was amazed how well I adapted to the cocked position. The offensive linemen didn't know where I was going to line up or what I was going to do. I could play one gap between the center and a guard or the other; I could sit there or come hard through either gap. If I switched from one side to the other when the quarterback was calling an audible to change plays, it would really screw them up. I was allowed to freelance a lot, but the guys playing behind me were in sync. Lance Mehl moved to inside linebacker in Carson's 3–4 scheme, and he was a very intelligent player."

Mehl had played outside linebacker behind Klecko when he was at end, so they understood each other very well. Kyle Clifton, the Jets' other inside linebacker, also was sharp at reacting together with Klecko and Mehl. "Joe was the same as he was at defensive end," Mehl says. "He wasn't concerned about making tackles or sacks; he worried about the offensive linemen coming out to block the linebackers. He'd grab a guard and pull him down if he got loose, and he'd get on the other defensive linemen to stop the offensive line. In 1985 and the first half of 1986, we were one hell of a defense. Joe would do things the defense didn't call for, and Kyle and I would adjust. Once when we were watching film, Bud saw us do something we weren't supposed to do, and he said, 'What's this? I didn't know we had another coach.'"

Carson recognized the ability of outstanding players to adjust according to their instincts within the scheme of the defense. He put Klecko in situations where he could be aggressive about rushing the passer. His only concern was that Klecko not become predictable, but Carson experimented freely with Klecko because he was so effective at driving blockers into the quarterback's face and collapsing the pocket. When he was with the Steelers, Carson sometimes put Hall of Fame defensive tackle "Mean" Joe Greene in the cocked position in a four-man line, but he told him just to take one gap. Klecko perfected the position, more or less, because of his ability to play two gaps. "Greene didn't play the same way as Joe Klecko," Carson says. "Klecko taught me a lot about the position because he had such great hands and did more penetrating and stunting. He was so good, I gave him more things to do. When you came to play the New York Jets, the first thing you had to do was figure out how to block Joe Klecko."

The Jets opened the 1985 season with a 31–0 loss to the Raiders in Los Angeles, but most of their problems could be traced to the absence of holdout offensive tackles Marvin Powell and

Reggie McElroy, who signed the next week. Klecko was uncomfortable in his first game at nose tackle but quickly settled in as the Jets went on a five-game winning streak.

"I didn't know anything about the position, but Bud gave me a lot of confidence," Klecko says. "He told me what he wanted me to do, but then, he let me find my own way to do it. He didn't make me take certain steps. Once I found what worked for me, he started pulling in the reins and showing me ways to play more sound. He taught me to switch things up coming off the ball. Because of my knowledge of the game and my ability to anticipate, I started to figure out how to play nose tackle."

In Carson's estimation, no center handled Klecko the entire season, which was the major reason the Jets allowed the fewest points in the American Football Conference. He had two big games against Miami's perennial all-pro center Dwight Stephenson and dominated Seattle's Blair Bush in a performance memorable for one play on which Klecko steamrolled Bush flat on his back and crawled over him to yank down quarterback Dave Krieg by the ankle. Bush said, "Some people call it the 'bull rush.' We call it 'The Klecko Skate' because, when he hits you, it looks like you're rolling backward on skates."

One of the best games Klecko ever played came in the final game of the regular season when the Jets beat Cleveland to finish 11–5 and clinch a wild-card playoff berth. After the game, Browns center Mike Baab said to Klecko, "Boy, I learned a lesson today." But the Jets' season ended abruptly the next week when they self-destructed with four turnovers in a 26–14 playoff loss to eventual AFC champion New England.

Although his statistics were not as spectacular as in 1981 when he was end with the Sack Exchange, Klecko was every bit as disruptive a force. When the AFC players and coaches voted him to the Pro Bowl as a nose tackle, he became the first defensive player in NFL history selected for the Pro Bowl at three different positions. "Being voted to the Pro Bowl by my peers was important to me," Klecko says. "Going to the Super Bowl and winning it is probably more important, but I was able to do something nobody else has done. That's pretty damn significant."

Whether or not it was related to Klecko's move to nose tackle is hard to say, but Joe Fields had one of his best seasons ever in 1985. It was the first time Fields and Klecko had gone nose-to-nose in practice on a daily basis, and even though most of the work was not full speed, it was productive because of the level of competition involved in trying to use their hands to outmaneuver each other and work on the tricks of the trade they had learned over the years. Fields wasn't called for a single penalty in 1,011 offensive plays, and he consistently handled every nose tackle he faced. Miami's Stephenson and Pittsburgh's Mike Webster were chosen for the AFC Pro Bowl squad, but *Sports Illustrated* named Fields as its all-NFL center because of his technical brilliance.

Beyond the time he spent studying the game, the secret of Fields's success was his capacity for recognition and recall. "Once I got in the flow of a game, I felt I knew what a defense was going to do and could take advantage of it," Fields says. "During a game, I could watch what was happening, and I had a good memory for those things. I was kind of like a huge antenna. I'd take it in and run it through my mind, and I would just recognize it right away. I could always adjust on the fly to things I heard or sensed. If I heard a defensive line call, I would remember what my opponent did to me the last time on that call, and I would be ready for it."

When Fields came into the league, Miami's Jim Langer was established as the top center, and Webster quickly gained a following as the center for Pittsburgh's four Super Bowl champions in 1974–75–78–79. They were the players Fields studied the most on film.

"I watched Langer and Webster to see what they did, and I fit the things I could do into my repertoire," Fields says. "I couldn't muscle people the way Webster did, but I could take something he did and adapt it to my style. I might have to get in a different position to do it. I understood how to get the best position for leverage and how to vary the speed at which I did things so they would work. Mostly, I tried to make guys think they could take advantage of me and then use my quickness against them. I used my hands and feet well. You have to work within your limitations and take the textbook moves and fit them to your abilities."

Position coaches can have a major positive or negative effect on a player's performance because they each have specific ways of teaching particular moves and often are inflexible in their insistence that a player adhere to the system rather than make the adjustments that work for him. Fields was fortunate to have a series of quality coaches in Bob Fry, Jim Ringo, and Dan Radakovich.

"Fry never lost his cool," Fields says of the coach he worked under for his first eight seasons when the Jets were known for their strong running attack. "He chewed tobacco, and when he talked to you a lot in a game, you knew it because you had tobacco all over your shoes. Radakovich was a master technician, a very smart guy. He put everything into physics as far as learning the positions where you were strongest and best-balanced. He compared pass-blocking to golf in the way you have to concentrate on doing the little things until they become natural. Some guys are so big and strong they can get away with not paying attention to the fine points for a while, but it will catch up to them.

"Rad said every single play is a physical struggle. You have to constantly fight to survive. That's why he believes in one-on-one pass-blocking drills. It's a survival thing."

Self-preservation certainly was a primary consideration for Klecko's opponents, to whom it must have seemed as though he was born with a genetic edge. Klecko was unusually fast for a man his size, and he had the quick hands of a trained boxer. But it was his natural strength, especially the power of his grip, that could set off the body's alarm system. Klecko was the Jets' enforcer, and his presence emboldened them all.

"Klecko had a reputation," says Jets quarterback Pat Ryan. "People in the league were scared of him. When Klecko snatches you, it freezes you up."

Once when a fullback named Dwayne Crutchfield challenged his authority in the Jets' locker room in a way that was only half-kidding, Klecko waited until Crutchfield turned to walk away and then quickly snatched the 245-pound player off the floor and deposited him on top of a locker. "Klecko picked Crutchfield up like a little kid," Ryan says, recalling the astonishing sight. "He did it in one movement. Klecko held him over his head and then put him on top of the locker. It wasn't a struggle. The whole thing took maybe three seconds. Crutchfield was screaming, and Klecko said, 'Don't fool with me, buddy. You better grow up.' "

"Later on, Crutchfield said to me, 'Man, now I know why not to mess with you,' " Klecko says. "I could have confronted him when he challenged me, but I showed him why instead."

It's amazing the effect a display of Klecko's strength could have on a gathering of unruly football players. "I intimidated guys by grabbing them," Klecko says. "They didn't want to fuck with me. There were times where I picked people up in games and threw them on their heads. I know how to get guys off balance, and I could pick them off the ground like candy. When you do that to somebody, it's an awakening. Nobody's really going to back down, but in fights, I could calm a situation down as fast as anybody. I did it when one of our linemen, Barry Bennett, got in a fight against Denver in 1986. He slammed down the Broncos' quarterback, John Elway, for a safety, and some of their guys went after Barry until I started pulling them away from him. We were in Atlanta the same year, and that rookie tackle Bill Fralic started something. I grabbed him by the front of his shoulder pads and picked him off the ground. When he saw who it was, he just said, 'Okay,' and went back to the huddle."

There was only one time Klecko didn't come to the aid of a teammate in a fight. In a 1983 game against the Los Angeles Rams at Shea Stadium, Mark Gastineau performed his sack dance, and the tackle he beat, Jackie Slater, chased Gastineau down the field, setting off a bench-clearing melee. "I grabbed one of the Rams, and he said, 'Let me go, let me go,' " Klecko says. "I said, 'So you can go fight and get thrown out of the game? What do you want to do that for?' "

"I wasn't thinking," laughs Fields. "I came off the bench onto the field and started fighting and got fined by the league."

Whenever Klecko spoke with fans, he invariably was asked to name the toughest players he ever faced. If he were to choose an all-star team, the names at the top of the list would be those of New England guard John Hannah, Miami center Dwight Stephenson, and Cincinnati tackle Anthony Munoz. Hannah earned an extra measure of respect from Klecko. Even though they didn't know each other well at the time, Hannah visited the Jets' locker room to wish Klecko well the day his patella tendon snapped in 1982 at New England.

"Hannah and I would beat the shit out of each other, never say a word, just kind of give a little nod or something," Klecko says. "There was respect between us. He wasn't going to give up, and neither was I. People told me John was never a big weightlifter, but he sure played football strong. He was a lot like Fields, who isn't a real strong guy; Hannah used leverage the same way. I used to literally throw guys out of the way, but I couldn't pick Hannah off his feet because he was so stout and positioned himself so well. When we played the Patriots, they'd run at me, and I'd stop them. On pass plays, I'd get there a little too late because

Hannah would hold me off. I don't know if I ever got a sack off Hannah, but if I hit the quarterback, Hannah would come back and kill me the next play. I don't feel he ever really beat me or that I beat him in a game.

"Without a doubt, Dwight Stephenson was the toughest center I ever played. When I played tackle before I moved to nose tackle, I faced Dwight a lot. You could ignore the game and just watch me and him. That's how good the battles were. He combated one of the things I do well with his hand speed and quickness. Dwight uses his strength well, and he's very smart. Anthony Munoz is a great player, too, a big, strong person. I heard that he once said myself and Lee Roy Selmon were the best he played against, and that's an honor."

Among the quarterbacks Klecko banged around, Houston's Dan Pastorini sticks out in his mind for his resiliency in a 1979 overtime victory against the Jets in Houston. "I had one or two sacks in the game, but I swear to God that I hit Pastorini seventy-five percent of the time he threw the ball. It seemed like I hit him every fucking play. I thought he was a real tough guy because I rocked that SOB big-time, and he kept getting up."

There were several other opponents Klecko respected for the clean, hard way they played the game, including Pittsburgh tackle Jon Kolb, Houston tackle Leon Gray, and Buffalo tackle Ken Jones, who had five holding penalties the first time he played Klecko. Jones changed his number the next game, and the memory of that day always seemed to inspire him to play his best against Klecko.

"Good athletes, like Leon Gray, were the type that gave me trouble," Klecko says. "Strong guys never bothered me because I was stronger. I remember playing against Mike Kenn of Atlanta. He could never block me because I had the build he couldn't combat. I was his worst nightmare. We became friends, though. An Atlanta reporter came to see me after one game and said, 'Don't you think Mike really played bad?' I said, 'Get the fuck out of here and leave that guy alone.' I didn't know it, but Mike was standing right there. When I hurt my knee in Atlanta in 1986, Mike came to see me in the locker room after the game. I didn't have to hate my opponent. Playing hard was good enough for me."

There was one player, however, that Klecko found it easy to detest. Surprisingly enough, it wasn't Buffalo guard Conrad Dobler, the so-called "dirtiest player in the NFL." It was the guy who lined up inside of Dobler, center Will Grant.

"Dobler was the kind of guy who would take a cheap shot; he wanted to get your mind off the game," Klecko says. "But Grant would grab you and kick you and do all kinds of things. I used to fight with him all the time. I hate him to this day. What really gets to me is that he thought he was good, but he wasn't worth a shit as a football player."

Referees didn't receive much respect from Klecko, either. His language was strictly X-rated when addressing them. "The referees in this league hate me because of the confrontations," Klecko admits. "I cussed 'em up one side and down the other. I've come as close as you can to cold-cocking referees because they wouldn't call offensive holding. I get so damn mad because it's so flagrant. They say, 'Well, you ran the guy over.' So what? It's illegal to hold. I've tried to take it easy on them, but I can't hold it back when I get to the boiling point. I remember Jim Tunney called me for a fucking penalty one time at Shea Stadium. He turned the field mike on just as I said, 'And you're a motherfucker, too!' It went all over the stadium, and he threw another flag on me. The greatest part of it is that a head coach has never said nothing to me when I come to the bench.

"I know a retired ref from Scranton, Pennsylvania. I was making an appearance in Scranton, and he came over to see me. He said, 'Joe doesn't know my name.' I said, 'Sure, I do. It's Ralph Moore.' And he said, 'No it ain't. It's motherfucker.'"

As vicious as the fighting in the trenches often becomes, it usually breeds respect between competitors rather than hatred. If they last very long in the NFL, opponents in the same division develop a kind of intimate relationship with each other. The mind game is critical because their moves are so familiar.

Fields had that kind of rivalry with Miami nose tackle Bob Baumhower, who played against him for the better part of ten seasons before injuries cut his playing time, and with Buffalo nose tackle Fred Smerlas, who opposed Fields for nine years in the AFC East. The competition was demanding because both Baumhower and Smerlas represented the AFC several times in the Pro Bowl.

"Freddie was a brute strength guy," Fields says. "Baumhower was strong, but he would try to trick you more often. He would act like he was going to jump offsides one way and then go the other way, and he'd use a head-butt and then pull you. I think Fred tried to use quickness more. He wasn't a great pass-rusher, but he could put pressure up the middle by getting loose.

"Fred and I got in a fight once. I thought he was piling on, and I said, 'Fred, what the fuck are you doing! Pile on me! I'll be over the ball all day! You know where to find me!' We were at the Pro Bowl together a couple years later having some beers with the guys, and Fred asked me if I remembered our fight. I said, 'Things happen.' He said, 'I know, I just wanted to see if you remembered.'

"I got to know Baumhower a little bit. He went to Alabama with Richard Todd, and we had a few beers together at Richard's wedding. Then, I talked to him at the 1982 Pro Bowl. We talked about how the Dolphins lost the Super Bowl to the Redskins, but we didn't talk about the AFC championship game we played in the mud that season at the Orange Bowl. He wasn't my teammate or friend, so why should I let him know how I feel about what happened in that game? We could be friendly to a point, but nobody was giving away any secrets. You develop a respect for each other, but I didn't want to know about his kids and his family or what he does in the offseason."

In the years Klecko and Fields spent with the Jets, they played on four playoff teams with an impressive collection of talented players. On offense, Fields was closest in every sense to right guard Dan Alexander, an ironman who never received enough recognition to make the Pro Bowl, though he was an alternate in 1986. "A lot of my success, I attribute to Alexander playing beside me," Fields says. "He played with pain, and I could always count on him to help me when I was hurt. If my shoulder was hurt, I'd ask him to watch out for anything on my right side, and I'd help him if he got knocked loose upstairs."

To Alexander's right was five-time Pro Bowl tackle Marvin Powell, but tackles often are alone on the offensive line, unless they're receiving help from a tight end. Guards and centers work in close coordination to cover the middle of the field.

"Marvin was a heck of a football player," Fields says. "He was huge at six-foot-five, two hundred and seventy pounds, and he was naturally strong even though he didn't do a lot of weightlifting. Marvin worked hard, but he relied a lot on natural ability. I always felt he could have been even better if he worked harder."

In his early years with the Jets, Fields always respected running back Clark Gaines, who was an offensive co-captain. "Clark was hard-nosed," Fields says. "He could put his head down and get five yards." But the most successful and, yet, most enigmatic running back the Jets ever had was Freeman McNeil. He had days best described by the Australian term "walkabout," meaning he wasn't all there, and then, he would put on brilliant, free-form running displays, such as the playoff game at the end of the 1982 season in Cincinnati when he carried 21 times for 202 yards and also threw a touchdown pass. "I felt we didn't have to block anybody that day in Cincinnati, and Freeman would gain yards," Fields says. "At times, eleven men couldn't tackle him, and at other times, Freeman would tackle himself."

The Jets always were known in those playoff years for the deep-strike threat posed by wide receiver Wesley Walker, who put the ball in the end zone more times than anyone in Jets history except Hall of Fame wide receiver Don Maynard. Fields admired Walker's talents, but if any Jets wide receiver is going to join Maynard in the Hall of Fame, Fields expects it will be Al Toon, who joined the Jets in 1985. "I told Toon he could be one of the best to ever play," Fields says. "Coupled with his great natural ability, he works on all the finer points of the game."

On the defensive side, linebackers Lance Mehl and Greg Buttle, who was with the Jets in Klecko's early years, stood out as players who knew the game, and free safety Darrol Ray and cornerback Jerry Holmes were the best in the secondary. "Ray was a player I liked, a real smart player," Klecko says. "Holmes I respected for what he had to work with at corner. He didn't have the greatest speed or size, but he played tough. Marty Lyons was above average on the defensive line, but Lyons gets wrapped up in a lot of his own hoopla in the locker room. He's always yelling and throwing stuff because he thinks that's what motivates guys. He cut his hand punching out a window in the locker room before our playoff game against the Raiders. It gets old after you beat it into the ground."

With such a varied store of talent on which to draw, it was hard for Klecko and Fields to accept the fact that their Jets never made it to the Super Bowl. It felt as though they were good enough, but something always went wrong—turnovers killed the 1981 and 1985 teams in wild-card playoff games at home against Buffalo and New England; the 1982 team got stuck in the mud at Miami one step short of the goal, and the 1986 team was burdened by injuries and blew a game it should have won in double overtime at Cleveland. It was hard not to wonder if the coaching change from Walt Michaels to Joe Walton after the Jets lost the 1982 AFC title game disrupted a team in its prime. What if the field had been covered in Miami? Did Walton fail to adjust the offensive game plan to the muddy conditions during that game? The questions could drive a man crazy, and if he knew the answers, they only could make him sick to his stomach.

They were team players, but the highest team achievement eluded Klecko and Fields. In the end, the Pro Bowl recognition they received was their greatest source of satisfaction because it came from other players and coaches. Brooding about the void in his career, Fields says, "A Super Bowl ring would be nice because it's a team sport, but I've got two Pro Bowl watches. I'm starting to think that's a lot nicer. I've seen some pretty bad football players wearing Super Bowl rings, but I haven't seen too many bad players wearing Pro Bowl watches. That's the way I feel, especially when I'm not going to get to go to the Super Bowl."

The only time Klecko and Fields went to the Pro Bowl together was after the 1981 season. Klecko was hurt most of 1982 when Fields made his second trip, and *Sports Illustrated*'s nomination as the best center in the game in 1985 didn't help Fields when the players overlooked his superb season and voted for old standbys Dwight Stephenson and Mike Webster. In a way, all the honors Fields received were just so much icing on the cake to him.

"I never really considered myself that good," Fields says. "I was flattered I went to two Pro Bowls and flattered *Sports Illustrated* picked me to be an all-pro. I never got a Super Bowl ring and I never played the perfect game, but I just really enjoyed playing. That was all the satisfaction I needed."

Because of the nature of the sport, pro football's all-star game is more of a celebration for the players and a chance for them to vacation in Hawaii than a serious sporting event. It can't be played at midseason because of the risk of injury, so it comes as a bit of an afterthought following the Super Bowl. Klecko can't think of the Pro Bowl without thinking of Raiders outside linebacker Ted Hendricks, whose nickname as "The Mad Stork" only hinted at his penchant for the inordinate pursuit of excess.

"Drinking with Ted Hendricks was like trying to kill yourself," Klecko says. "I remember my first trip to the Pro Bowl. I was in the front line during jumping jacks at the beginning of the first practice, and Hendricks said, 'Klecko, I've heard a lot about you. I'll meet you in the bar after practice.' He left right then, and I went on practicing. I didn't see him until I went to the bar. He was a great guy. We drank all week long. His wife was mad at him, but Debbie wasn't too mad at me. She said, 'This is your time.' After we played the game on Sunday, we were in the hotel restaurant eating, and Debbie said, 'Joe, there's Ted. He's looking for you.' I dove under the table because he was looking for me to go drinking with him, and I just couldn't take it anymore.

"Hendricks and I became pretty good friends. We were at the Pro Bowl again after the 1983 season when the Raiders won the Super Bowl. Debbie and I were standing in the check-in line, and Hendricks, drunker than hell, walked in and started screaming about us beating them in the 1982 playoffs. He said, 'Last year, you SOB, I bought you your snowmobile. Now, you've got to buy me something.' He turns to Debbie and says, 'Check him in. We'll be at the bar.' We stayed out that night. Chuck Knox, the Seattle coach, was coaching the AFC team. The next day at practice, Knox told us to run two laps. Ted and I looked at each other and walked in. There was no way we were going to run. Ted retired after spending all of the '84 season on injured reserve, but when I was at the Pro Bowl in '85, he was out there looking for me.

"There were a lot of good times at the Pro Bowl. I got to know Howie Long, the Raiders' best defensive lineman, at the Pro Bowl. At the '84 Pro Bowl, I took Mark Gastineau's helmet without Mark knowing it and gave it to Howie as a souvenir. We opened against the Raiders the next season, and Merlin Olsen, who was announcing the game, revealed it on TV after talking to Howie and me. That's how Mark found out. Mark never said anything to me, but evidently he said something to Howie because Howie sent it back."

In 1985, Klecko took his mother and father with him to the Pro Bowl because he knew how much it meant to them, especially his father. But it was an awkward time. Joe Sr. never could contain his pride about his son's achievements. He had been a sandlot football star in Chester, Pennsylvania, but never had the chance to pursue his dreams further. As Klecko's mother, Josephine, explains, "Dad sort of tried to live in Joe's shoes. It was something he wanted to do but couldn't do. He's so proud of Joe that we have to watch him when we're tailgating at games because he's always off introducing himself to people as Joe Klecko's father. He was in his glory at the Pro Bowl, but he put us all on edge."

The father who once was so ashamed because his son failed to play in his first high school football game now wanted to share the spotlight with him. He wanted to know what it was like to be as good as the son he once said "wouldn't make a pimple on my ass." The sandlot star, "Shea" Klecko, suddenly found himself vastly overshadowed by the achievements of his son.

"Marcus Allen and Freeman McNeil were there, and Dad was talking about girls with them at the hotel pool," Klecko recalls. "The ABC cameras came around and started taping Freeman while he was taping everybody else. Dad jumps up and stands next to Freeman and says, 'Hey, Freeman, how are you?' He wanted to be on TV. It was the toughest week we ever spent on vacation. I get him around other players, and he embarrasses me to death. It's not enough for me to be his son. He has to try to live it.

"It was a problem for me and my mother. I was hesitant to take him anywhere in my career because he acted so overbearing about being my father. I always shunned publicity, but my father loved the accolades. I'm Joe Klecko, not him."

The game of football gave to Joe Klecko, Sr. some of the happiest and most rewarding moments of his life. He was touched with the warrior spirit and reveled in everything about the game from the contact to the camaraderie with his fellows. To think he had a son who not only played pro football but was recognized in 1981 as the best defensive player in the NFL filled Joe Sr. with an inexpressible sense of pride. "I wanted everybody to know who I was, see," he explains. "How would anyone feel if they had a son like that?"

The feeling reminded Joe Sr. of the thrill he experienced the time he sneaked onto the sidelines during an Eagles game at Franklin Field to grab a football for his son and took the opportunity to shake hands with Dallas defensive lineman Bob Lilly. It meant everything just to touch a real pro. "It was so great to be near a football player," Joe Sr. remembers. "I was so proud. Now, I've got a football player for a son, and he won't let me be near him as much as I'd like. He doesn't understand how much I love to stand near him."

12

The Wives:
Debbie's Story

Once when he was at a christening party, Joe Klecko heard a female acquaintance say with regard to his wife, Debbie, "Yeah, some day, I'm going to marry a rich man, too." That comment perfectly defined the stereotype with which the wife of a successful professional athlete must live. People just naturally assume Debbie landed Joe Klecko, NFL football star, not Joe Klecko, long-haul truck driver. They picture her throwing herself at Klecko in a bar full of groupies or enticing him in some more glamorous setting, not meeting him at a pizza parlor where adolescent boys and teenage girls try to work up the courage to speak to each other. If the stereotype is sometimes accurate, it's more often misguided. The person comes before the celebrity, the real life before the public facade.

The woman's remark, tinged with envy, was in keeping with human nature, but still, it rankled Klecko, who says, "My wife and I were together way before I amounted to anything. Debbie went through the hard times. She was in high school, and I was driving a truck when I asked her out. She used to ride in the truck with me on some of the long hauls."

So much for glamour. Klecko wore shaggy blond hair and long sideburns in keeping with teenage fashion trends, and though he looked as big and strong as a Clydesdale, he was a little soft around the edges, since his baby fat had not yet been shaped by year-round weight training. Debbie saw beyond the tough-guy image he presented, and she found his shyness attractive.

"He was sort of cute," she says. "He never dated much. He was kind of afraid of girls, and that was a challenge to me. I liked his nature. He was very kind, and he always tried to help people, even if he had to go out of his way. I admired that."

Maybe Klecko was destined to have a football career, but it was Debbie who recognized how much he missed the game after high school and who gave him the push he needed when he was dragging his heels after the semipro Aston Knights invited him to a tryout. She talked him into going and then drove him to practice to make sure he didn't give in to a last-minute case of stage fright.

Laughing at the thought of where that day led, Debbie says, "In a way, I guess I'm responsible for it. Joe had only played six games in high school and received all kinds of honors, and I knew he had just touched the surface, really. But even though I knew he was a good player and really enjoyed it, I never thought he would be a professional football player. For where we lived, he was making decent money driving a truck. I really expected we would get married, he would drive a truck, and we would live like his parents and my parents. No way did he want to go to college. He hated school."

When Klecko decided to attend Temple University on a football scholarship, the transition to college life threatened their relationship because he was leaving the familiar small-town atmosphere in Chester. They even broke up for a while, and Debbie thought for a time that they would go their separate ways. But they got married at the end of Klecko's junior year and moved into a small, dingy apartment that was poorly furnished. Klecko continued to drive a truck and work as a bouncer at the same time he was trying to play football and spend enough time in school to pass his courses. Debbie worked in Philadelphia as a computer programmer, and they were lucky if they saw each other more than twice a week. When the Jets drafted Klecko in 1977, it was exciting not because they were sure he would make the team but because the $12,000 signing bonus allowed them to move to a nicer apartment.

At first, life with the Jets was an adventure. They socialized with other young couples like themselves from the team. It was more exciting than most jobs, but still, it was just a way to make a living like anything else. Klecko never made more than $31,000 in base salary his first three seasons. But then came his first small movie role in *Smokey and the Bandit II* in 1980, followed by the full-blown success of the New York Sack Exchange in 1981. Suddenly, Debbie Klecko was married to a star football player who only pretended to be a truck driver in the movies.

"I can see where the attention Joe received could put a strain on a marriage," Debbie says, "but Joe didn't become Mr. Hollywood. He enjoyed it, and he always seemed to have time for people who came up to him. It didn't really faze me at all. I liked reading about him in the newspapers, but I didn't get caught up in it. We didn't spend a lot of time in New York City; we stayed home most of the time. Joe always stayed the same, so, that helped me. I've been secure enough that the attention he received didn't bother me.

"I went with him when he did his first movie. We drove to Jupiter, Florida and stayed for a couple of days. We sat there all day and watched while they set up a stunt that took about three seconds in the movie. Joe asked if I wanted to meet Burt Reynolds, and I said no. I would have felt stupid doing that. I sat back and watched, but I know he loved it. He said it was an easy way to make money."

The movies were about as far removed as anybody ever imagined they would be from the reality of life in a working town like Chester. The phenomenon of celebrity status in general bears little connection to reality. Joe and Debbie enjoyed the benefits, but they never really took it seriously enough to forget they were the same kids who met over pizza and rode together in Klecko's truck to make deliveries. Debbie observed it all with a down-to-earth sense of humor and a cool head, which was helpful at those times when they were out in public and other women—the groupies with their hooks set for a rich and famous man—wanted to brush up against her husband.

"I've had girls walk on my feet to get at Joe to meet him," Debbie says. "I laugh because I know that if Joe were a truck driver, they would not be walking over me to get to him. He knows it, too. That's the one thing that's kept us from fighting. He's always kept his head. I'm sure there have been times I've been jealous, but not many. It's my nature to be easygoing and laid-back. The other women make me mad sometimes, but most of the time, my anger doesn't last, as long as he doesn't act like a jerk and get too impressed. If I couldn't handle it as a wife, I'd be upset all the time."

Another woman might have been jealous of the celebrity that Klecko achieved, might even have tried to compete with him. It's not unusual for that to happen, but Debbie wasn't like that. "Debbie's been around it a long time, but there is no resentment in her," Klecko says gratefully. "A lot of times, wives resent the things their husbands get. Debbie works at making me happier when that stuff happens, not because she's afraid of losing me, but because she really wants me to be happy."

It varies from team to team, but football wives also face certain expectations related to their husband's career. Some wives' groups are heavily involved in charity work, which may lead to considerable social responsibilities and political game-playing.

"When we first came up with the Jets, Joe was making twenty-one thousand dollars," Debbie says. "Nobody could be snobby or act sophisticated because it wasn't that much money. Now that the players are making a lot of money, it seems like their wives are a lot different. A lot of it is political. Everybody was trying to look good for their husband so he would be thought of well. Either you go along, or you feel like there's going to be some resentment toward you. I don't like being involved in it. I missed several of the wives' luncheons."

At one of the luncheons during the 1987 season, Kay Fields reported to Debbie that Ginger Walton sang and called the other wives up to join her on stage. The wife of Jets coach Joe Walton once had been Miss Washington, D.C. and was runnerup in the Miss America contest and she still was playing the role. "It was unbelievable," Debbie says. "She had all the wives holding hands and singing like it was some big Girl Scout thing. Luncheons are nice, but who needs that other stuff?"

In 1985, when the social atmosphere on the Jets began to change in ways that Debbie found less appealing, she and Joe decided it would be best if she and their two sons lived year-round at their home outside of Philadelphia, since the boys had reached school age. It helped Klecko, too, because he could stay late at the complex and lift weights until about 7 P.M. without worrying about getting home in time for dinner. He could stay focused on football, which became even more important as he grew older. The Kleckos were used to time apart when Joe was driving a truck, and the adjustment wasn't difficult for someone as self-sufficient as Debbie.

"I kind of enjoyed the time to myself," she says. "I said to my friends, 'How can you stand having your husband around all the time?' Joe had his freedom. I wasn't the kind of wife who was possessive, and that helped us last. If anybody tries to sit on Joe, he runs. He cannot stand to be told what to do.

"I look at my friends and say their lives are so boring. They look at mine and say it's so hectic. I used to really enjoy moving. We'd pack up at the end of summer and go up to New York, and it was exciting. Then, we'd come home at Christmas. I liked the change. It's been a lot of fun. How many women get to go and watch their husband do his job and cheer for him? Kay Fields and I have been close friends, and we get together pretty often. When we both lived up on Long Island, we were about three blocks from each other, and we had a ball. We've helped each other a lot. We went to games together, and she baby-sat for me when I needed it. She and I come from similar backgrounds, so, we felt comfortable with each other. We always could talk about how to deal with our husbands' problems with the Jets."

Debbie and Kay were good company for each other because they were living with two of the more dominant male egos on the Jets. Kidding around one time with tight end Rocky Klever about the "wimp scale" on the Jets, Debbie and Klever rated Klecko and Fields as typical male chauvinist pigs. "There's some truth in it, but you just have to know how to manipulate him," Debbie says of her husband. "It helps that Joe and I came from the same background. He went to an all-boys Catholic high school, and I went to an all-girls Catholic high school.

"Joe is really pretty gentle at home. He's rarely very aggressive. It's almost funny to watch him play and be so mean on the field. Sometimes, it takes him a few hours to wind down after a game, and on Monday mornings, it's tough. I'll be glad when it's over so he won't be hurting all the time."

Klecko's level of pain in his post-NFL years, of course, is problematical. He expects to have arthritis by the age of fifty, if not sooner. He's undergone major surgery on both knees and taken numerous injections of cortisone, and the general wear and tear of a long pro football career may be expected to exact a physical toll.

As dramatic as Klecko's snapped patella tendon was in 1982,

it was easier for Debbie to handle it because Joe was in the prime of his career and the doctors were able to give her strong reassurances that he would be all right. He was able to make it back the same season in time for the playoffs. But the damage was worse in 1986 when Klecko underwent arthroscopic surgery on his left knee at midseason in a desperate attempt to keep playing and collapsed after one quarter in his first game back, necessitating a full reconstruction job.

"The second one was harder to deal with because of his age," Debbie says. "The doctors never said, 'He's going to be fine.' They said, 'Well, Joe's not your average thirty-three-year-old.' When he tried to go back after his arthroscopic surgery, I could tell he wasn't going to be able to play. When he went down, I was kind of relieved it happened then instead of the next season. After the surgery, the doctors told me everything went well even though they did a lot more things than they would for anyone else because they knew he still wanted to play. He was so depressed watching games on TV after the surgery. We had friends over, and he wouldn't even talk to them."

Living with Klecko as he struggled with injuries during the last half of the 1986 season and fought to come back in 1987 was no easy task. "I was a bear for a couple of years, and Debbie handled it like it was nothing," Klecko says. "She never bothered me with her problems. A lot of women would put all the burden on their husband. She's unique. Like when the kids were born. She thought it was great, but some people think they're the only ones who ever had kids. Debbie wasn't like that, but one night when our oldest son, Michael, was sick and couldn't sleep, she sat down and cried. Debbie doesn't cry about anything, but she cried because Michael felt bad. When I get hurt, she knows I don't like pity. She'll help me and sympathize, but she will never pity me because she knows I think that's weak."

In Klecko's early days with the Jets, Debbie was like him— she thought he was invincible. Going to the games was the same as going to a party with their good friends. But Klecko's injuries, problems the team had adjusting to Walton, and, finally, the prospect of retirement changed all that.

"The games got harder and harder to watch every year for me," Debbie says. "I'd be covering my eyes on defense. I'd watch Joe to make sure he got up after every play. I couldn't even watch on TV because it would make me so upset. I used to relax and enjoy it, but after so many injuries, you just start to hold your breath.

"Joe Walton put a lot of pressure on my Joe and Joe Fields. Even when they were getting along with Walton, he would call them into his office, and the pressure was on them to do something about the team if it wasn't playing well. It changed Joe's personality; he became a lot more serious and stressed out. He didn't bring a lot of it home, but it was more than he thinks. Sometimes, he would sit there and think he was being fine, but I could tell when he was upset."

In some ways, the most practical thing would have been for Klecko to retire after his second major knee surgery at the end of the 1986 season, but Debbie realized how difficult that would be for him to do. In fact, it wasn't a consideration because he was determined to prove he could come back again. When he struggled and the Jets played poorly as a team in 1987, all the signs indicated he would be asked to retire. It would have eased her concerns for his health if Klecko wanted to go that route, but Debbie knew he wasn't ready and she wasn't going to add her voice to the others trying to goad him into retirement.

"Joe and I have always been on the same wavelength about his playing," Debbie says. "I understood what the Jets were trying to do to him. If he retired after the surgery, it would have affected him forever. It was important for his mental health to come back and play even if he couldn't have a great year."

When he was president of the Jets, Jim Kensil said players should think of football as a stepping stone, not a career. It sounds logical enough, but Kensil's reasoning ignores the deep physical and psychological investment players make in order to succeed in the sport. It's not a simple pastime; the game is a source of identity and self-respect. It's intense. It forces a man to stretch to find his limits. It has all the properties of a meaningful career except one—longevity.

The problem with being a professional athlete is that it guarantees an early-to-mid-life crisis. Debbie recognized the symptoms with Klecko as he approached the end of his time with the Jets. At times, they argued over insignificant things when the real problem was the anxiety Klecko felt because of the mounting pressure on him to give up football.

"It was scary," Debbie says. "Joe wasn't as carefree. He had to think more about the future and mature. He puts a lot of pressure on himself to succeed, and I could see the wheels turning constantly. He was always looking for a deal. He wasn't a happy person. He couldn't relax and say, 'The hell with it.' "

Debbie did what she could to take the pressure off Klecko. "She said, 'Joe, we don't need to live in a big house,' " Klecko recalls. "Things like that put your mind at ease. If I sold all the cars and the boats, I know my wife would be just as happy."

Klecko always spoke of football as a kid's game and found it hard to believe he could be paid so well for doing the thing he loved. He could recite those clichés and mean it because of the pleasure the game gave him, but at the same time, he understood that NFL football truly is a dangerous man's game that has become exceedingly big business. It wouldn't be easy to leave that life and start a new one.

"Now, he has to go into the real world and earn a living," Debbie says. "He has to stop and think: 'What am I going to do?' He has investments, so, he's made a good start. But he has to worry about what he's going to do day-to-day. I dread the first football season he doesn't play because I know he's going to be depressed. After that, I think he'll be okay."

So, it seems, will Debbie Anderson and Joe Klecko of Chester, Pennsylvania, whose marriage survived and came out stronger for the experience. Life in the NFL can't last forever, but life goes on.

The Wives:
Kay's Story

Football hero marries cheerleader—"The old story," Kay Fields says with a warm smile. It was a cliché, but that didn't stop Kay and Joe Fields from getting married before his second season with the Jets. The only new wrinkle in the plot line was that Fields was a center, not a quarterback. After all, how many times does a center get the girl?

But at Division III Widener College, the center was the best player on a very good team. In 1975, Fields was just the second Widener player ever chosen in the NFL draft. He wasn't picked until the fourteenth round, so he knew his work was cut out for him if he wanted to make the Jets' roster. But if a compulsion for hard work meant anything, the situation was made to order for him. Fields was a workaholic, even if the term wasn't invented until the eighties. He had one opportunity, and he was totally committed to making the most of it. Since he didn't have great natural athletic ability, it meant long hours of training and practice when he wasn't working at his regular job. That's the part of being a football player they never show in the movies or on TV. Too tedious.

"I was so dedicated to football, and I was such a workaholic that, in the offseason, I was gone seven days a week working construction," Fields says. "When I came home, the first thing I did was go to the gym and work out for three or four hours. I was gone from six A.M. to ten P.M. every day. Football put a lot of strain on us then. We almost split up in the first three or four years of our marriage. It was because of me being a workaholic."

"Joe couldn't incorporate football and his wife," Kay says. "He kept the two separate. I didn't even live with him on Long Island. He couldn't emotionally be there for me and deal with me. He had to keep me away from football so he could have one hundred percent concentration on football. He completely excluded me."

Everyone who achieves a level of success has a method and believes in it. Single-minded dedication is what always worked for Fields before he and Kay were married. It was the only way he knew, and Fields was a guy who always was willing to believe the worst about himself as a football player, who always figured he was expendable. "I felt so much pressure," Fields explains, "that I thought that's what I had to do to stay in football."

At Widener, football had been fun for Kay. It was a vital part of the social fabric of college life. Football games on Saturday afternoon and parties on Saturday night. The anticipation built all week during the fall. It was exciting. But that casual atmosphere disappeared once Fields went from playing football as a passionate avocation to a fulltime occupation.

Kay Weeks was the second of six children, five girls and one boy, in a family that lived in La Plata, Maryland, where her high school graduating class numbered thirty-four students. Her parents and their six children all shared one bathroom in a tiny house with three small bedrooms and a cramped kitchen. She was used to holding conversations with more than the walls, and the long periods of solitude after she was married represented a dramatic change in her life-style.

"At one point, I hated the way Joe isolated our lives," Kay says. "I gradually accepted that fact and told myself, 'You better sink or swim.' Football was fun in college. I guess I expected to be a big part of his life with the Jets because he didn't exclude me in college. But it was like a night-and-day change when he went to the pros, and that caught me off guard."

Once Fields was established with the Jets, Kay moved in with him during the season, and their domestic troubles began to smooth out. But in 1983, the story of Saturday's hero and the cheerleader took another unexpected turn that defied the stereotype that said they would have 2.5 kids and a blissful life. Joe and Kay learned they couldn't have any kids of their own.

Coming from a large family, Kay says, "Kids were really the only thing I wanted out of life. When we found out we couldn't have children, it shook everything. Joe didn't want to adopt. I thought, 'If he's not going to change his mind, I've got things I want out of life.' I couldn't live alone."

While he wrestled with his own feelings about adoption, Fields used Joe Klecko as his sounding board and discussed his relationship with Kay and the differences they were having. When Klecko and his wife, Debbie, went to the Pro Bowl after the 1983 season, they left their sons Michael and Danny with the Fields to give them a sample of family life. "Klecko was a good ear," Fields says. "He just said, 'Think about Kay and what she's thinking about.' I think that really helped me."

Kay was doing some soul-searching of her own about the fact that she shared Fields with his mistress, football. She was jealous of the time he devoted to staying in the game and felt neglected by comparison. But after all the time they had spent together, she didn't want to give up on their relationship or the idea of finding a way to have a family.

"I had to take into consideration his feelings," Kay says. "I listened, and I understood what he was going through. At that point in life is when I really let go of football. I realized it wasn't life; it was just a job. All the time he was putting into it was a benefit for me and our future, and that's when I stopped rivaling with football."

At first, Fields had a closed mind on the subject of adoption, but his attitude began to change as he and Kay talked more about it and she exposed him to the literature on the subject. He was surprised to discover that an acquaintance at the gym where he trained during the offseason was adopted, and he came to realize there was nothing wrong with adoption.

On May 29, 1986, he and Kay attended a meeting arranged by an adoption agency. "After listening to stories from other people, I knew it was for me," Fields says. "I said, 'I can adopt.' From that day forward, I never had another qualm about it. I think it was just looking at the pictures of all the other couples in this album the agency had that convinced me. The problems I had accepting it disappeared, and I became one hundred percent gung-ho."

Once he decided that he could adopt, Fields didn't limit his choice to perfect babies. He and Kay agreed they were willing to accept a child who might be handicapped in some way because they wanted to take the same chances they would if they were having a baby naturally.

"We didn't think we could handle emotionally a severe handicap, but we felt we could take someone with a learning disability or a slight physical handicap," Fields says. "Yes, the fact that I have a brother with Down's syndrome was an influence, and Kay's always been real close to my brother, Robert. There was a feeling we could handle that."

Fields was ten years old when his only brother was born in 1963 with Down's syndrome, which also is known as mongolism and results in a degree of mental retardation. In that era, doctors commonly advised parents of such children to institutionalize them. Yet, Fields's parents resisted that suggestion and worked hard to help Robert learn to function as best he could in life.

"All the advice was negative, but that made us more determined not to put Robert in an institution," Joe Sr. says. "Robert made Joey more self-reliant because we couldn't devote as much time to him and the other children individually, but they didn't resent it. I think Joey learned some compassion because of Robert. We're just as proud of Robert's achievements. You know, he never forgets a phone number."

Helen Fields brought in tutors three times a week to help Robert with his speech and basic reading, writing, and spelling. "We raised Robert like we raised the other kids," says Helen. "Robert was very easy to raise. He was always pleasant and never demanding. He was very satisfied with whatever you could do, and he could entertain himself. Robert became a blessing."

Caring for Robert was a much bigger job than Helen Fields makes it sound. Joe's older sister, Cheryl, says, "Robert took longer to do everything. A normal baby would take twenty minutes on his bottle, but Robert couldn't suck strong enough. My mother put bigger holes in the nipple and sat with him an hour at a time to give him his bottle. Unless you have a retarded child, you don't understand that little baby isn't going to do things on time, isn't going to speak on time. But everybody loved Robert because he was a lovable kid. We all made a fuss over him, and he was accepted. He wasn't shut in a room. If other kids said something mean, we stood up for him. Our friends always knew we loved him. We pretended he was normal and took him along with us wherever we went. My mother would dress him and fix his hair just so."

Fields's youngest sister, Sandy, eventually wound up tutoring Robert for an hour a day after she got home from school. When she was in high school, Sandy's girlfriends often included Robert in their outings. The experience was so rewarding that Sandy became a special education teacher. "Sandy graduated from Florida Atlantic University on the same day that Robert was competing in a Special Olympics swimming meet," Joe Sr. says. "Sandy told us, 'Go there, and don't worry about coming to my graduation.' "

Sacrificing to help Robert, who has a job in a shelter for mentally handicapped persons and lives with Sandy and her family, was a way of life in the Fields family. Joe felt he and Kay could be as strong as his parents had been, and they told the adoption agency they had no restrictions regarding the baby's health.

On their way home from the adoption agency meeting, Kay asked Joe, "Did you feel they were looking at us for something or treating us differently?" He agreed that he had a similar feeling.

One month later, the agency contacted Kay and Joe and told them a baby boy was available, but he had undergone a rare medical procedure called ECMO, which means extra corporal membrane oxygenation. The boy's lungs were not oxygenating the blood, so it had to be cycled through a machine that did the job for him.

"At the time, we thought the only handicap would be physical weakness on the left side of his body, no mental problem," Fields says. "With me being a football player, they felt there would be nobody better than us to help him learn to do physical things. It was between us and another couple. Once you knew about him, how could you put this child's life in somebody else's hands? Maybe they couldn't handle it. We felt we definitely could handle it."

Joe and Kay picked up the boy on July 9, 1986 and named him Christopher. He was two months old. Two weeks later, Fields reported to training camp, leaving Kay on her own to care for Christopher.

Fields was in the best condition of his life and was excited when the Jets got off to a fast start, including a thrilling 51–45 overtime victory against the Dolphins in the third game of the season. The Jets were on their way to their third win in four games when Fields suffered a severely sprained knee the next week at Indianapolis. The injury was the most serious of his career and put him out of the lineup for seven weeks. At the same time, the Jets continued on a nine-game winning streak, the longest in club history, and Guy Bingham played well at center in Fields's absence.

"There started to be some talk about how the Jets didn't need Joe Fields," he says. "These things start to work on your mind. I was depressed, and the writers were always making little jokes, 'Seven-and-oh with Bingham at center.' I was still going to meetings and making suggestions about the way I thought things should be blocked. After seven weeks, my knee still wasn't one hundred percent, but I felt I had to get back."

Fields's timing for his return to the lineup couldn't have been worse. The Jets took a 10–1 record, the best in the NFL, to Miami for a Monday night game and got clobbered, 45–3. The magnitude of the loss shook the confidence of the whole team, which had been playing superbly despite injuries to several key performers.

During October, when Fields was sidelined by his knee injury, Kay began to notice the first signs that Christopher's problems were more serious than originally believed. "Christopher was very weak," Kay recalls. "He never extended himself up. He made very few sounds and didn't move much. He was very much into himself. Sometime in late October, I started noticing him jerking. I didn't know what it was."

Because of his injury, Fields was home on weekends, and he noticed the same symptoms, "I was outside with Christopher one day, and I saw he was really jerking." Fields says, "It was eighteen times. I counted. I knew this wasn't just a muscle spasm."

After a few such incidents, their pediatrician scheduled an EEG test for Christopher the day before Thanksgiving, which was two days after Fields had rejoined the Jets for their disaster in Miami. Since Fields was back with the team on Long Island, Debbie Klecko made the one-hour drive to come and help Kay.

"We had to get Christopher up at five-thirty in the morning and keep him awake so he would fall asleep during the EEG," Kay says. "I'm trying to make light of all this, and Debbie's hanging over the backseat and shaking his car seat and shouting, 'Wake up! Wake up!' Christopher didn't want any part of her and was trying to get away. After the EEG, we went to Debbie's house to pick up her kids and then went back to my house because we were going to drive to New York the next morning to spend Thanksgiving with the guys.

"At seven-thirty that night, the pediatrician called. He said, 'Christopher has serious problems. I don't know how to get this across to you. There's probably a seventy percent chance he's mentally retarded. He's on his way to major convulsions and seizures. You've got to put him on medication right away. You need to seriously consider whether or not you want to go through with the adoption of this child.'

"Immediately, we put him on six teaspoons of phenobarbital, which is the worst-tasting stuff you ever imagined. Debbie and I tried to syringe it into his throat, but he was spitting it all over. I'm thinking he's going to go into convulsions, but we finally got him to sleep. When Joe called that night, I just said I'd tell him all the details when I saw him the next day."

After she and Debbie drove to Long Island on Thanksgiving morning, Kay told her husband that his long-awaited son had serious medical problems. The news came at a time when his knee still was bothering him, and he knew he couldn't be home to help her deal with this crisis in their lives. "The biggest question had to do with my job," Fields says. "Most of the pressure was going to be on Kay."

"The doctor told me Christopher probably never would recognize me, never would walk, never would potty-train, and probably would be a vegetable the rest of his life," Kay says. "He was going to be a big child when he grew up. I really questioned whether I was strong enough to handle that."

"I got a little pissed off and called the pediatrician," Fields adds. "He told me we should think about giving Christopher up, and I said, 'First of all, that's not a consideration. What we need from you is to help us in any way you can. He's our child, and that's it.' I told Kay we'd been through a lot in ten years, and we could handle this, too."

"How could you not form an attachment to him?" Kay asked. "I thought maybe he wouldn't know the difference, but I'll know that he's taken care of."

Kay and Joe spent most of Thanksgiving Day in tears. Klecko went out to a convenience store to pick up some food for them, and then he and Debbie took the kids and left them alone. After a sad Thanksgiving dinner of roast beef sandwiches with melted cheese, Kay and Joe just sat and talked about what they were going to do.

In the months that followed, they learned more about the rare ECMO procedure that Christopher underwent as an infant before Kay and Joe adopted him. When he was connected to the machine that oxygenated his blood and distributed it to different parts of his body through a shunt in his neck, he had to be given drugs to immobilize him as if he were still in the womb. The blood to the right side of Christopher's brain was cut off for a brief time while it circulated through the machine, and that may have caused the damage leading to his mental problems.

"We took Christopher to a neurologist, and she immediately gave us a report that was more grave than the first one," Fields says. "She said we should give him up. We said, 'No way. We're coming to you for help.' It was December ninth; we kept a diary."

The next day, Jets coach Joe Walton announced a sweeping series of lineup changes and said he hadn't yet decided if he was going to replace Fields as his starting center. Between Thanksgiving and Fields's consultation with the neurologist, the Jets had managed to extend their losing streak to three games with losses to the Los Angeles Rams and San Francisco. Still favoring his knee, Fields played poorly against the 49ers' Pro Bowl nose tackle Michael Carter, which is what caused Walton to threaten his starting job.

The gods must have been angry with Fields. As if his problems with Christopher and the Jets weren't enough, he and Klecko were having troubles in business because one partner wanted out, and it was going to cost Jetgroup half a million dollars to buy him out. Not only that, but Fields had just been audited by the Internal Revenue Service and hit with an order to pay substantial back taxes that put him under an even greater financial strain. The only positive note was that Walton decided to leave him in the starting lineup, but a back injury suffered in practice put him in worse physical shape. The Jets went on to lose their last two regular-season games to finish with a five-game losing streak that dropped them to 10–6, but they still qualified for a wild-card playoff game.

"The news about Christopher really hit me like a sledgehammer," Fields says. "He was the main thing on my mind. But we were losing, and I was having troubles in business. A lot of things were working on my head. I couldn't keep football separate from the rest of my life anymore. Everything was all together. My job was being threatened, and I wasn't playing the way Joe Fields can play."

While Fields tried to play on through his troubles, it was Kay's full-time job to deal with Christopher's day-to-day problems. She tried to offer emotional support for Joe and, at the same time, relieve some of the pressure by downplaying the effect Christopher's condition was having on her.

"I kept Joe aware of the medical facts about Christopher, but I didn't tell him I was depressed or that I cried myself to sleep one night," Kay says. "I couldn't burden him. I knew how bad I felt. What was the sense in making him feel that way, too? Phenobarbital sometimes makes kids lethargic. At other times, it makes them grouchy, and they cry and cry and cry. I was home alone with Christopher, and I think that helped. I spent hours and hours holding him and talking to him, and I could always talk to Debbie."

The medication brought Christopher's seizures, which were similar to petit mal seizures, under control before they could develop into convulsive seizures. Then, he started to learn. Most likely, he was having seizures that weren't so obvious before the doctors recognized the need for treatment. There was a marked contrast in his behavior after his problems were properly diagnosed. Christopher began to make eye contact and show signs of recognizing his parents, and he also started making more of the happy-baby noises that bring joy and reassurance to parents.

"He actually reached for his first toy on his first Christmas Day in 1986," Kay says. "He knows his daddy, and he knows when daddy's not here, too. He knows me, and he's very clingy to the two of us."

Christopher's progress after Christmas helped lift Kay's and Joe's spirits, but the Jets' season ended badly when they blew the double-overtime playoff game at Cleveland. By April, Fields was completely healed from his knee, back, and rib injuries, but he still was worried about his future with the Jets. The insecurity he felt in his early days in the NFL was back, and he was putting himself through two strenuous workouts a day just to prepare for veterans minicamp in May.

Kay thought Joe was working too hard. They were lying in bed talking about it when the telephone rang. It was 11:30 on a Thursday night.

"The call was from an attorney wanting to know if we were interested in adopting a baby boy through a private adoption," Kay says. "We had put out feelers all over before we got Christopher, and we never told any of the people we had contacted that we already had adopted a baby. We just didn't think about it. These people called to tell us there was a healthy two-day-old boy available, but they needed an answer by nine the next morning.

"My first instinct was, 'No way.' With all of Christopher's problems, I didn't think I would have the time to care for another baby. Joe and I stayed up all night talking about what we should do. At nine A.M., I called the man back and told him we couldn't take the baby."

After Kay hung up, she and Joe sat there looking at each other without saying anything for several minutes. Finally Kay broke the silence. "You know, we may never get this opportunity again," she said. "People wait years and years for this chance."

At 9:10 A.M., they called the attorney back and said they had changed their minds and decided they wanted the baby boy. Two hours later, Kay and Joe went to court to sign the papers finalizing their adoption of Christopher. When they returned home, the attorney called to tell them they had to pick up their new baby on Monday. They sent the papers that day by overnight delivery service and spent all day Saturday buying baby furniture and putting together a room for the son they named Sean.

About the time he was nine months old, Sean's physical abilities surpassed those of twenty-month-old Christopher, who was able only to pull himself across the floor using his good right arm. His condition now is described by doctors as a form of cerebral palsy classified as hemi-paresis, which means his mind doesn't control the muscles on the left side of his body, and he is considered an epileptic because of the seizure disorders. He also is mentally delayed for his age.

But Kay and Joe organized their own team, including a neurologist, a special education teacher, a speech therapist, an audiologist, and two physical therapists, to work with Christopher. Kay began taking him to physical therapy sessions three days a week to work on stretching and learning to use the left side of his body. Gradually, Christopher began progressing far beyond the original worst-case scenario painted by the doctors.

On September 5, 1988 at the age of twenty-eight months, Christopher took his first step with the aid of a brace he wears on his left leg. By the time he was three years old, Christopher was walking and climbing stairs. He still couldn't use his left arm and his left leg remained a little shorter than the right, but his mobility helped speed the learning process. He even had developed a vocabulary of about thirty words.

"It's hard enough when God gives you a handicapped child, but when you choose one, that really says something," says Fields's older sister, Cheryl. "You can see the way Christopher loves his parents. Joe is happiest when he makes Christopher smile."

Whatever questions they once had about adoption and about their own relationship have been resolved by Kay and Joe, who have reached new levels of understanding with Christopher's help. "I think Christopher has just made us more appreciative of things," Kay says.

"When Sean and Christopher play together, it's such a joy to see," adds Fields "I think Sean will learn compassion at an early age, and I think he will help Christopher learn physical things. I'm so proud of Christopher right now that it's unbelievable. I tell Kay all the time, 'You should really be proud of everything you've done for him.'"

Pain

The 1986 season began as the best in Jets history and ended with one of the most stunning and disastrous reversals ever seen in the NFL. At midseason, the feeling was euphoric because the Jets were winning in dazzling fashion with repeated touchdown bombs from quarterback Ken O'Brien to wide receivers Wesley Walker and Al Toon and a defense that smothered most opponents until the offense could work its wonders. The Jets were described by club president Jim Kensil and radio announcer Randy Rasmussen as equal to or better than the 1968 Joe Namath-led Super Bowl champions. Rasmussen was an expert on the subject because he had spent a decade blocking for Namath and wore a Super Bowl ring.

But after winning a club-record nine straight games to reach the zenith of 10–1, the Jets imploded, collapsing because of an unbelievable series of injuries to key players. They made it into the playoffs as the home wild-card team in the AFC despite losing their last five regular-season games by a combined score of 183–61. The Jets momentarily pulled out of their nosedive when Pat Ryan replaced O'Brien at quarterback and led the wild-card victory over Kansas City, one of the weakest playoff teams in memory. But the next week in Cleveland, the Jets expired, completely spent after their truly courageous fifty-six-minute effort gave them a 20–10 lead they couldn't hold in the double-overtime disaster. Four minutes of solid football was all they needed to wring from their battered bodies to reach the AFC championship game.

It may have looked to some as if the Jets choked, but the truth is they played better than they had any right to expect in the first eleven games when the injuries were piling up. By the end of the season, coach Joe Walton was flogging a dead horse. Judging by the desperate moves he made, Walton didn't seem to respect his players' efforts, but they tried to respond because they were well-conditioned to the idea of playing with pain and finding ways to get by without injured players. Unfortunately, they had little or nothing left to give.

"If you take the New York Jets team that started the season in September and put it out there in January against that Cleveland team, the Jets probably would have cleaned up the Browns," Joe Klecko says. "But if you take the Jets team that was all beat up going into January, they weren't so hot. But when you're out there at that time of the year, you have no idea what it was like back in September. Ask a player if he's fatigued, and we're going to say, 'No. I'm fine.' It's not a question of whether you are or aren't fine. Because of the way football players have a makeup to play through the season, you don't even come to realize how badly beaten up or mentally fatigued you are. Your head can take over. It really can. Even though you're a step slower, you think you can do it."

No one lasts very long in the NFL without developing a high tolerance for pain, especially the offensive and defensive linemen whose bodies take on the load of equally large and strong opponents on every play of every game. The injury rate is 100 percent, which means that survival depends on learning how to play hurt. That ability is one of the primary criteria by which players are judged by coaches, trainers, and each other.

"You may see one guy play with an injury and another guy not be able to play with the same injury," Joe Fields says. "But you never know what pain a guy is feeling. It's different for different guys. But once you're out there on the field, you mentally eliminate injuries as an excuse. It's your job to play. You picture yourself playing the same as if you were healthy. When you get beat, you say, 'How the fuck did that happen? I must have done something wrong.' You never think, 'It's because I've got no strength left in my shoulder or my knee is hurt.' To survive, that's the mentality you develop."

The incessant struggle to improve in some way or to gain an edge against the competition leads many NFL players, especially linemen and linebackers, to use or at least experiment with anabolic steroids, which promote the rapid growth of muscle tissue but also have harmful physical and psychological side effects. Steroids also may be used to help speed the healing process for injuries involving damaged muscles. That is a compelling reason for some players to use steroids, while others hope steroids will give them the strength to get through the season.

The use of steroids, it seemed to Klecko, became commonplace in the NFL in the late seventies and increased during the next decade to the point where it became a major health issue. "I would guess that sixty-five to seventy percent of all linemen were using steroids by 1987," Klecko says. "I can't prove it, but based on my experience, I'd say there were a high number of steroid users. I think there are some misconceptions about abuse. Steroids help some guys and hurt others. There are different levels of users; a lot of guys are scared to use too much. People have proven steroids are a depressant at some times and a stimulant at other times. They're a big mental thing because they make some people very aggressive, which is a benefit in the NFL, but guys can develop a psychological addiction when they're using heavy doses. Steroids work in different ways for different people."

At various times in their careers, both Klecko and Fields used steroids. "When I came up with the Jets, there was quite a bit of steroid use by our linemen," Klecko says. "I used steroids when I wanted to be bear strong for the three NFL Strongman contests I entered in the offseason from 1979 through 1981. I took them for six weeks at a time, and I had doctors watching me to make sure I was safe. There was never any change in my structure. I didn't take megadoses because I was afraid of the harmful side effects. The doctors I know say the amounts I took probably didn't help me that much. Some guys get in trouble with what is called 'stacking,' which is taking different kinds of steroids at the same time. Steroids definitely can be dangerous if they aren't used properly, and I'd say ninety percent of the guys who take steroids get them illegally rather than through a doctor's supervision.

"I really don't think steroids help you win football games. They help some injuries heal faster, and they keep you stronger longer to help you get through the season. There was never any pressure on me to try them, but I did because I felt steroids might give me an edge. I don't think I made any dramatic strength gains, but they made me feel stronger, which is a psychological edge.

"I quit taking steroids after 1981 because I was worried about the long-term consequences of using them. A few years later, I got into an amino acids program, using high-grade aminos. They make your body-repair system work better naturally. Aminos are *the* alternative to steroids. They can help you build muscle, but not in the same way as steroids. Nothing is as good as synthetic testosterone to build muscle tissue, but the risks are so high because of the side effects. My bench press went down from five hundred twenty-five pounds to four hundred eighty pounds, but how much do you need?"

Former Jets coach Walt Michaels once said of Klecko that he not only was an exceptional weightlifter, but also he knew how to play football. The point Michaels was making is that it takes more than weightlifting to succeed in the NFL. There are plenty of players who come to NFL training camps pumped up on steroids, but they get cut because they can't play football.

Fields proved his ability to handle bigger, stronger players because of his knowledge of how to play the game. He built himself up to average weight and strength levels for his position without chemical aids. But after nine seasons in the league, he looked around and saw how many players were using steroids, and it made him wonder if there were something more he should do. He decided to try steroids before the 1984 season and again before the 1987 season. In both cases, his cycle of use lasted a month.

"I wanted to see if it would help me get stronger," Fields says. "I thought it might give me something extra on top of what I already had. It wasn't important to me to be real big or to have that real hard look like it is to some guys who use steroids, and I didn't need them to survive. I had been to the Pro Bowl, and I knew I was good enough to play in the league. But I saw how many guys were using steroids, and I wanted to see if they would do anything for me.

"Steroids didn't work for me at all. I didn't want to take a lot of something, no matter what it was. The doses I heard some guys were taking were ten or twenty times greater than what I took. I wasn't willing to commit to steroids because I wasn't convinced they would work."

Of all the problems with steroids, one of the most serious in

Klecko's estimation, is their increasing use by kids at the high school level, whether they are football players or strictly body-builders. Steroid use at any level is a controversial practice, but there are some important distinctions that should be noted by youths following what they regard as the NFL example. "I don't think steroids should be used by younger people," Klecko says. "High school kids' bodies are nowhere near mature enough. In professional football, you're getting paid to play. That psychological edge is such a tough edge to keep that it makes you do things you wouldn't do otherwise."

The amount of money at stake is one of the forces that drives players to take chances with their bodies whether by taking steroids or by playing hurt. But there's more to it than that. The big-money era in professional sports has been accompanied by a matching cynicism, but still Klecko always left the impression he would play as hard and put as much effort into the game if his only reward were all the beer he could drink, which is exactly what it was with the Aston Knights.

"The greatest risk I took was in 1986 when I came back from arthroscopic surgery to play against Pittsburgh," Klecko says. "I didn't have to do that. I was getting paid. I can understand why some people might say I wanted to keep playing for the money. There's no doubt it would have been hard for me to walk away from the eight hundred and twelve thousand dollars I was going to make in 1987. But that's not what I play for. It really isn't."

It's hard for fans and even coaches to see past the big dollars, but most of those who make it to the NFL are there because they were competitive enough to want to play with the best. "I'm a pride guy," Klecko says. "I know what it is to dominate and then go out and have fun that night. Walking on the field is a thrill, but it's not the thrill of a game where you were dominant and everybody wants to talk to you because you were it. That's what it's all about, being spent after the game and knowing you won and kicked ass big-time.

"Like in '86 against Denver, I was in charge of that game. A lot of us played a big part, but I really felt I controlled everything on the line of scrimmage that night. That was a very satisfying game for me, but there's only a few like that. Denver's center, Billy Bryan, who once played for our offensive line coach, Dan Radakovich, told Rad, 'I played against Joe Greene, and he couldn't hold a candle to Joe Klecko the way he played tonight.' When someone puts you in the company of a great player like Joe Greene, that's a very satisfying feeling."

The Jets' 22–10 Monday night victory over a Denver team that would go on to represent the AFC in the Super Bowl was the midpoint in their nine-game winning streak in 1986, but it was just one in a series of superb performances. The Jets opened the season by spoiling the home debut of Buffalo quarterback Jim Kelly in a 28–24 shootout victory. Klecko's shifting caused Bills center Kent Hull to back up into Kelly and knock him down a couple of times and confused rookie guard Will Wolford. "Kelly was having trouble with my size fourteens," Hull admitted. "When Klecko's jumping around like that and the quarterback is calling signals, it throws the whole play off-kilter."

Jets starting left cornerback Kerry Glenn suffered a season-ending foot sprain in the opener. Four days later, the Jets lost running back Freeman McNeil for four games with a dislocated elbow in a 20–6 Thursday night loss to New England. Three of the Jets' starting defensive backs left the game with injuries, including safety Harry Hamilton, whose forehead split open in a bizarre accident when his head collided with the artificial turf at Giants Stadium, where the Jets play their home games.

Then the winning streak began with a wild 51–45 overtime victory against Miami in which Dolphins quarterback Dan Marino threw six touchdown passes. O'Brien connected on a TD pass to Walker as time ran out to send the game into overtime and then took the kickoff and won the game with another touchdown pass to Walker, their fourth of the game. Klecko felt a twinge in his left knee, which he had injured in a preseason game, and came out briefly against the Dolphins, and running back Johnny Hector suffered an injury that put him out for the next game at Indianapolis.

The next major injury occurred when Fields suffered a severely sprained knee in a 26–7 win at Indianapolis. He would miss the next seven weeks. "I was blocking the nose tackle, and my right knee was locked," Fields says. "Reggie McElroy, our right tackle, came down the line and went to cut his man, but he landed on my knee. I tried to play four or five more plays, but I couldn't go any longer."

O'Brien was the next victim, going down with a mild knee sprain in a 14–13 victory over Buffalo. Ryan replaced O'Brien in a 31–24 upset win at New England in which Hector carried forty times for 143 yards. McNeil returned for the Jets' victory over Denver, but McElroy suffered a knee injury that put him out for the next seven weeks. A hobbling O'Brien had to take over when Ryan's ribs were injured. In week number eight, wide receiver Al Toon caught three touchdown passes from O'Brien as the Jets beat New Orleans, 28–23, but inside linebacker Lance Mehl was lost for the season with a knee injury that required reconstructive surgery. Klecko also left the game after reinjuring his left knee, and it was decided to rest him for the next game at Seattle.

Tom Baldwin replaced Klecko in the starting lineup, saying, "The only way I would know how to play is the way Klecko does. He's taught me everything I know. I want to be a graduate of the School of Klecko." Acknowledging that he lacked Klecko's level of strength, Baldwin added, "He's got a black belt in whup-ass, so that helps."

The Seattle game was the high point of the Jets' season. They quieted a Kingdome crowd of 62,497 with a dominating 38–7 victory in which O'Brien passed for 431 yards and hit touchdown passes of 50 and 36 yards to Toon, 83 yards to Walker and 1 yard to tight end Mickey Shuler. It was after that game when Kensil and Rasmussen compared these Jets to the 1968 Super Bowl champs.

Klecko returned for a 28–14 win at Atlanta, but his knee failed to hold up and defensive end Marty Lyons also was lost with a shoulder injury. "I hurt my knee in preseason, and then I got clipped by Colts tackle Kevin Call," Klecko says, reciting the accumulation of damage to his left knee. "I hurt it again in the New Orleans game and should have had arthroscopic surgery then, but I wanted to play Atlanta. Against the Falcons, I collapsed on a double-team block. The pain was so intense that it couldn't support me. We had such a good chance of going to the Super Bowl that I decided to have it 'scoped instead of reconstructed right then." Klecko underwent arthroscopic surgery the next day, hoping to return to the lineup in five weeks.

The Jets returned home and scored a 31–16 triumph over Indianapolis to reach the 10–1 mark, but they lost defensive end Mark Gastineau with a torn anterior cruciate ligament in one knee. He underwent arthroscopic surgery following that game and did not return until the playoff game against Kansas City. Gastineau's injury meant the Jets had lost their entire defensive line, linebacker Mehl and cornerback Glenn on defense, along with Fields and McElroy on offense. McNeil, Hector, O'Brien, and starting right cornerback Russell Carter were out for shorter periods of time, and several others on the offensive line and in the defensive backfield were playing hurt.

Considering their physical condition, the Jets were defying gravity by remaining for so long at the top of the NFL. But a trip to Miami would take care of that. Recognizing the need for some inspiration, Walton welcomed Fields, "The General," back to the starting lineup even though Guy Bingham had played well as his replacement. Walton also had Klecko put on a uniform and stand on the sidelines like an empty threat. Knowing he couldn't play, the sight of a lame Klecko probably did more to inspire the Dolphins. The dimensions of Miami's 45–3 rout exposed the fragile underpinnings of the Jets' success. It was comparable to Toto pulling back the curtain to reveal the Wizard of Oz as nothing more than a flim-flam man. The loss scared the Jets because they were up so high, and it sure looked like a long way down.

Playing at home against the Los Angeles Rams and needing a win to settle their stomachs, the Jets lost 17–3 as the offense failed to score a touchdown for the second straight game. Then, they traveled to San Francisco to play the dangerous 49ers.

The situation was so critical that team physician James Nicholas gave the go-ahead to allow Klecko to test his left knee a week early. Explaining the move to reporters, Klecko said, "Nicholas said, 'If you win against L.A., I'd like to not play you [against the 49ers].' It changed the view of things because we lost. You lose confidence when you lose. No doubt, this is a very big must game for us."

But the cross-country flight caused Klecko's knee to swell, and he spent another game on the sidelines as the Jets lost in much worse fashion than the 24–10 score indicated. The defense missed eighteen tackles and allowed a season-high 198 yards rushing; receivers dropped balls right and left, and O'Brien appeared glassy-eyed and was virtually speechless in the locker room after throwing three interceptions for the first time in his career and being sacked four times.

The 49ers' Pro Bowl nose tackle Michael Carter roughed up Fields about as badly as he'd ever been beaten at center, sacking O'Brien once and getting pressure up the middle when O'Brien threw a key interception that sailed far over his receiver's head into the lap of Niners safety Ronnie Lott. "Michael Carter overpowered me a few times and beat me for a sack," Fields says. "The Jets weren't used to Joe Fields getting beat for a sack. I could probably count the sacks that I had ever given up in one season on one hand, and he beat me clean. It was a '41 pass.' I guessed with him, and I guessed wrong. Carter sacked Kenny, and the game went downhill from there."

The following Tuesday was the players' day off, and that was the day Fields and his wife, Kay, were advised by the second neurologist not to go through with plans to finalize their adoption of seven-month-old Christopher because of the severity of his medical problems. When Fields showed up for work the next day to begin preparations for a home game against Pittsburgh, he got more bad news.

"The trainer, Bob Reese, said, 'Joe wants to see you,' " Fields recalls. "I went to Walton's office, and he was very grave. He knew Christopher was having problems because I had asked Reese to call some doctors for me, and Reese mentioned it to him. No one knew about the business problems I was having or the back taxes I owed the IRS."

"Are you having problems with your son?" Walton asked.

"Yes, I have problems with my son, but I've never used anything as an excuse about my play and I'm not going to now," Fields replied. "I know I played shitty."

"Yeah, you did," Walton said. "We didn't play well as a team, you in particular. Bingham was playing real well. I haven't made up my mind, but I'm thinking about starting Guy."

"I just want a chance to show that game wasn't Joe Fields," Fields said. "It was a bad game, an aberration."

Fields left Walton's office not knowing whether he was going to start or not. He had graded out in the high nineties against the Rams the week before the loss to the 49ers, but it was clear one poor game was enough for Walton to identify him as part of the problem on a team crippled by injuries.

Later, at the general team meeting, Walton asked if any players had anything to say. "I stood up and said I'd like to be given another chance to play," Fields said. "Our fullback, Tony Paige, did the same thing. It was a very uncommon thing to do, but it wasn't hard for me because I've always been honest. It bothered me that I played poorly."

At the very least, Walton had embarrassed two starters into

standing up in front of the team and publicly confessing their sins. But to some players, it seemed as though Walton butchered them with his heavy-handed methods.

In quarterback Pat Ryan's view, what Fields did was unnecessary. "I don't think Joe had to apologize or ask for anything," Ryan says. "Everybody in the room had bad games. I'd seen him do too many good things. For a stretch of four or five years, there wasn't anybody better.

"Joe Fields was one of the main team leaders. He took everything that happened to the team personally, and he thought and worried about it a lot. He had a body that shouldn't have been playing football. He stayed beat up, but he never missed much time. At the end of that year, Fields was playing hurt. It's kind of sick, but guys look up to that. There's not a lot of people who can do that and perform."

It was because of his ethical commitment to his job and the team that Fields was able to stand up and ask for forgiveness. He wasn't worried about losing face. He had a track record of missing only nine of a possible 163 regular-season games in his first eleven seasons before 1986, and anyone who knew him knew how often he played hurt and played well in that time.

But the pressure had gotten to Walton. He was in his "Tailgunner Joe" mode, his squat body hunkered down in the tail section of a B-25 bomber, exposed to the flak coming up from the ground and exploding around him, firing away indiscriminately.

At his news conference that day, Walton announced outside linebacker Charles Jackson had gone from the starting lineup to the street via waivers. Paige and guard Ted Banker, who was playing with a shoulder injury, lost their starting jobs. When asked if Bingham would replace Fields, Walton left him twisting in the wind, saying, "Anything is possible." When reporters asked Fields about the shakeup, he just said, "I respectfully take the fifth. I heard that on the Iranscam hearings."

Fields decided to stop talking to reporters because he felt there was too much emphasis on the angle that his return to the lineup coincided with the losing streak. "I thought Peter Finney of the *New York Post* really started to attack me," Fields says. "He mentioned it every time I had a screw up. I felt like he was after me."

Now Walton was singling him out, too, and that was galling

because his leadership and effort never had been questioned. "If somebody has to badger you about losing or playing poorly, you ain't worth a shit," Fields says. "It pervades your whole life." As it turned out, Fields was in the starting lineup against Pittsburgh, and he graded out in the high nineties. But you could add Walton's shabby treatment of him to his list of injuries.

On the same day he announced his deletions from the lineup, Walton also made some additions. Lyons, who was wearing a shoulder harness, and Klecko and McElroy, who had two good knees between them, came off the injury list and into the starting lineup.

"They're going, they're going," defensive coordinator Bud Carson said, proclaiming the return of Klecko and Lyons. "This is stand-up-and-be-counted week." Asked if they had recovered sufficiently from their injuries to perform, Carson said, "I'm not fully aware of that, but I'm fully aware they're going."

Even though he was dead, El Cid, the eleventh-century hero, once was suited up by the Spanish, who tied him to his horse before a battle with the Moors because it was thought that his presence would inspire them to victory. It did. Klecko was in considerably better health than El Cid, but it was folly to think he could mount up and play against the Steelers. At the same time, the move was dramatic proof of his value to the Jets.

"If Joe hadn't been hurt in '86, he would have written all kinds of records for a nose tackle," Carson says. "He was a great leader. That was his highest asset on the field. Everyone knew that come Sunday just having Joe there had an effect. He was physical like a real warrior. A player like that gives a whole team confidence. He didn't do a lot of screaming, but he did all the little things for me, the backup things I wanted done. Sure, it was ill-advised for him to try to play against the Steelers, but Joe was a guy you wanted back."

Klecko also was a guy who wanted to be back and was willing to take the risk to see if he could put a stop to the losing streak and get the Jets pointed back in the direction of the Super Bowl. He played well in practice that week, but nobody was trying to tear his head off.

After hobbling around gingerly through most of the first quarter against Pittsburgh, Klecko steeled himself to play as he normally would. Either the knee would hold up or blow out. "I told Marty Lyons in the first quarter that I was really hurting us,"

Klecko says. "Then, I said, 'The hell with it. I'm going to play on this son of a bitch.' That's when it happened."

Two minutes into the second quarter, Klecko's left knee collapsed under him like a vacant apartment building when the demolition charge is set off. The knee twisted out from under him as he was rushing quarterback Mark Malone on the artificial turf at Giants Stadium.

When trainer Bob Reese reached him on the field, Klecko looked up at him with a smile and said, "Well, I guess it didn't work."

The Jets lost to the Steelers, 45–28. McElroy's leg gave out once in the third quarter, and he went down for good in the fourth period. A few days later, Dr. Bart Nisonson performed reconstructive surgery on both Klecko and McElroy.

As cruel as it appeared for Klecko to offer up his left knee as a sacrifice for the good of the team against the Steelers, his case was a classic example of the harsh medical choices faced by so many NFL players. The anterior cruciate ligament in his left knee was completely torn, and the joint was unusually loose because some of the ligaments had been stretched. But tears in both his medial and collateral cartilages had been repaired during arthroscopic surgery almost five weeks earlier, and the muscle strength in his left leg was equal to that of his right leg, indicating he might have the support necessary to play without reconstructive surgery. Some players are able to perform for years without the anterior cruciate ligament in one knee.

Despite the odds against Klecko's survival, Reese and Nisonson both were convinced they acted in the best interests of a thirty-three-year-old football player with two bad knees and one last shot at reaching the Super Bowl. "Quite frankly, we all knew deep down it wasn't going to hold up," Reese said at the time. "He had less than a fifty-fifty chance because the knee was so unstable, but we didn't want to go through reconstructive surgery if we could avoid it. We weren't using him. Joe Klecko knew what was going on. We owed it to Joe to find out if he could hold up. He could've said, 'I want my knee right. Let's fix it now.' I told Joe he owed it to himself to try to get by without it so he wouldn't have to go through rehabilitation at thirty-three. If I said there was no risk of further damage, it wouldn't be entirely truthful, but the risk was so minimal. We said, 'What harm can it do? What's the difference if you have to reconstruct the knee anyway?'"

Klecko's only choices besides playing were to rest his knee until the next season, when it almost certainly would have collapsed in the same fashion, or to undergo reconstructive surgery immediately without first testing it. Klecko's age, the Jets' playoff chances, and the remarkable recovery he made in 1982 from patella tendon surgery on his right knee all were factors in the decision to allow him to play.

"We treated Joe as a mature individual," Nisonson said following the reconstruction. "He wanted to play the odds because of the consequences. What is good judgment for one person is not necessarily good judgment for another. Klecko loves the game. He doesn't feel fulfilled without football. I don't know if it's fair to deny someone that. Once he knew this was the only way to go, he made up his mind to give himself as good a physical chance as he could. There always would have been a question in Joe's mind if the Jets made the Super Bowl and he didn't try to play. You would have had a destroyed human being."

The loss for the second time that season of Klecko and McElroy crushed whatever was left of the Jets' spirits. Hope vanished. The heady success of a 10–1 record was a fast-fading memory that taunted them. Humiliated and afraid of what might lay around the next corner, the Jets traveled to Cincinnati for their final regular-season game.

"I hurt my back in practice that week," Fields says. "The trainers had to shoot it in two places with a total of five ccs of Marcaine so that I could bend over to snap the football."

After the Jets lost to the Bengals by the grossly embarrassing margin of 52–21, it seemed the humane thing to do would be to anesthetize the whole team to end its misery. But the Jets were required to take part in the playoffs. After failing to pull O'Brien in the middle of games earlier when he was going into a slump with the rest of the team but still had time to regain his perspective, Walton now decided to make a change to Ryan as the starting quarterback for the playoffs. The burden of blame came down heavily on O'Brien, just as it had on Fields two weeks earlier. As he nearly always has in such situations, Ryan responded by establishing his decisive control of the offense and infusing the Jets with some badly needed confidence in their victory over Kansas City. But he also suffered a groin injury that badly restricted his mobility the next week at Cleveland. After throwing an early touchdown pass to Walker, Ryan was forced out of the game with the score tied, 7–7, in the second quarter, and O'Brien returned.

It was all the Jets' offense could do to manage a couple of field goals for a 13–10 lead at the end of the third quarter. Then, cornerback Jerry Holmes intercepted a Bernie Kosar pass at the Cleveland 25-yard line, and the Jets' offense finally made a big play when Freeman McNeil broke loose on first down for a touchdown that gave the Jets a 20–10 lead with four minutes left.

As Fields and right guard Dan Alexander were walking to the sidelines, Fields turned to his friend and said, "This game is far from over, Caj."

When the Browns got the ball, a holding penalty and a sack by Lyons put them in a second-and-24 situation at their own 18-yard line, but when Gastineau smashed into Kosar after he had thrown an incompletion, it gave the Browns a first down and new life. The cumulative effect of rushing Kosar and covering his receivers on each of 64 pass plays that day was too much for the Jets' weakened defensive line and haggard defensive backs. They were slow reacting as the Browns scored 10 points to send the game into overtime. After McNeil's touchdown, the Jets' offense gained a net of 6 yards in its final four possessions, one in regulation and three in overtime before a Mark Moseley field goal gave the Browns a 23–20 victory after 77 minutes and 2 seconds of play.

"I didn't feel like we played well on offense the whole game," Alexander says. "We got slaughtered in overtime. Injuries could've had something to do with it. I was the only healthy offensive lineman. When the Browns tied it up, the whole tempo of the game changed. It was typical of the second half of the season. It sticks with you quite a while."

The way the 1986 season ended and the fact they would be coming off the most serious injuries of their careers, Klecko and Fields knew, did not portend well for them. They would not be valued for the things they did to try and play when the Jets needed them but would be viewed as damaged goods with an expiration date that nearly was up. Fields was putting himself through two-a-day workouts by spring, and Klecko began pushing his knee as soon as it came out of the cast.

Linebacker Lance Mehl, who underwent reconstructive knee surgery almost two months before Klecko, was amazed by the workload to which Klecko subjected himself from the earliest stages of recovery. "It was February before I was doing much of anything, and I was just doing little things to strengthen my leg," Mehl says. "Joe was working out at home, but he came into the complex one day to have his knee examined. I was thinking we had it made because we wouldn't have to do much in training camp, and I said to Klecko, 'We're going to have a blast in camp.' He said, 'We're going to do two-a-day workouts, and each session is going to last from two to two-and-a-half hours, just like practice.' Working out with him, I got as strong as I've ever been in my life. Joe gave me goals to shoot for. We not only worked our legs, but he made everybody in rehab do upper-body work, too. He always tried to keep a hundred pounds ahead of everybody. It was like a game we all played."

Once he came out of the depression he was in as he watched the Jets lose in Cleveland, Klecko convinced himself he could make it back. Rather than do a straight repair job so Klecko could use his knee the rest of his civilian life, Nisonson did extra things to try to stabilize Klecko's knee sufficiently for him to play pro football again.

"I had all the faith in the world in Bart Nisonson," Klecko says. "As far as I'm concerned, he's the greatest thing ever as a surgeon."

To Nisonson's skill, Klecko added the force of his will to push himself throughout the offseason in the home gym he outfitted with almost a ton of free weights. "It's mentally hard, not physically hard," Klecko says of the dogged discipline of his training regimen. "But I have that grind-it-out need to do it. I don't blow it off unless I'm sick. I work six days a week. A lot of people work harder at getting out of it than at doing the work. I train until I don't have any energy left in my body. I know what it's like to be in great shape. The thing that kept me going was the thought of Sunday afternoons and what I once was and what I felt I could be again."

Two Strikes
and You're Out

To almost everyone on the Jets except their few remaining contemporaries, Joe Klecko and Joe Fields must have seemed very "old world" in terms of the values they represented. Certainly, they were more conservative than most in the sense they felt a strong identity with and commitment to the Jets organization. Neither of them had come out of a big-time football environment in college, unlike many younger players who had grown accustomed to special treatment in such places. Klecko and Fields entered the NFL making barely a tenth of the average salary of $220,000 in 1987, so it was not surprising they felt as if they had worked their way up from the mail room.

They were aware that some players didn't care for their old-fashioned style of hard-nosed leadership and resented their physically intimidating presence. But their leadership went largely unchallenged because they clearly were in charge on the field. Klecko and Fields understood football and the need for discipline, and their muscle lent a certain force to their words, an important quality in a physical sport.

Describing the position of strength from which he and Klecko led, Fields says, "People knew who backed up Joe Fields. You've got to have strong people who are going to do what you say whether they agree or not. If it should ever get down to physical force, you know they're going to side with you. Bring it down to the basic thing—the presence or threat of the use of force. The players know who's in control. They have to ask themselves, 'If I step out of line, am I going to get any repercussions?' If there's no threat, there's no steel in what you say."

Fields was in a position that demanded leadership. The popular conception is that only the quarterback can lead the offense, but while a quarterback has the most control over what happens to the ball, the center runs the show in the trenches. Klecko was in a different situation on defense. He could make an impact with big plays, act as an enforcer, or do the little things to make everyone around him better.

"Fields and I were looked to for answers and leadership," Klecko says. "If there was fighting or dissension, I would get involved, but I never preached. When someone got out of line, I told them about it, but I tried to do it subtly. The only guy I blatantly told to shut up was Chris Ward, who played left tackle for us from 1978 to 1983. He usually was out of shape, and he didn't play as well as expected for a number-one draft choice. One day in practice, he was running his mouth, and he stuck me with his helmet. I walked over to him, and he told me, 'Don't fuck with me, man. I'm from the ghetto.' I put my arm around him just as cocky as could be and said, 'You motherfucker. I was born in the ghetto. You ain't telling me nothing, punk. You want a piece of me right now? Here I am.' I pushed him, and the offensive line coach, Bob Fry, stepped in between us. I said to Ward, 'You ain't nothing but a big-mouth lard-ass.' I gave him every opportunity to take a shot at me, and he backed down.

"But that was just one incident. Walt Michaels appointed Fields and me team leaders. When Joe Walton became head coach, he always talked to us. But I never did things for Walton that I didn't feel. Mostly, Walton questioned us—'What's the matter here or there? What can we do different?' But I never asked the players to do something for the coaches. It was "us." Coaches are Monday to Saturday, and on Sunday, it's us, the players. My role developed because of who I was and how I played. I never worried about trying to be a leader. It was there."

But as the 1987 season approached, it was obvious Klecko and Fields were vulnerable. There were questions about Klecko's ability to recover from knee surgery, and Fields's job security had been threatened by Walton the previous year. Because of the NFL Players Association strike that was brewing, the prevailing political forces at work also had the potential to undermine them since they both opposed a strike. The Jets took a strike-authorization vote during veterans minicamp in May, and everyone was in favor except Klecko, who voted no, and Fields, who abstained. At the time, they didn't think the vote would affect football matters, but it did isolate them from many of their teammates. As they would find out, the players committed to the strike didn't recognize a separation of politics and football.

The Jets got the 1987 season off to a flying start with a win at Buffalo and a 43–24 home victory over New England in a Monday night game that was the last played before the strike became official at the final whistle. Mark Gastineau was the only veteran who remained in camp when the strike began. The rest of the team met the next morning at a baseball diamond at Hofstra University, a few hundred yards from the Jets' training complex, to take another strike vote. The previous night, Klecko and Fields discussed the situation and agreed it would be best for Klecko to cross the picket line because he was at a crucial stage in the rehabilitation process. After two months in a cast, his left thigh had withered terribly, and he was working at his usual ferocious pace, trying to push his rebuilt knee to overcome the lack of tangible support. But during the course of the meeting, the two of them changed their minds.

"As we sat there and listened to everybody and took the vote, Klecko and I looked at each other and decided it was best he stay out for a little bit and hope that it would be resolved quickly," Fields says. "We didn't go on strike in support of the union and its demands; we went on strike to show our teammates we were behind them. But I didn't know how long I could support something my heart wasn't in."

Their decision to support the strike figured to cost Klecko slightly more than $50,000 per week and Fields more than $29,000 per week for a cause they felt was misguided. But both stayed out and missed their first paychecks when the NFL canceled the third week of games.

Fields, who kept a diary of the strike, made this observation of the situation: "The union tells us the owners are definitely going to make this game up, that the owners want the TV money as much as we do. They say, 'Don't worry. You're going to make your game checks.' I'm starting to get a little skeptical because some of the teams that weren't bringing in scab players at the beginning have decided to get on the ball and get ready for a game. A lot of the players think they're not going to play this game. I think they are. The owners don't have any qualms about putting on scab football. That's going to infuriate the players."

As the strike entered its second week, Jets team physician James Nicholas dropped a bombshell on Klecko during a routine examination of his knee, indicating for the first time that he might pull the plug on Klecko's career. "Dr. Nicholas checked my knee, and then he made all three doctors check my knee," Klecko recalls. "He told me, 'Your knee is very unstable, and I might not pass you on the physical next year. If I don't pass you on the physical, you can't play here, and I don't know if anybody else would pass you on a physical with a knee as loose as that. You'd probably be out.' "

Klecko blew up at Nicholas, saying, "How could you possibly do that without giving me a chance? What are you afraid of, a lawsuit?"

He wasn't going to give up his career without a fight; he wanted the chance to live or die on the field, not in the trainer's room. If his rehabilitation program were going to stay on schedule, Klecko had to go in. "Dr. Nicholas is the kind of guy who has to be involved in decisions affecting the team," Klecko says. "I think it was his way of saying he had something to do with my future as a Jet. It made me mad that he would suggest I had to quit without giving me a chance."

The significance of Nicholas's words sank in overnight, and Klecko went to meet with his striking teammates the next day to explain his decision to cross the picket line. It was a Thursday, and the Jets had assembled a replacement team that was preparing to play the Dallas Cowboys' strike team that Sunday at Giants Stadium. "The way Nicholas talked right then, I was not ever going to play again, and that's what I told everybody," Klecko says. "It would have been pretty stupid for me to stay out. I was in a different situation because I could not make an impact on the games since I wasn't playing."

The money Klecko was losing also was a factor in his decision, and he admitted that to the rest of the Jets. "The fifty thousand dollars a week made a very big difference," Klecko says. "I had only been at that level a little while."

Despite the condition of his knee, the threat from Nicholas and the fact he wasn't healthy enough to play in any replacement games, Klecko's decision found little understanding among the

Jets. The hard-line strikers argued that they, too, might have played their last game.

Looking back on the situation, Klecko suspected Nicholas chose that time to apply pressure in order to force him to cross the picket line and give a boost to Jets management. "I don't think so; I know so," Klecko says of that scenario. "I know how those bastards operate. They knew I wasn't in favor of the strike. I wasn't planning to go in then, but I probably would have in another week or two when it dragged on. The money was important."

Klecko crossed the picket line on Friday, and defensive end Marty Lyons became the second veteran to cross that same day after meeting with the team in the morning. Lyons encountered even more resistance than Klecko had because he was healthy. He said he wanted to help the Jets win, and that comment led to arguments with several players who said the replacement team wasn't the real Jets. When the meeting ended, tight end Mickey Shuler, who had assumed a role as spokesman for the strikers along with player representative Kurt Sohn and assistant rep Reggie McElroy, asked Fields when he was going to cross. Fields told Shuler he couldn't stay out much longer. That afternoon, Fields drove to the complex to get a look at the replacement team and to speak to Walton, who was worried because Dallas had several veterans on its strike squad. But Fields decided to remain on strike at least through the Dallas game.

Once Klecko and Lyons crossed the picket line, the generation gap dividing the Jets became more obvious. When a reporter asked McElroy if he expected more players to go in, he said, "We kind of expect Joe Fields to go in. Joe Klecko and Marty Lyons are good friends. They're like the Three Stooges—what one does, all do."

When Fields heard about the insult, he confronted McElroy and the rest of his striking teammates. "I told them, 'I can understand you getting hot and saying stuff about players who have crossed the line, but I've been out here picketing with you every day. I've been to every meeting, and I voiced my opinion, which is not to be out on strike. But I'm still out here with you.' At that point, Reggie stood up and apologized. I told them I didn't want to go in, but I wasn't going to continue to picket because it wasn't me anymore."

That Sunday, the reality of the strike hit home when Dallas whipped the Jets, 38–24, in the first week of nonunion games.

There were only 12,370 customers in the seats, but the TV cameras were turned on, which is what mattered most. The amateur Jets permitted 11 quarterback sacks, and 3 of 6 Cowboys pass completions went for touchdowns. It was a sad display all the way around. The spectacle may not have been real football, but the owners definitely were playing hardball.

"After the first scab game, I started thinking the union was in serious trouble if it intended to stay out until it got free agency," Fields says. "I'd already forfeited two paychecks, amounting to more than fifty-eight thousand dollars, and I had worked long and hard for that contract. It seemed I was giving it away so easily. I always felt I was the ultimate team player. My team was on strike, so I was on strike with them, even though I never voted for the strike. By striking, I was changing my principles and looking at my personal goals differently because of the team. I started thinking that staying out was going against what I wanted to accomplish. It wasn't a Joe Fields type of strike."

Fields preferred to keep playing while the union negotiated on issues he felt were attainable, such as improved pension and disability benefits and guaranteed contracts. "In 1977, we won free agency in court, and the union gave it back at the bargaining table," Fields says. "It wasn't worth me losing another dime over it."

Maybe it was because he had come so much further in the game than most others. The thought of making a salary of $467,500 was beyond comprehension when he joined the Jets. That was Namath money, and he was throwing it away. The young guys, it seemed to Fields, took it for granted that the money always had been there. Fields had taken part against his will in a wildcat walkout in 1975 and the league-wide strike in 1982 when the players were locked out both times. This time around, Fields had tried to take one for the team against his own beliefs, but now, he had to follow his conscience. On Wednesday of the third week of the strike, "The General" broke ranks with his troops and reported for duty with the Jets' strike team.

Quarterback Pat Ryan, who was in his tenth year at the time, said of Fields, "He's been through three strikes and given his bucket of blood." But the younger players on the picket line, some of whom received rookie signing bonuses that were more than Fields earned in his first five or six seasons combined, weren't willing to put things in that historical perspective. Their resentment toward Fields would manifest itself later.

Practice already was under way when Fields showed up at the Jets' complex. "One of the loneliest walks I've ever made in my life was from my car to the end of the practice field to tell Joe Walton I was in," Fields remembers. "It seemed everybody kind of stopped and watched me. I was a little down, but Walton was supportive. He said, 'Marty and Mark went through it. You don't feel like you're part of it, but this is football. If you don't get your head on straight and do things the right way, you're going to hurt yourself.' He asked if I thought there would be hard feelings when the rest of the players came back. I said there would, but it would be short-lived because everyone was there to win. All through this, Klecko never tried to persuade me to come in, but once I did, he said, 'I wish you'd done it last week. You may feel bad the first day or two, but after you get in here, everything is going to be like it was before. Don't worry.' "

The next morning, Fields met with the strikers to explain his decision. "It wasn't as nerve-wracking as I expected," Fields says. "I told them it was a financial decision. Sohn asked how I felt about the players out there, and I told him, 'I'm going in to get paid, but my heart is out here with the guys on strike.' I was going in to play football with some people I didn't know and leaving a bunch of guys I respected. It was a hard thing to get ready to practice."

In his first practice with the replacements, Fields made the mistake of going full blast after laying off for more than two weeks. He popped the hamstring in his right leg, an injury that would sideline him for another three weeks and ultimately spare him from actually playing in any replacement games.

Although the issues were serious, some of the events of the strike were almost comical. On the first day of picketing, striking Jets loaded up with eggs and bombarded the vans carrying replacement players. The Jets switched to buses the next day, and when the strikers threw more eggs, the club added a police escort that included several motorcycles and squad cars. "These officers on motorcycles almost ride right through you," Fields said in his diary. "I was standing near the curb and almost got hit. It seems like they're ready for a war or something."

Hofstra University set aside one entrance for use by all Jets personnel and picketing strikers. Anyone wishing to reach the complex in a private car had to stop at that checkpoint and receive a pass that was turned in at the gate to the Jets' parking lot. Gastineau stopped to get his pass one day and became involved in an altercation with several out-of-work teammates. One striker spit on Gastineau through his open car window, and a brief fight erupted when he came out swinging. County policemen on duty at the gate moved in to break it up.

When Gastineau discovered he was going to receive his game check of $45,312.50 for the game that was canceled the first week of the strike, he told a reporter from *Newsday* that he planned to donate the entire sum to a charity for terminally ill children. "When Mark said that, it left ninety-nine percent of the team extremely skeptical," Fields said at the time. "I don't think he'll donate it to charity. Why he comes out and says these things, I'll never know." As it turned out, Gastineau did make a relatively small donation after some prodding by the charity in question, but it wasn't remotely close to $45,312.50.

On his first day with the replacement team, Fields said, "There was a very nice gentleman in my locker, a long snapper named Martin Cornelson. He offered to move out of my locker, but I told him to keep it. I was dressing in the racquetball court with Klecko. Martin was a story in himself. He was a heck of a long snapper in college at North Carolina State, and he also was a textile sales-man. The Jets called him up just to do the long snapping. He wasn't big enough or fast enough to play any real position. The last two weeks of the strike, he'd come to practice one day a week and then snap on Sunday. The couple days he had to come to practice, his company docked his pay for playing football even though he still did a lot of business for them.

"Before the strike ended, a couple of guys came up to me and said, 'I watched you as a kid, and it's exciting to meet you.' I thought that was kind of funny."

Although he couldn't play because of his injury, Fields traveled to Indianapolis with the replacement Jets for their second game. Out of superstition, Fields took his regular seat on the charter flight and put his jacket and travel bag on the seat next to him, which usually was occupied by placekicker Pat Leahy. Instead of leaving their hotel at ten the next morning for the bus trip to the Hoosier Dome, the Jets' strike team left at seven A.M. to avoid a picket line that never materialized, and the players ate their pre-game meal at the stadium.

Describing the locker-room scene for his diary, Fields said, "A funny thing happened while the guys were getting dressed. Jim Haslett, a veteran linebacker from Buffalo who was with our team, came up to me and said, 'Joe, you're not going to believe this, but there's a kid who has his thigh pads in the wrong way.' It was kind of hard to imagine. Marty Lyons and Haslett went up to the kid and told him that, if he got hit, he could get hurt. The pads might pinch his balls. The kid looked down and said, 'Oh, yeah.' He took them out and put them back in upside down. When he did that, the three of us really cracked up. I felt sorry for the kid, but Jim and Marty showed him how to put them in."

Thus equipped, the imitation Jets went out and lost to the nonunion Colts, 6–0, in one of the most inept and deadly dull performances ever to wear the NFL label. Even though they were strikebreakers, the replacement Jets were depressed because they felt they had let the real Jets down by losing two straight to fall to 2–2 in the standings.

Meanwhile, out on the picket line, things were getting tense. Rookie defensive lineman Gerald Nichols crossed the line on Monday because it was obvious the replacement at his position, Scott Mersereau, was in the process of earning a permanent job. The reporting deadline set by the owners for those who wanted to be eligible to collect their check and play was one P.M. Wednesday. After a heated meeting the previous night, quarterback Pat Ryan, offensive guard Ted Banker, and defensive linemen Barry Bennett, Don Baldwin, and Don Smith crossed over. As Ryan explained, "I guess you could say it's financial—not in the sense that I had to have the money, but in the sense we're throwing good money after bad. The only way we're going to get a favorable agreement is if the owners decide to toss us a bone. I felt it was time to cut my losses." At the mention of his popularity with his teammates, Ryan snorted and said, "Hah! Used to be."

On Thursday, October 15, the NFLPA called a halt to the twenty-four-day strike. Just one minor detail—the weekly reporting deadline had passed, and the owners decided to force the strikers to miss another paycheck. There was a bitter scene in the Jets' parking lot when the strikers were turned back after they attempted to reclaim their locker room.

"That disappointed a lot of players," Fields says. "Bob Crable, one of our linebackers, said the union assured them they would be paid for the week and they would be able to play. It was very hard to swallow when they were turned away. Now they were losing one-fourth of their contracts. There was going to be a lot of anger toward the guys who crossed the line anyway, but I think that raised the degree of animosity even higher. The players who stayed out on strike are upset because they think the players who crossed the picket line led to the collapse of the strike. But I don't think that's right at all. The strike collapsed because the union really wasn't ready for what the owners did, and it didn't prepare the players. Even if no players crossed the line, I think the owners would have continued to play with replacement players. There's no question in my mind. A lot of players started to see that, and that's why they came in."

The replacement Jets had one game left to play against Miami at Giants Stadium, and it turned out to be a wild affair that was tied 31–all at the end of regulation time. With thirty-four seconds left in overtime, Ryan threw his fourth touchdown pass of the game to secure a 37–31 victory that left the Jets in a first-place tie in the AFC East coming out of the strike. Ryan's performance was special because he was suffering from a rotator cuff injury that prevented him from throwing a single pass all week in practice.

"I'll tell you something about Pat Ryan," Fields said when the game was over. "He had a cortisone shot for his shoulder problem in the middle of the week. Before the game, all he got was a shoulder massage. He had to put up with the pain and play. I don't think he was able to throw the ball more than twenty-five or thirty yards the whole game, but he's a pretty tough son of a bitch. He may not be able to do all the things some other quarterbacks can do, but Pat has proven he can win. Miami coach Don Shula looked mighty pissed off when he walked off that field. Joe Walton said he was going to give game balls to everybody and one special one for Pat Ryan. Then, I sat and watched as Pat paid the price. He got his shoulder injected so it would heal faster. Sometimes, a little cortisone on those inflamed areas really helps because it goes where it's supposed to be right away, but it's painful. The next day after the shot, it's more painful."

The strikers returned to work the following day, but the Jets also kept fifteen of the replacement players in case the regulars went back out at a later date. When the strike began, the picketers were throwing eggs, but now that they were reunited under one roof, everybody was walking on eggshells. Whatever personality conflicts had simmered below the surface for the sake of team harmony were brought into the open by the strike. The issues went much deeper than the winning and losing of football games, and the emotional response of the players seemed to liberate them from all the rules they had lived by in the locker room. There was an uncivil war going on in terms of the way strikers acted toward those who had crossed the picket line.

After attending his first meeting with the veterans, Fields said, "There's a tremendous amount of animosity, more than I thought there would be. There's probably six or seven players not talking to me right now. I'm not pissed off because they weren't on my side, but if they want to be pissed off at me, that's okay. Five or six years from now, I'm not going to see more than one or two of these players. They're not going to tell me how I'm supposed to take care of my family. Joe Walton tried to appeal to the players' desire to win and make the playoffs and also to the goodness in each of them. That approach isn't going to work. In the next few days, he's going to have to come up with a much tougher approach."

The back-to-work date was Monday, October 19, 1987, which wasn't such a hot day for a lot of other people outside the Jets' small world, either. "Funny thing," Fields said in his diary, "the stock market dropped a record five hundred and eight points today, and the New York Jets reported back to work. Just a thought."

In their first game back from the strike, the Jets traveled to Washington, where they lost a 17–16 decision on a field goal with fifty-four seconds remaining. Fields was unable to play because of his hamstring, but he made the trip. "In the locker room before the game, it was quiet," he said. "Everybody played hard, but still, there is animosity in that locker room. Mickey Shuler is one of the guys really holding a grudge against me personally. I don't know why. Guys like Kurt Sohn seem to be getting back into playing football. Pat Leahy is still my good friend. I don't think our relationship has been strained in the least. We had a nice, long talk about the strike on the plane ride home from Washington.

"Maybe I'm naive, but I figure the guys I was friends with before the strike are still going to be my friends. The strike was a loss for everybody, and the funny thing is I lost a lot more money than most of the guys. What really hurts is that some of the guys acting pissed off toward me are the same people that, years ago, I talked to and maybe helped a little bit. That bothers me."

Fields was scheduled to return to the lineup at right guard in the next game at home against Indianapolis. Since right tackle McElroy was recovering from knee surgery, it was decided in training camp to move right guard Dan Alexander to McElroy's position and Fields to right guard so that Guy Bingham, who had filled in capably for Fields when he was hurt in 1986, could play center. That's the way it stayed when the regular season began.

"Tuesday after the Washington game, Walton called me in for a meeting," Fields recalls. "I didn't talk to the team like I usually do in pregame warmups before we played the Redskins, and he said I needed to go back to being Joe Fields. He also told me I was going to play right guard, and Guy Bingham was going to play center. By his own admission, Guy played a very bad game against Washington, but Walton said he still deserved to play center. When I had a bad game at San Francisco the previous year, Walton threatened to bench me. I guess he thought Guy had problems because the strike still was on his mind. But I don't think Walton realized who he was talking to. When I had a bad game, my mind was away from football because I had just been told my son should be institutionalized. It's strange how Walton treats some people, and someone like myself, who has been consistent over the years, gets treated harder after a bad game."

Just two days before they played Indianapolis, there was a meeting of the Jets' executive committee, which is composed of senior players from different segments of the team. The purpose of the committee is to facilitate communication between coaches and players and to discuss club rules and other situations affecting the team. During this meeting, Shuler said Fields should step down as team captain because the majority of players didn't support him. He wanted to hold a new vote. Walton cut off the discussion before it got started, saying, "No, I won't consider it."

But the sentiment Shuler expressed didn't go away. "There was a definite decision made by a lot of guys who stayed out on strike to bring their own guys in as leaders," Fields says. "When I called everybody up to huddle on the sidelines so I could talk to them before my first game back against the Colts, I could see several guys hang back. There was a lot of hesitancy and none of the excitement there had been in the past. I took it personally. The players had always called me 'The General.' It meant I had a lot of respect because I came from nothing, and I went somewhere. Now, there was a conscious effort to make things different than they were before the strike. I knew then things would never be the same with some guys. My role was diminished. It also was hard to be the leader Joe Walton wanted when I was switching positions and struggling myself.

"Toward the end of the season, Mickey came up to me and said he didn't want to revote the captain, that he was just speaking for the other guys. I think that's bullshit." The next season, Shuler was named as one of the offensive captains.

The Jets played an apathetic brand of football in their 19–14 loss to the Colts, and their record fell to 3–4. It seemed to Fields they were just going through the motions, and he wondered as he came off the field if they still had the ability and the desire to be able to come from behind. Walton was upset with the effort, as well, but he only succeeded in making the players who had remained on strike to the bitter end angrier by accusing them of "stealing money" and "backing up to the pay window."

In the next week, Walton called in each player for a one-on-one conversation. "Walton talked to me for thirty minutes about the crazy things going on," Fields says. "His attitude was that he wasn't going to let the inmates run the prison. His theme all year long whenever we lost was that there was no leadership. I think he figured Klecko and I couldn't help him anymore as leaders. I remember one time in a meeting, he yelled out, 'Where's this new breed of leaders that was going to come in? Where are they going to lead us?'

"It was obvious the strike had created divisions that were going to last the rest of the year. We were more affected than most teams because the older guys, who were the leaders on the field, were the ones who went in. The younger guys wouldn't look up to us anymore. I always put everything else behind me when I went on the field. If I hated a guy before I went on the field, I could hate him when I came off. But during a game, I was going to try and help him kick somebody else's butt. Everybody has different values. It's important to stand up for what you believe, and I respect that. But in this strike business, it seemed like nobody respected anybody else's opinion."

After his first ten years in the league, Fields began to notice that it was becoming more difficult to relate to the new players coming in each season. Every time he looked around the parking lot at the assortment of expensive automobiles, he couldn't help but think of the beat-up Mustang he drove as a rookie. He finally sold that car for $96 and figured he'd made a good deal. The young players seemed spoiled and self-centered by comparison. During the strike, it didn't appear many of them made the effort to understand his situation. They saw him more as a symbol of another time, not as a person like themselves.

"As I look back on the strike, I ask myself how many guys, when something bad happens or you get cut, call to see how you're doing," Fields says. "I've got a handicapped son. How many of those guys ever asked me about him? The guys who knew about Christopher understood one hundred percent when I went in. The other guys don't give a shit about you, anyway. During the strike, I thought, 'What if Christopher should need something and, because I lost all this money, I can't provide it for him?' That would be a horrible thing when I had the ability to do it and pissed it away for something stupid. I'd feel I let him down. Thank God, nobody else on the team has those problems. When you don't have those problems, you don't think about them."

The great irony of the 1987 strike and the effect it had on the leadership roles of Klecko and Fields is that, of all the Jets, they had two of the strongest union backgrounds. Both spent their first few years in the NFL working as union laborers during the off-season to augment their football earnings. Fields was an iron-worker until one day in January, 1982 when he found himself 135 feet off the ground, welding plates on top of a water tower in a snowstorm accompanied by a howling wind that reduced the chill factor to minus-60 degrees.

"I was hanging on the side of the tower, and the wind kept blowing the weld out," Fields remembers. "We had to build tents around us so we could get it done. It was so cold that we had to come down every thirty minutes to warm up. I was up there on the tower thinking, 'Ten days from now, I'm going to be in Hawaii for the Pro Bowl. This is crazy. I have to stop doing this.' That was my last year as an ironworker."

While the strike was on, Fields went home for a few days in south Jersey, and he took Kay and Debbie Klecko to a little bar frequented largely by union laborers. As Fields recalls, "One guy said, 'I don't mind you guys being on strike, but when you start recruiting the Teamsters and painters and ironworkers and NBC technicians to walk the line, you should be union all the way. Don't cross their lines, and don't go on NBC and give interviews when their technicians are on strike. Don't be union just when it fits you.' He was right; there are a lot of hypocritical football players who don't understand what it's like to be in a real union."

Fields and Klecko knew the reality of unions and strikes, and they had seen enough to understand the power of the owners to turn the NFLPA strike into a big loser for the players. Even after he reached the $100,000 salary level in 1980, Klecko continued to drive tractor-trailer rigs for two more years as a member of the Teamsters, which he had joined at the age of sixteen.

"My local had a guy running for office that was put in there, but he still had to run," Klecko says. "I was put on the picket line to protect him at one time. I was young and dumb, and they wanted to use me as a strongarm guy. There were people who wanted to kill this guy. The police were there because we had some fights, so nothing more happened. I've worked the ignorance of a picket line. When you get guys who are fighting for something they don't understand, they forget the whole picture. It's who you're fighting against, what you're fighting with, and the reality of whether or not you're going to get it. The owners were ready to disband and form another league before they gave us free agency."

"I told Kurt Sohn, our player rep, 'Don't believe everything they tell you. Don't become a puppet,' " Fields adds. "That's exactly what he did. He believed it to the hilt. He took everything that was fed to him by the union and reiterated it to the players. It takes a strong person to stand up to Gene Upshaw, the executive director of the NFLPA, and say, 'That's wrong.' Kurt was one tough SOB of a football player, but he couldn't do that. It was so sad."

In the aftermath of the strike, the generational conflict deepened as Walton waffled in his search for answers between the traditional leaders and the younger players who emerged as leaders of the strikers. The Jets' coach felt the pressure as acutely as anyone. He had another year remaining on his contract, but after the collapse at the end of the 1986 season and the way his players clearly were fractured by the strike, Walton seemed to sense a loss of his control over the team. His own security appeared to be in question, and while no one in the front office ever said that was the case, the speculation weighed on him.

The concept of the "new breed" of team leaders was a lifeline Walton could embrace. But quarterback Ken O'Brien, the most prominent candidate to succeed Klecko and Fields as leader of the Jets, still was struggling to establish himself on the field as the consistent performer the Jets needed. His benching at the start of the 1986 playoffs didn't look too good on his résumé. As well as he played when things were going right for the team, O'Brien hadn't shown he could lift those around him in times of trouble the way Ryan seemed able to do whenever he came out of the bullpen.

"It's not that Pat Ryan gets the guys fired up when he comes in; it's that he does whatever it takes," Fields says. "He drops back, and if he's got a pass called to beat a '6 zone,' which is the name we have for a specific pass defense, and it ain't a '6 zone,' he ain't going to sit back there and screw around. He's going to run right now. He makes a decision right away. You don't have to be able to add two and two to play football, but you have to understand the game.

"I think Kenny changed during the strike. He tried to bite off a bigger chunk than he could handle, and Walton tried to push it on him when he came back. The leader of the new breed—it cracks me up. The new breed of what? I laugh my ass off thinking about it. If these younger guys took over, they did a pretty shitty job."

The lack of respect Fields felt from the hard-core strikers wounded his pride and angered him at the same time. It was bad enough that the forces of nature were creeping up on him and the coaches insisted on playing him out of position. The mutinous air on the Jets made it that much worse because his authority was eroding quickly and he could see, distinctly now, the end of his career on the horizon. Maybe the Jets weren't his team any-more, but Fields wasn't convinced anyone really had earned the right to replace him in his role as "The General."

"No question, I have lost touch with the young guys," Fields admitted to himself. "The money and the way guys are looked at today exaggerates the differences. A guy like Russell Carter, the cornerback the Jets drafted number one in 1984, made $2.1 million in four years. All he did was make the team. Guys who just make the team haven't accomplished anything. It means getting your paycheck, and that's all. It teaches people it's okay just to make the team without reinforcing the idea that the objective is to make the Super Bowl and the Pro Bowl.

"It's different today. There are no company people left. In football, a company person will take a shot if the guys need him to win. When Richard Todd was our quarterback, he was like that. I remember him getting a shot in the ribcage and wearing a flak jacket so he could play against Miami in 1981 because he knew we needed him to win. In the restaurant business, I can see the problem when you don't have company people. When I was union with the boilermakers, I never worked so hard in my life, but I was still a company person. I believed it was important to do a good job, not just get paid. A job well done lasts with you long after the money's gone.

"Maybe I feel that way because I'm in business and in sports. My attitude has always been that, if somebody gives you a job, he deserves to get all you can give him. There aren't enough company people left in football, not enough company people in the restaurant business, not enough company people anywhere."

In time, Fields would discover there aren't enough "people companies" in the world, either. But that insight was a few more games down the road.

The End (Part I)

After two straight losses following their return from the strike, the Jets received a heavy dose of the Walton Method, the main ingredient of which is fear. Running back Freeman McNeil's name apparently came up in trade talks with the Los Angeles Rams, and when a deal failed to materialize, McNeil simply was demoted to second-team status. Walton's message to his players went down like castor oil, but they responded with a 30–14 Monday night victory over a strong Seattle team at Giants Stadium to reach the midpoint of the season in a five-way tie for first and last in the AFC East at 4–4. When it was over, defensive lineman Barry Bennett neatly summed up the situation by saying, "What was on people's minds was the unpleasant working conditions. Fear is a great motivator, isn't it?"

Certainly, fear had become Walton's motivational tactic of choice over the years, but for the Jets' next game at Kansas City, Joe Klecko provided a more inspirational theme by returning to fulltime action eleven months after the complicated surgery on his left knee. Expressing his reservations about whether Klecko's knee would hold up, team physician James Nicholas said, "It's like a fighter's scar. Is he able to take a punch again?"

Admittedly, Klecko's wounded knee still was loose. The operation had left Klecko with some instability when he swung his lower leg forward, which is common. But he also had a "medial translation," meaning the joint slides from side to side. "I've never seen a knee quite like his," said Jets trainer Bob Reese, "but I've never worked with anybody like Joe Klecko."

Since there was damage to both medial collateral ligaments and the posterior collateral ligaments, Klecko's thirty-four-year-old knee wasn't worth much as collateral for borrowed time, but with the help of some tape and a steel brace, he thought he could get by on it. He felt some pain, but nothing he hadn't overcome in the past. The main thing was that he had none of the swelling the doctors had expected. In fact, Klecko was ready to resume his regular role *before* twenty-seven-year-old tackle Reggie McElroy, who had surgery at the same time and was scheduled to play in a backup role at Kansas City, and twenty-nine-year-old linebacker Lance Mehl, who underwent knee surgery seven weeks earlier than Klecko and had to wait another week longer for his comeback.

As the Jets were preparing to catch their charter flight to Kansas City, Mark Gastineau added his own special dramatic touch to an eventful week by missing the team meeting Saturday morning. He showed up later at the airport, and when Walton threatened to leave him at home, Gastineau unburdened himself about his impending divorce and other personal problems. The head coach decided to let Gastineau make the trip, but when the Jets got to Kansas City, Walton called Klecko, Joe Fields, and Marty Lyons into a hotel room and told them, "You've got to help him. I really think Mark would have committed suicide if I left him home. He broke down and cried like a baby in front of me."

"Mark was such a good liar," Klecko says. "He always had Joe Walton baffled. He's lied like that all along." The ironic kicker to that incident came a year later when Gastineau quit the Jets in the middle of the 1988 season in order to maintain his relationship with actress Brigitte Nielsen. But special treatment for Gastineau was nothing new. "Year in and year out, the coaches always said, 'Joe, accept him. He can help us.' Every coach, Walt Michaels and Walton. It was always, 'Baby Mark, take care of Mark.'"

The Jets made allowances for Gastineau, but Klecko, the player defensive coordinator Bud Carson described as "the guts of this team," went to Kansas City with Nicholas's threat to fail him on the postseason physical exam hanging over his head. The physical exam that mattered most to Klecko was the one against Chiefs center Rick Donnalley. In the first quarter, Klecko was tentative, trying to find his way.

"A lot of the time, I was in no-man's land with my leg because I didn't know how it would react, but getting into the game resolved a lot of that," Klecko says. "Being able to get mad at an opponent helped. I started out very apprehensive, but I told myself, 'Screw it. You've got to go after it.' And I did."

In the second quarter, Klecko began to exert pressure up the middle. It appeared that Donnalley wasn't sure how to block a nose tackle in the cocked position, so Klecko was able to line up to his left of the center most of the game and drive off his good right leg. Just before halftime, Klecko flashed his old quickness, blowing past Donnalley the instant he snapped the ball to sack Chiefs quarterback Frank Seurer.

"I anticipated the snap correctly," Klecko explains. "When I got the sack, it was a real confidence-builder. After that, I started to disrupt things, and it felt pretty damn good. I had been building up to that moment for eleven months. Just being able to come back when people said I couldn't was very satisfying."

Klecko's presence had a remarkable effect on the whole defensive line, which totaled 5 sacks. McNeil also experienced a rebirth that day, coming off the bench to rush for 184 yards as the Jets beat the Chiefs, 16–9. The Chiefs' Donnalley was so impressed that he compared Klecko in his first game back to Chicago Pro Bowl defensive tackle Dan Hampton, saying, "Klecko's the best nose tackle I've gone against all year. I'd rather block Hampton than Klecko. His initial move is very quick. His second move is something that will work better once his knee is one hundred percent."

Savoring a chew of tobacco like fine wine after the game, Klecko was beaming as he told reporters, "I'm so damn happy, I can't explain it. If I couldn't play football anymore, I'd probably die."

Walton was equally delighted. Every time someone mentioned Klecko's name, a smile sprang to his lips, and he had to struggle to suppress it. "Klecko's presence has always been big for us," Walton said. "He's a guy who can rally people strongly."

For the moment, Klecko had succeeded in ignoring the medical risks and the actuarial tables that said a thirty-four-year-old with two surgically repaired knees couldn't take the punishment of playing nose tackle in the NFL. If Nicholas were Mr. Jordan come to claim him, Klecko said retirement can wait—*this* is heaven.

"It's the greatest thing in the world to be an athlete," Klecko said, trying to describe his immense sense of fulfillment. "When I look down the road ten years, whether I'm walking right or I'm in a lot of pain, I don't worry about that. Hell, the average football player only lives to be fifty-five years old. I'm going to live it to the hilt."

Marveling at his best friend's will to continue playing, Fields said, "Some people put too much emphasis on age. It's what kind of heart you have and what kind of mind. This is what he loves. When people tell him they're going to take it away, well, you just don't do that to a guy like Joe Klecko and not expect him to fight back."

The era of good feeling lasted one week until the Jets were beaten up in a 17–14 home loss to Buffalo. Once again, Walton blamed the Jets' problems on a failure of leadership among the players. His Monday talk with the team lasted less than sixty seconds instead of the usual fifteen or twenty minutes. He walked into the general meeting and, with a mixture of sarcasm and anger, simply said: "Did everybody get their paychecks? Okay, now get the hell out of here!"

In the next few days, Walton spoke of how the players had to learn to "push their own buttons," and he made it clear he still was waiting for some players to step forward and take control of the team on the field. Klecko and Fields always had been the ones to do it. But now Klecko was under pressure to prove he could play like the Klecko of old, and Fields was being asked to change positions for the second time before the Jets played a home game against Cincinnati. McElroy was ready for fulltime duty at right tackle, which meant Dan Alexander could move back to right guard. By then, Fields had grown comfortable at right guard, but offensive line coach Dan Radakovich shifted him to left guard instead of restoring him to his center position.

At first, Fields directed his anger at Radakovich. Their problems dated back to training camp when Fields, rather than Bingham, was asked to move to right guard. "There was one time in training camp when I was ready to punch Rad out," Fields says. "He was riding me unmercifully in pass-rush drills, and I told him, 'Fuck off,' three times in a row. Later on, he asked the guys, 'If Joe Fields was to jump me and hit me, would you stick up for me?' He told me, 'You lost it a little bit this morning.' I said, 'Yeah, you don't know how close you came to really getting hurt.' He said, 'Well, you never know until you push.' As I look back on it,

I think Rad was busting my balls to get me to work harder or do something so that Walton wouldn't get rid of me. I think it was Joe Walton pushing Rad to put pressure on me."

Trying to learn a new position made it difficult for Fields to be an effective leader during a game. He was concentrating so hard on doing his own job that he couldn't help those around him in his usual fashion. After the battering the Jets' offensive linemen took from the Buffalo pass rush, they were beginning to look a little war-weary, which made the negative atmosphere created by Walton that much harder to bear.

"We never heard positive reinforcement from Walton," Fields says. "He always attacked us: 'You sons of bitches, you're all a piece of shit.' Not quite in those words, but that was the feeling he conveyed. He was a very good offensive coordinator, but he's not a good head coach because he affects too many people."

"You know what he loves?" Klecko adds. "He loves to have his ass kissed in the papers. Matt Monger, a backup linebacker, said in the papers that Walton talks from the heart. Geez, we heard that fifteen times. He was talking about leadership one day, and he said, 'Some guys think I talk from the heart. You'd think that other guys would stick up for what I was saying when they hear people talk in the locker room and say, 'Did you ever think Joe Walton is right?' But how can you talk to a bunch of guys who feel Walton is abandoning ship on them? He never gave anybody a bit of confidence ever."

The classic example of Walton's instinct for survival and penchant for shifting the blame took place in 1984. The Jets reached midseason with a surprising 6–2 record and were scheduled to face the Patriots in New England the week that head coach Ron Meyer was fired as the result of a player uprising and replaced by Raymond Berry. Everything should have been upbeat for the Jets because New England figured to have some turmoil created by the coaching change. But Walton came into the Wednesday team meeting and made an angry speech about how he would never let his players get him fired. For forty-five minutes, he ranted and raved, saying such things as "The prisoners aren't telling this warden what to do." It was unreal. The Jets just sat there shell-shocked and wondered what had possessed Walton to go on this tirade. What was the point of upsetting his own players, who had nothing to do with the firing of Meyer? But he just kept raging about how players had no loyalty and shouldn't get the coach fired. The Jets lost that game at New England, and the season went downhill from there.

With his continual harping on the problems created by the strike and his constant references to players showing up just for their paychecks, Walton indicated he was determined not to let them drag him down. Rather than try to unite a divided team, his remarks were calculated to plant the fear of losing jobs. He communicated his own sense of insecurity with repeated comments about players taking bread off his family's table.

Walton's search for leaders before the Cincinnati game overlooked the primary fact that leadership is implicit in the job description of any head coach. But he was up and down like a yo-yo following the strike, and so were the Jets.

"You don't need that kind of pressure when you're going bad," Klecko says. "You can't play with a tight asshole, and nobody gets a tighter asshole than Joe Walton. It's a fact a team takes on the personality of its head coach. Those guys were trying not to let it get to them, but they were taking on his personality."

The strike may have diminished their role as leaders, but Klecko and Fields decided before the Jets took the field against the Bengals that they would have their say to an audience that had been largely hostile to them since they crossed the picket line. It was time to step in and try to prevent Walton from inflicting any more psychic damage.

"I told Walton to get out of the locker room because we needed it to ourselves," Klecko says. "He likes to talk before a game. I said, 'Joe, it ain't working. You get out, and we'll talk to them.' I told the players, 'We ain't playing for the fucking coaches; we're playing for ourselves. You've got to realize that. You're trying to kick the other guy's ass. Nothing else matters.'"

Fields added, "The coaches kicked us out [of the Monday meeting] this week. They can kick you out at the end of the year. You're playing for the guys in this room, and that ultimately comes down to number one. And you're playing for pride in yourself."

"We didn't say, 'You no-good SOBs. How could you not believe in Joe Walton?'" Klecko says. "You don't say that. That's not the kind of thing guys respect because they see right through it."

The Jets pulled out an improbable 27–20 victory over the Bengals by scoring the winning touchdown on a blocked field goal return in the fourth quarter. Klecko had been getting penetration up the middle on earlier field-goal attempts, but this time, he was caught flat-footed when Bengals nose tackle Tim Krumrie, who was playing left guard, fired out to block him. Barry Bennett went through the spot vacated by Krumrie to block the kick, and safety Rich Miano returned it 67 yards for the TD that gave the Jets a 6–5 record and put them in a three-way tie for the AFC East lead.

After the game, Walton said, "We played hard all game—not well all the time—but they played damn hard today."

Klecko and Fields were dressed and on their way to the stadium parking lot when Walton stopped them. The head coach wanted to know the magic words they had said before the game, the secret of leadership that he couldn't unlock.

Klecko told him, "Joe, I didn't say a goddamn thing. I just told them what they were playing for."

Walton told both Klecko and Fields, "I don't know what you said to them, but this team is yours until you leave."

"Talk about a guy who will turn tail and run on you," Klecko says, recalling that moment. "The next week after the Miami game, he tells me I suck and my career is over. One game. That shows how quickly he changes. Walton has no idea what a leader is all about."

• • •

Some days at the office are bloodier than others. It was Monday night, December 7, 1987, in Miami—Pearl Harbor Day—and a sense of insecurity pervaded the atmosphere in the Jets' dressing room at Joe Robbie Stadium. There was a feeling of everyone looking over his shoulder, believing Walton wouldn't hesitate to swing the executioner's blade wildly if he thought it would save his own head.

A civilizing shower following the Jets' 37–28 loss to the Dolphins only served to open up the pores and let the impact of the game seep deeper into Joe Klecko and Joe Fields. Over the course of their careers with the Jets—thirteen seasons for Fields and eleven for Klecko—how many truly awful games had either one played? A handful. No more. But at that moment, none of their past deeds or sacrifices counted. They couldn't draw on a savings account of accumulated experience with the Jets to see them through lean times. There was just this game, this dreadful game, the worst either ever had played in all those years in the NFL.

Klecko dressed and answered the murmured questions of reporters. Somehow, the quiet of a losing locker room always serves as a reminder the NFL is a high-stakes business, not a game. "Oh shit," he thought to himself. "What a bad time for this to happen to both of us."

It was just one game, but it evoked haunting overtones of the 45–3 blowout the Dolphins inflicted on the Jets the previous season, when they came to the Orange Bowl with a 10–1 record and then collapsed into the rubble of a 1–6 finish. Now, here they were a year later in a brand new stadium that looked like a South Florida shopping mall with its softly lit exterior and aqua-and-orange interior-decorating scheme. It was another disturbing symbol of change on a night when both Klecko and Fields looked old and felt out of place.

Once Klecko resumed playing on a knee that literally was bolted together in the absence of the usual connecting cartilage, it was inevitable that muscle fatigue would set in after a few weeks. The Dolphins game was his fourth after eleven months of rehabilitation. Physically, it was impossible to be the Joe Klecko who tore up the middle of the line with hurricane force, driving opposing linemen back into the quarterback's face. But that's the player Walton was counting on to pick up his directionless team. Klecko had been effective, if not overpowering, in his first three games, and Walton credited him the week of the Miami game with improving the pass rush. Yet, Klecko knew he still was very much under the gun, especially because it was the hated Dolphins and quarterback Dan Marino and he was facing perennial Pro Bowl center Dwight Stephenson, the one opponent against whom Klecko measured himself.

"This was my big test, and I failed," Klecko thought. "Stephenson had his way with me all night. I didn't come close to Marino. I know how it's going to be handled. I looked like a world-beater against Cincinnati, but this game was so bad, it changes everything. It's the nail in the coffin."

Fields's problems weren't as obvious to the people in the seats, but they were just as real. The Miami game was his second at left guard. Even though his debut at the position against Cincinnati had been satisfactory, the switch fed his growing anxieties. On the surface, it appeared a simple move, but at the NFL level, the picture he saw was so foreign it needed subtitles. He and Alexander had played well at right guard and right tackle. At left guard, all the moves were just the opposite of what Fields was used to doing. Out of position, he felt like a thirty-four-year-old rookie.

"Are they just using me to plug the hole, and when the hole's filled, I'm gone?" Fields wondered when the change was made. "That's the scary part, the insecure part. When they pencil in the starting lineup at the end of the season, will they pencil me in, or am I just a fill-in guy? Do they say, 'If this guy is healthy or this guy signs a contract, do we still need him?' I told Walton after the Cincinnati game I didn't realize how much harder it was to play left guard than right guard. The left side is a whole different world."

When he finished dressing, Fields joined Klecko in the tunnel outside the locker room, and they spoke quietly while waiting to board the buses for the trip to the airport. After so much time together, they could practically read each other's mind.

"This is it," Fields said. "We're out of here."

Was it really possible their careers could come down to this one horrible game? They didn't have to think too long to answer that one. "We knew how Walton was going to react when things got bad," Klecko says. "We got our asses kicked. At that time and place, he wasn't the type of guy who would just say, 'You guys played terrible; we're going to throw this film away.' He was look-ing to point fingers all over the place."

The worst-case scenario was unfolding. The Jets were losing; Walton was the target of boos from the home fans and harsh questions from the media, and the team was riddled with dissen-sion resulting from the strike. Klecko and Fields looked bad against the Dolphins, but they had plenty of company. The Jets didn't know it at the time, but they were on the verge of falling apart for the second straight season in a grim four-game losing streak. Walton needed answers, a place to shift the blame. As symbols of the post-Namath era, Klecko and Fields knew they were it, the designated scapegoats.

"My theory is we had a core of this team from 1982 when we went to the AFC championship," Fields says. "When you put your faith in a group of guys, like Walton did, you should stay with them until it's over. You don't question their leadership through good times and bad. You picked them. You live and die with them. He changed his mind near the end, and we lost four games in a row."

If it was evidence Walton needed to get rid of them, it was all there on videotape. Stephenson and the Dolphins went right after Klecko on the first play of the game, sending running back Troy Stradford up the middle for a 15-yard gain. The Dolphins were just about the worst running team in the NFL, but they were pounding it up the gut.

"Miami came after Klecko with a different scheme," Bud Carson says. "They had people come right after his knees. The strongside guard cut him bad. You can't play that way. The first drive was nothing but running. They shocked us with that first drive, and I don't think we recovered."

It didn't help that Klecko was playing with a broken finger for which he had taken a painkilling injection before the game. "I had lost the feeling in the top of my hand," Klecko says. "When you play defensive football, the use of the hands is essential. I couldn't feel anything; I couldn't grab. Playing against Dwight Stephenson, who is the best center I ever played against, that was pretty damn hard."

But that wasn't what worried Klecko the most. Whenever he tried to run a "game," looping around one of the defensive linemen next to him, Stephenson was on top of him almost before he could move. The quickness on which he relied wasn't there, and the frightening part was that Klecko didn't understand why it was happening.

"Usually, I would come around clean as a whistle," Klecko says. "The only person who could block me would be the offside tackle, and it would be hard for him because he wouldn't expect me. But I was getting stymied on the line, and that hardly ever happened to me. Stephenson was getting on me before I could run the game, or I'd get to the hole and get pushed by instead of sitting down in the hole and taking everybody on. I had no clue what was the matter. In other games, I would always go back to the basics, but I couldn't even do that in this game. I stunk, and I've never stunk. I couldn't explain this one to myself, and that bothered me.

"Part of it was that I wasn't into the game mentally. I thought I could turn up the intensity when I got into the game like I always had, but I couldn't do it this time. I'm sure some of it had to do with Stephenson. He was prepared for the Joe Klecko he always played against, and he came after me with his usual tenacity."

The sight of Klecko giving ground was shocking to all those on the Jets who had come to expect him to perform superhuman feats as a matter of routine. He was the John Henry of defensive linemen, a real steel drivin' man. For years, he walked with a painful-looking rolling gait, but then, that beer-barrel body would explode out of its stance with a powerful surge. His explosive quality was missing, and the way the Dolphins were pushing him around made Klecko look mortal.

"It was an experience I never had, so I didn't know how to combat it," Klecko says. "Of course, I started thinking about my leg and questioning myself again and again. Thoughts about the pain or the possibility of injury didn't enter my mind. I was thinking, 'Jesus, everybody's going to think it's my leg.'"

Mehl, who was in his third game back from knee surgery and was playing inside linebacker behind Klecko, knew exactly how Klecko was feeling. The Dolphins had sent a lead blocker at his knee on the first run by Stradford. "Neither of us should have been out there," Mehl says. "We weren't a hundred percent. We didn't have a strong leg to stand on. It was too early to make a comeback. I felt, 'Geez, what am I doing here?' Your legs are dying. We were in the lull period. You don't have the burst, and you're struggling mentally."

On the other side of the ball, Fields was having a similar experience. The first quarter hadn't ended, and the Jets were down, 14–0. But they got the ball back at the Miami 49 and had a chance to get in the game. Quarterback Ken O'Brien called "25 Lag Draw." Fields was supposed to invite Miami defensive end John Bosa inside by the way he set at the line of scrimmage, and if Bosa tried to come inside, Fields would turn him in that direction so the ballcarrier, Johnny Hector, could run through the vacated hole.

"I was sitting too wide, and when Bosa came inside, I didn't get enough of him," Fields says. "He had an angle directly to Hector and hit him for a three-yard loss. I went to the sidelines thinking I did everything exactly right. But really, I was lined up wrong."

Embarrassment gave way to desperation as the Dolphins built a 27–0 halftime lead. Klecko began taking shots, trying to guess the snap count and get off the ball before Stephenson. One offsides penalty gave the Dolphins a chance to score a touchdown when they would have been forced to settle for a field goal. Another in the third quarter wiped out a Jets interception and allowed the Dolphins to kick a field goal. In the past, the coaches had trusted Klecko's instincts and winked at his offsides penalties because his style so often led to big plays, but by that time, they were telling him to play the position by the book and recording each offsides as a black mark against him.

"Sometimes, I go off and play the position the way I want and make a big play because I can get away with it," Klecko says. "I was trying to get that edge and compensate by taking shots because I was under such scrutiny. But I wasn't getting away with anything against the Dolphins."

Carson, always a supporter of Klecko's, was upset. "Joe started freelancing too much that night," Carson says. "It was the only time in my life I was disgusted with Joe. He was destroying himself. The whole club was a shambles."

The offense managed a comeback in the second half, but still, Fields continued to get his wires crossed at his new position. In the fourth quarter, he was supposed to pull to his left to block outside linebacker Mark Brown. Fields was looking for a stunt to the inside by Brown, who caught him by surprise by blitzing straight at him. "I hesitated, and Brown hit me when I was off balance and sacked O'Brien," Fields says. "I saw Brown coming, and Jim Sweeney, who was playing left tackle, did me a favor and put a hand on him to try to slow him down. But Brown beat me like a drum. I was playing a new position, and I was thinking too much. So many things were going wrong that every play was a struggle, whether I blocked the right guy or not.

"Later in the game, there were two guys blitzing on one play. I knew we couldn't pick them up, so, I tried to block them both. I tried something I couldn't do. It was frustrating."

Finding themselves together on the sidelines at one point, Fields told Klecko, "Joe, the harder I'm trying, the worse I'm getting."

"I'm the same way," Klecko said. "I'm trying to get my hands inside on Stephenson, a simple thing, and I'm getting killed."

The damage was extensive when the Monday nightmare ended. Klecko had four offsides penalties, one assisted tackle, and the feeling that much of the Dolphins' 139 yards rushing had come through the area where he normally stood as stout as a brick wall. "If we had been winning and everybody else was playing well, I wouldn't have been under such a microscope," Klecko says. "I would have been accepted for what I was as a role model. Because we were going bad, I still was expected to carry everybody and do the extra things I always did to make the big plays.

At that time, I didn't have the physical ability to do that, so, everybody said, 'Joe, what's wrong?' I can't believe everything I had done for the Jets would come down to one game. Take that game away, and what does my career look like?"

After giving up 2 sacks and blowing the play where Bosa nailed Hector in the backfield, Fields wasn't looking forward to the tape review and the criticism he knew was in store. "I can remember having games where my name never was mentioned when they looked at the films," Fields says. "All of a sudden, I miss a block and they say, 'What are you thinking about?' We gave up a lot of sacks all year, but I was responsible for six and didn't have a holding penalty all season. That was more sacks than I ever gave up in one season. They were at left guard and right guard, but they weren't looked at that way. I'm Joe Fields; I've been around thirteen years, and Joe Fields shouldn't get beat."

The Jets' charter flight returned to New York in the wee hours Tuesday morning, and the players headed home for their day off. By the time they reported for work Wednesday, Klecko and Fields were outcasts. Nothing was said, but they recognized the changed order in their familiar locker-room environment almost immediately. Live in a place long enough, and if a picture frame is tilted, something feels wrong even before you know exactly what is out of kilter. Their sixth sense was telling Klecko and Fields decisions already had been made. They read it in the body language of assistant coaches who walked past without speaking, their eyes averted. Teammates shied away. Paranoia is a communicable disease.

The "leper syndrome" Fields called it, and Klecko knew exactly what he meant.

"The coaches don't talk to you, and you feel like a leper," Fields explains. "Because I played like shit in Miami, they go by me and don't say hello. I'm unclean. They don't want to associate with me. It's a weird feeling, a strange feeling, but it's not one I'm imagining. The same guy who was my buddy last week isn't talking to me. When you're on shaky ground, nobody—assistant coaches and other players—wants to be associated with you because they don't want the head man to think they're siding with you. I say let's bring bells and ring them as we go down the hall."

It was instinct and Walton's track record of shifting the blame that told Klecko and Fields they soon would be ex-Jets. When Walton replaced Walt Michaels as head coach in 1983, he took over a team that had reached the AFC title game the previous season and went 7–9 with it. After that season, Walton got rid of quarterback Richard Todd, whom he had nurtured the previous two years as offensive coordinator. Another 7–9 record in 1984 prompted Walton to fire four assistants, including defensive coordinator Joe Gardi, a friend with whom he shared a ride to work nearly every day for four years. The Jets went 11–5 and made the playoffs in 1985, but they lost the wild-card playoff game, in part because they couldn't provide pass protection for O'Brien. Offensive line coach Bill Austin was fired after the season, and five-time Pro Bowl tackle Marvin Powell was traded. When the Jets fell apart in 1986, Walton forced O'Brien to bear the brunt of the blame by waiting until the playoffs to replace him at quarterback. Not all of those moves were unwarranted, but it was remarkable how Walton never stepped up and took any responsibility. Clearly, Walton's excuse for the Jets' problems in 1987 would be old age, rather than his own poor handling of the team after the strike, and Klecko and Fields were at the head of the senior-citizen class.

The first harbinger of bad news on Wednesday following the Miami debacle was trainer Bob Reese, whose judgment Klecko trusted. Reese told Klecko, "You weren't protecting your leg; you just couldn't fucking play. You better think about retiring if you can't play. If you can't do better than that, you could get killed."

The conversation scared Klecko because Reese was talking to him as a friend. Later that day, Klecko was in the locker room when assistant coach Mike Faulkiner told him the head man wanted to see him. Walton, wearing a mask of grim concern, was sitting behind the desk in his dark-paneled office, and he motioned Klecko to a seat at the side of the desk. They were about five feet apart.

"You know, Joe, you're not going to make the decision about retiring," Walton began. Ticking off the names of the Jets' defensive coordinator, defensive line coach, and team physician, Walton continued, "Bud Carson's not going to make it; Ray Callahan's not going to make it, and Dr. Nicholas isn't going to make it. So, I'm going to have to do it. Some guys who play this game have to be kicked out of it. They don't always know when they've had it, and other people have to make the decision for them."

Klecko could feel his blood beginning to boil, especially when Walton then suggested he thought of putting Klecko on injured reserve or the inactive list for the final three games of the season, but he held his tongue because he didn't want to fly off the handle and give Walton any more ammunition.

"I'm going to give you a chance to play," Walton said.

"That's all I can ask," Klecko responded.

"But I want you to watch the film," Walton said. "Tell me what you think. I think you were protecting your leg."

"Coach, I'm telling you I wasn't," Klecko said, rising to leave.

Before Klecko reached the door, Walton called after him, "And by the way, son, you make a lot of money."

Until that moment, Klecko hoped the end of his career with the Jets would be handled with a certain grace and dignity because of the part he played in the revival of a franchise that had subsisted on nothing more than memories of the Joe Namath glory years. He thought there would be consideration of the painkilling shots he had taken, the operations he had survived, and the body parts he had donated along the way. But the name "Joe Klecko" apparently meant nothing. He was just another piece of meat—at $812,000, an expensive filet at that. Klecko's salary just made it that much easier for Walton to cut him loose.

After watching the film, Klecko concluded he wasn't protecting his leg. He poked his head in Walton's office and said, "You're totally wrong." The two of them held each other's stares for a moment. Without another word, Klecko left.

"I knew he'd already made the decision," Klecko says. "There was no use arguing it."

That evening, Klecko went straight home after practice rather than staying to lift weights, as he usually did. His wife, Debbie, had come up to Long Island from their suburban Philadelphia home to take part in a charity fashion show put together by the Jets' wives. Grabbing a six-pack of beer, Klecko and Debbie took a walk to a nearby beach, where they sat talking until the beer was gone.

"I knew when I got back they were going to expect 'Joe Klecko,' and I can't be that this year," Klecko told Debbie. "I thought they would give me the benefit of the doubt because it was such a severe injury. It's not easy playing without all your tools and getting no recognition for it from the coaches. When you're losing and everything becomes magnified, there are no excuses. A lot of people have construction, but nobody has reconstruction like I had. The surgery was so bad; there was so much damage. Just by making it back, I'm way ahead of the odds. My knee X-ray looks like a Sears hardware store. I've got a three-eighths bolt that's five inches long and runs from one side of my knee to the other. I don't have the stamina I know I can have with an offseason of training. I didn't have training camp to get in shape. There's no way I can get any stronger this season. But I'm asked to play to save my soul, and it's a fucking battle.

"I thought I could do it because of my skills and knowledge of playing, but I haven't been able to. I'm looked upon as losing it because I'm not playing to Joe Klecko's level. Maybe I should retire. Is it worth it to be kicked constantly after I've just about given my whole heart and soul for something I really believe in? You talk about being loyal to a football team, and in return, you get *nada*. You get shit."

"Joe," said Debbie, "you can't change Walton's attitude."

"You're right," Klecko said. "The only thing I can do is play as hard as I can."

Word of Klecko's little tête-à-tête with Walton made the rounds of the team, and in no time at all, the "leper syndrome" began to manifest itself in a more tangible way. It was easy enough to see what was happening from the alignment of bodies on the practice field. Dan Alexander, who had lined up next to Fields in games and dressed next to him in the locker room for eleven seasons, stood firmly by him. But Marty Lyons, Klecko's closest friend on the defensive line once known as the "New York Sack Exchange," stood apart from Klecko, apparently hoping to maintain that distance in Walton's eyes. There were others who separated themselves from Klecko and Fields by their body language, but Lyons was the one whose decision to turn his back on them hurt the most and best defined the insecurity and fear sweeping the team.

"It was so blatant with Marty because we hung out and partied together so much," Klecko says. "We had the same style. We liked to have our fun during the week and then go out on Sunday and just kill people. The religious guys would come in for Bible study on Saturday morning, which was all well and good, and Marty and I would joke about having our Bible study on Friday night. I remember one time Bud Carson really got mad at me and Marty coming in hung over on a Saturday before playing Seattle in 1985. We said, 'Bud, don't worry about a thing.' After we won the game, we saw Bud in the locker room, and we said, 'See?' He laughed. Bud never carried a grudge."

Day after day, Klecko and Lyons knelt on one knee shoulder-to-shoulder during practice when the offense was working against the scout team. But now, a wedge had been driven between them. "Walton made a point of trying to win Marty over, telling him he was a great leader and had a lot of football left if he didn't stay under my influence," Klecko says. "Walton used to talk to me on the field a lot, and now, he was talking to Marty."

As soon as he saw what was happening, Klecko confronted Lyons. "You know what?" Klecko said. "You're an ass-kissing son of a bitch."

"Hey, Joe, the ship is sinking," Lyons replied. "It's every man for himself."

"After all we've been through," Klecko said, "you turn out to be like that?"

"You've got a point, I guess," Lyons admitted. But he didn't move closer to Klecko on the practice field.

Except for the moments he spent talking with Fields and Alexander during practice, Klecko felt like a deserted island. Before Walton put him on his "least wanted" list, Klecko's rough-edged charisma put him at the center of the daily byplay with players and coaches. He always was kibitzing, often testing teammates to see how they would react. All of a sudden, players who once sought his company simply stopped coming around in the locker room and on the field.

"Everybody is in a paranoia situation," Klecko said at the time. "But they have no backbone, and I'm not kidding one ounce. I can understand doing anything to keep your job as far as playing, but to abandon your friends you've been around for years ... I respect people that stand by you. If I knew somebody was going down, I'd pat him on the ass and say, 'Pick yourself up, guy.' It's sad, but I guess you could say it's part of human nature.

"It's not that I don't like them. They're great guys. But they're not the kind of friends I'd put up against my back to go to war. It has evolved to this: I stand completely at the other end from what's happening at practice by myself. I don't want to get them in trouble. I don't want to talk to a young kid and have Joe Walton see him laughing with me."

The End (Part II)

One week, one game. The Miami game was history and so, it appeared, were Joe Klecko and Joe Fields. One week, they were Joe Walton's leaders-for-life, and the next, they were his fall guys. Under the circumstances, a little gallows humor seemed in order for the condemned men. They decided to hold "Joe and Joe's Last Drink Party" on the Friday night between the Miami and New England games at the Long Island night club owned by Klecko. The party was open to everyone who had his leprosy shots. Soviet premier Mikhail Gorbachev returned to Moscow from his visit to the United States that week, and there was a newspaper headline that lent itself to the occasion of the impending departure of Klecko and Fields: GOOD-BYE UNTIL NEXT TIME. One of the equipment managers cut out the headline, pasted pictures of Klecko and Fields over those of Gorbachev and Ronald Reagan and attached it to the party announcement posted in the locker room.

In the playoff years of 1985 and 1986, it probably would have been a raucous gathering. But few players were in a party mood. A total of seven players, including Klecko and Fields, showed up. Dan Alexander dubbed the partygoers "The Magnificent Seven."

"The party was a sad one, a bum feeling," Klecko says. "Walton had set the mood for the rest of the year. Everybody was worried about their job, every single one. I was joking, even to the wives that came, 'Hey, we're out of here.' Alexander said, 'No way.' I said, 'Man, you've got a rude awakening coming. There's no way

245

they're keeping us here.' It was like we were trying to convince people, and no one would believe it."

The party was meant to inject a note of levity into a grim season, but when Klecko and Fields arrived at the training complex the next morning to join the team for the trip to New England, they discovered it had the opposite effect on Walton, who had a rule that team parties had to be approved by him. It was related to his desire to control, as much as possible, the lives of his players.

Before Walton became head coach, Marty Lyons sponsored an end-of-training-camp party called the "Swarm Party," which was named after then-defensive coordinator Joe Gardi's constant admonition to his players to "swarm to the ball." It was held at a park near the Jets' training complex, and players invited friends and business associates, as well as their families. "Walton changed that," Klecko says. "He said it had to be held at the complex, and it's only for the players' families. It's a day off and a fun thing, but you better be there. It's not that he was making it more family-oriented; he was putting everybody under his control. Walton got mad at Alexander and Guy Bingham once for having a Mexican party on a Friday night before a Monday night game. He wants a bunch of 'yes men.' "

Apparently, Walton was upset by the implications of a lost cause in "Joe and Joe's Last Drink Party" because he asked around, trying to find out who put up the sign. "The party started as a joke," Alexander says. "It wasn't like Klecko and Fields went out and recruited people to come to the party. I go out to dinner every Friday night. They asked me to come by, and I brought my wife with me. Everybody sat on the couches and told old stories. We talked and had a few drinks and didn't stay too late. It was very quiet, and I think everyone went home about eleven-thirty that night. All of a sudden, a party that started as a joke got blown up into a big Friday night drinking deal. It wasn't like that at all. It was highly misunderstood."

That Saturday night at the team meeting in the hotel, Walton staged one of his most mean-spirited performances ever, calling his players "pea brains who will never amount to anything after football" and telling them they had no character. Klecko and Fields were certain their party was one of the things that set him off, even though Walton didn't refer to it directly in his speech.

"Guys came out of that meeting saying, 'I can't believe this fucking guy,'" Klecko says. "He couldn't find answers, so he started blaming people. It was the most negative goddamn thing you ever heard. He had all the excuses built in for losing before we even started, and that's what the guys read. He condemned the whole football team at one time or another in that speech."

"He was personally attacking guys, not the football player, but the entire person," Fields says. "Guys really started to resent Joe Walton. You couldn't stick up for him on the field because, if you did, guys would tell you that you were full of shit."

During the course of Walton's "Pea Brains Speech," the coach at first implied he was upset at everyone and then said he wasn't talking about everyone. Citing examples of poor play by unnamed players, he said, "You know who you are." In some cases, everybody knew who he meant, and in others, it was a puzzle.

"When Walton says he's not talking to everyone, the players ask themselves, 'Who's he talking to? He's got to be talking about me,'" Klecko says. "Walton is creating paranoia among the players, but he doesn't understand that. He's a guy with all the answers, but he doesn't know how to handle people. He's so scared. He has no confidence in himself at all, and that's very evident."

Numb from Walton's constant browbeating and undermanned because their top three cornerbacks were on injured reserve, the Jets lost to the Patriots, 42–20. Pats quarterback Steve Grogan threw four touchdown passes and ran for another to make the halftime score 35–6. Thanks to the kindness of New England coach Raymond Berry, a religious man, the Pats threw just two passes in the second half to hold down the score.

Lost in the chaos was the fact that Klecko came back from his miserable performance in Miami and played pretty well under the conditions. "Nobody ran up the middle, and twice when Grogan threw touchdown passes, I was right in his face," Klecko recalls. "I hit him one time and knocked him down the other time, and he still hit the passes. There's no explanation for that. New England came after me hard as far as cutting me and double-teaming me, and I did fine."

The next day, Walton eased up in his criticism of the players and told the media the responsibility for the Jets' problems belonged to him. But on Thursday before they played a home game against Philadelphia, Walton ripped into his players again, saying they had "too many fighters and not enough football players."

If nothing else, Walton had succeeded in uniting his players for the first time since the strike ended—they were united in their distaste for the Walton Method. Five players representing various segments of the team were quoted anonymously in an article in New York *Newsday* in which they criticized Walton's handling of the team. Their comments were supported by other teammates who spoke only on background. The article was published on Sunday before the Jets played the Eagles and lost their third straight game, 38–27. It revealed not only Walton's remarks before and after the New England game, but also that he went into a tirade about "job security" hours before the Monday night game in Miami.

The tenor of the article was best expressed by one of the players quoted in *Newsday*. He said of Walton, "He tries on Friday and, sometimes, on Saturday to instill fear. It's not conducive to playing relaxed football. . . . He tries to pump people up, but he tears them down. . . . He walks around in his own world the day of a game. I wonder if he realizes what he did [to the team's mental state] the night before."

The following Thursday before the season finale against the Giants, Walton called a team meeting to clear the air. The coach, who heard "Joe must go!" chants from the fans at three distinct junctures of the Philadelphia loss, told his players that Jets owner Leon Hess had assured him he would be allowed to fulfill the two years remaining on his contract at that time. Then, Walton said he wanted to have a "heart-to-heart" talk with his players.

To some, this team meeting was the scariest in which they ever had been involved. After ten minutes, it almost seemed as though there was going to be blood on the walls before it was over. Walton clearly was stunned by the depth of anger and emotion expressed by his players. It was a wild scene that quickly put him on the defensive.

The tension in the room increased dramatically when Klecko stood up midway through the meeting and challenged Walton's authority and leadership. "Everybody was supposed to air out their feelings," Klecko says. "I got up and started to speak my mind, but I got cut off real quick. I asked Walton, 'Do you feel you breed confidence in this team?' He said, 'Yes,' but instead of giving me a chance to explain why his methods weren't working, he brought up the 'Last Drink' party."

"Do you think that's part of being a leader?" Walton asked, referring to the party. Walton then began asking players he knew hadn't attended, such as quarterback Ken O'Brien, wide receiver Al Toon, and tight end Mickey Shuler, "Were you there? Were you there? Were you there?" Turning back to Klecko, he said, "Nice team party. Nobody came to it, did they?"

"I just shook my head," Klecko says. "He went to somebody else right away, and I didn't pursue it. I was talking in an even tone, trying to make sense to him, but he took it personally and never really answered anything I asked."

When Fields and Mehl raised their hands, Walton ignored them, but Fields got up and just started speaking. "I said, 'Joe, I think I speak for the majority. I don't care if you attack me football-wise; that's your job. But you don't do that. When you attack us after a loss or like in that speech where you called us pea brains, you attack the whole person. A football player is made up of a lot of things. He's a football player, a father, a husband, a salesman, a businessman."

Walton apologized for the remark, saying he didn't mean for it to come across that way. Some players remained silent when Walton called on them to speak, figuring they had nothing to gain. But others spoke out strongly.

"Lyons brought up the point about how guys are so paranoid around here it's unbelievable and about how he doesn't want players talking to the media," Klecko says. "Then, you get guys like Tom Flick, a third-string quarterback who never played a down for the Jets. He's very religious, and he says, 'I don't think guys should go out on Friday night. I take it personally because it hurts me.' Well, who the hell is Tom Flick to be controlling other people's lives? I never wrung anybody's neck to go out with me. If someone didn't have enough sense to go home if he couldn't handle it, I can't help that. Everybody is supposed to be an adult."

"I've never asked anybody not to be themselves," Fields adds. "Just play your ass off on Sunday. That's the bottom line. In all the time I was in the league, I was never able to sleep on Friday and Saturday nights. I always took Valium on Saturday nights so I could get my sleep, and on Fridays, I had a few beers to help me sleep."

As the meeting grew wilder, tight end Rocky Klever stood up and blasted Walton for his 'pea brain' remark. "When you tell me I'm nothing without football," Klever said, "I just wanted to stand up and tell you to go fuck yourself." Walton reacted as if Klever were telling him to do just that at the moment when, in fact, he was explaining how he felt at the time of Walton's ill-conceived insult.

Union representative Kurt Sohn also got into it with Walton about the way he handled the aftermath of the strike. Sohn complained that it was a mistake to force players to bury their feelings rather than allow them to get everything out in the open right away.

Most everything was out in the open when the meeting ended. To Klecko and Fields it seemed the purpose of Walton's "heart-to-heart" talk was not so much to clear the air as it was to identify the sources of the criticism Walton had received so he could add the offending players to his enemies list and earmark them for removal.

"I often said to Walton," Klecko recalls, " 'You don't give these guys a chance to be a man. You want to lead them by the hand and make them do things your way.' "

"Joe Walton is very, very paranoid, and the sad part is he doesn't realize who is on his side," Fields adds. "Take Klecko and me. We didn't agree with a lot of things he did, but if he asked us to do something, we did it. In that respect, we were on Joe Walton's side. But his attitude was: 'You guys are against me.' "

When they pictured the end of their careers, Klecko and Fields always assumed they would be the ones to make the decision. No one would have to tell them they couldn't do it anymore because they would recognize the loss of quickness and skill. The team would give them time to make up their minds, possibly reward them with an extra year for their faithful service and the value of sharing their knowledge with younger players. It would be a rational process based on mutual respect. Maybe there would be a ceremony before their last home game, something special. Look at the Raiders, they carried quarterback Jim Plunkett for an extra year because of all the injuries he endured to lead them to two Super Bowl titles. Lowly Atlanta did the same for longtime center Jeff Van Note. For linebacker Steve Nelson's last game at the end of the 1987 season, the Patriots introduced only Nelson before the game, rather than the whole starting lineup, and made it a special occasion.

Klecko and Fields hoped it would be like that for them, but after the Miami game, they knew it was foolish to think the Jets would treat them any better than they did Joe Namath when he asked for one more year. Their end, they realized, would be bitter.

The jerseys were being torn from their backs. Sometimes, they joked with each other about how the Jets would have to send a team of guards to remove them from the locker room—maybe the Jets could hire the same police escort they employed during the strike. Since they would be clinging so fiercely to their lockers, the easiest thing would be to come in with chain saws, cut out the whole locker and carry it out to the street with them still in it. Laughing at the thought of the fight they would put up, Klecko and Fields then would chant in unison: "They can have my gun when they pry it from my cold, dead fingers."

"Now that we've seen a few guys go out with style this season, you think it would be nice to do the same thing," Klecko said. "I thought maybe they'd have a dinner or something, and it would be on a very good basis."

"If you've given them your blood and played double figures in years, it merits that opportunity," Fields agreed. "There are only three guys in the history of the Jets who played longer for them than my thirteen years—Randy Rasmussen, Winston Hill, and Pat Leahy. I would think they would come to me and say, 'We think this should be your last year.' If I agreed, I would announce it either before or during the season, and I would go out with some class. That's how I always hoped to do it."

So much for the ideal. The reality was something else. On the Saturday morning before the Jets met the Giants, Fields's right elbow, which he hyperextended against Philadelphia, was in such bad shape that he couldn't do a pushup.

"I suggested to Bob Reese, our trainer, that we should shoot it," Fields says, referring to the use of painkillers. "He said we'd have to shoot it too many places. We called one of the team doctors, Elliott Hershman, and he wouldn't allow it because it would leave me with no strength in my arm. So, they put me on injured reserve for what I thought might be my last game as a Jet."

When he phoned Kay to tell her what happened, Fields said, "It's a lousy way to end it, being on IR with an elbow that feels like shit. I don't know what's going to happen next year, but I'm not going to retire.'"

"Think back," Kay said. "Don't you think they were trying to get rid of you from the beginning this year? They kept changing your position until they found one you couldn't play."

The Jets had three other linemen with experience at left guard,

Guy Bingham, Ted Banker, and Mike Haight, but they chose to play Fields out of position rather than use him in the spot where he once was one of the NFL's best. "Bingham came up to me when they moved me to left guard and said, 'I don't know why they didn't move you back to center,'" Fields said. "He admitted to me that he was playing poorly. He felt it. Dan Radakovich, the offensive line coach, told me he doesn't keep veteran players as backups. I don't think I'm going to be around here next year."

Because of his injury, "The General" stayed at the Long Island house he shared with Klecko and left tackle Jim Sweeney, ordered a pizza, and cracked open a few beers and watched the game on TV like any other civilian. The Giants won easily, 20–7, and the Jets' offense gained just 70 yards and three first downs in the second half. The defense gave up 420 yards, and the Giants were able to run up the middle on several occasions as Klecko struggled manfully to fight off their double-team blocks and got little help from the inside linebackers in plugging the holes.

"I was upset before the game because I knew I had no power over the decision," Klecko recalls. "I told myself, 'This could be my last game as a New York Jet. Try to go out in style.' It would have been easy to fake an injury to get out of the game. But I got mad when Ray Callahan, the defensive line coach, took me out for one play."

Twice during the game, Callahan asked Klecko, "Do you want to come out now?"

"No, I'm here to play football," Klecko replied the second time. "That's why I get paid."

After the game, Fields met Klecko, Alexander, Bingham, Leahy, and a few other players at the Long Island restaurant owned by former Jets linebacker Greg Buttle. It was a sad farewell. Fields complained to Leahy about the Jets' lack of tradition.

"Pat became the eleventh player in NFL history to score a thousand points this season," Fields said, "You would think they would make a presentation to him or something. There's no recognition. I've seen the Jets' owner, Leon Hess, at games, but I don't know him. I think he hires people and puts his faith in them to do the job. I don't think he's really involved with tradition. The Jets have won the Super Bowl. There should be reminders of that everywhere. There's just a trophy in the lobby at the training complex."

The rest of the evening was spent reminiscing. Alexander tells the story of the rookie lineman in training camp who asked him how long he'd been playing in the league. "I told him I'd been playing eleven years and Fields was in his thirteenth year," Alexander recalls. "The guy says, 'Wow! Unbelievable.' Then, I said, 'That's nothing, Fields played three years in Canada before he came here.' The guy bought the whole story."

Leahy and Fields always had a special relationship. It wasn't that they had a lot in common, but the time they spent together working on placekicks and the fact both of them lasted so long with the same club created a bond. "We sat in the same seats together on the plane for thirteen years, and we'd replay every game on the way home," Leahy recalls. "Joe snapped for more than six hundred of my career points. He would say that our relationship reminded him of Pavlov's dog—every time he saw me coming on to the field, he knew he had to stick his head between his legs and let three guys beat his brains in.

"I used to keep an eye on Fields, Klecko, and Lyons before games. It was funny. You could tell when they were going to snap and start their pregame shouting. There was yelling, cursing and, sometimes, pounding on the nearest chalkboards and chairs. Then, we would have a quiet prayer. Klecko and I didn't really become good friends until later in his career. We were at a party one night, and I kiddingly questioned his strength. Joe picked me up and pinned me on the ceiling—with one arm! And I weighed about two hundred pounds.

"Joe and Joe both were players that meant a lot to the history of the Jets. When you talk about 'tradition,' it's hard to define. Tradition comes from winning and having recognizable players. We haven't won too many big games, and we were a floundering team in the seventies. Our two most recognizable players in team history were Joe Namath and Mark Gastineau. One drove the franchise to the Super Bowl, and the other drove it crazy."

The season had been a long one, so the party was short. Klecko and Fields were home by eleven that night. Klecko was trying to accept the inevitable, but he told his friend he still was looking for that one ray of hope that would bring him back. Maybe someone in the organization would stand up for him. Defensive coordinator Bud Carson was the only one who went to bat for Klecko, and that wasn't good enough.

"Everyone knew what I thought of Klecko," says Carson, who became head coach of the Cleveland Browns in 1989. "I love Joe

Klecko, and I'd back him to the hilt on anything. But when they decided to release him, I was the last one to find out. I didn't know of any decision being made; I wasn't involved. I fought for him when it counted during the season. I said he should be brought back. I'm not knocking Joe Walton or the New York Jets because they were very good to me, but my personal opinion is that Klecko should have been allowed back to play. There was nothing for me to do but accept the decision.

"Really, he should have stayed out in '87 and been given the time to heal. When he came back in '88, he would've had some kind of shot to play the way he can."

Klecko had received the same advice from assistant coach Mike Faulkiner during his rehabilitation period. "Faulkiner told me I was a fool for trying to come back and play that year," Klecko says. "But I always put the team in front of myself. The stories everybody wrote about me going out there with one leg—that's the way I felt I could help the team. I felt when guys were around me, they played better and had a better understanding of what was going on. When it came time in rehab where I was able to start doing football things, boy, I wanted to be out there. It was eating me alive."

For doing everything he could to make a difference for the Jets, Klecko was ushered out as quickly as possible when the season ended. There was no consideration of giving him a chance to come back for another training camp. Team physician James Nicholas manipulated Klecko's left knee in the postseason physical exam the day after the season ended and advised him to retire. It wasn't the final word, but that was just a formality.

"I haven't given my life and half my limbs to be tossed aside for some dumb reason," Klecko said to reporters. At the same time, he made it clear salary, age, and his disputes with Walton were significant factors on a par with the health risks in the Jets' decision-making process. He even said he would take a salary cut based on playing time.

"Nicholas was playing God," Klecko says. "Don't tell me I'm going to be grateful for failing me on a physical after all I've done for this team and after I've come back from a serious knee injury."

There was nothing Klecko could say or do that would change Walton's mind. The plain fact is that Walton wanted to get rid of Klecko and Fields and anyone else he felt posed a threat to his authority and credibility. The Jets' coach made that abundantly clear in his final remarks to the team. Still feeling the sting of the previous week's criticism from the players, Walton told them to "clean their own doorsteps" and "look in a mirror" before they challenged his leadership. He suggested they all go home and think about all the things he said during the season, and they would see he knew what he was talking about. The message was "conform or else."

Mark Gastineau, of all people, hit the nail on the head—inadvertently, no doubt—when he defended Walton's position. "Some of the players have forgotten who is the boss, and that's the coach," Gastineau said. "If we were all rookies, not as many [critical] things would have been said. We just would've been happy to be here."

That was Walton's strategy. Bring in as many rookies as possible. The Jets needed an infusion of youth, and rookies are too scared and inexperienced to question the coach. It even would give Walton a chance to start over with a new group and, possibly, to learn a little patience and tact.

For Klecko, there would be no second chances, no patience to see if his knee would improve with a full offseason of training. He took off on a brief hunting trip after Nicholas examined him. Shortly after he returned home on New Year's Eve, Klecko received a call from Walton. He had been expecting it because Walton had called earlier while he was away. Walton said he had been advised by Nicholas that it wasn't in Klecko's best interests to continue playing football. He told Klecko the Jets wanted him to retire or they would place him on waivers as having failed the postseason physical examination.

"I went off like a roman candle," Klecko says. "I was yelling at him. I said, 'Why the hell did you leave me out there for seven games to get beat up when everybody in the world was cutting me? Why didn't you tell me then instead of feeding me to the lions and possibly exposing me to further injury? Now, all of a sudden, you're doing this for my own good? Bullshit! It's a copout, and you know it!' "

"Well, that's not the way we looked at it," Walton replied. "We felt we owed you the opportunity to play. Nicholas doesn't want you to wind up a cripple."

"That's bullshit!" Klecko shot back. "I don't like not even being considered in this decision. I wasn't conferred with. Who the hell is Dr. Nicholas to say I can't play football? I thought we had an understanding that, once I got through this year with no complications, I'd be okay for next year."

Klecko then asked Walton what he thought of the conclusions drawn by Nicholas, and the coach began lavishing praise on Klecko for his performance in the past and for all the things he had done to help the Jets. "If I'm such a great player, how come I'm not given a chance to continue playing?" Klecko asked. "Is it my salary?" Walton denied that inference, overlooking the remark he made about Klecko's salary in their meeting after the Miami game.

"I told Walton I wanted him to tell the press I can't play football, and the decision had nothing to do with my knee," Klecko says. "He asked me why, and I said it was evident. He said, 'I can't do that because it's part of the decision,' I said, 'Don't tell me what you can do and can't do. I'm no fucking idiot! If you release me because I can't play football, I'll bow out like a man and leave you alone. If you do it because of my knee, it ain't going to end there.'"

The idea that Nicholas simply walked into a meeting with Walton and the front office staff and said he wasn't passing Klecko on the physical didn't ring true, particularly since Walton had emphasized he would be the one to kick Klecko out. But every time Klecko mentioned how he had played hurt for the Jets or made some other sacrifice to help the team, Walton said it had no bearing because of the decision by Nicholas to fail Klecko on the physical.

"I deserved the truth, which they didn't give me," Klecko says. "I think they wanted to do whatever they could to get rid of Joe Klecko, and the easiest way was for Nicholas to take this position. I was his scapegoat. I didn't fit in with Walton's plans, and he didn't have the guts to tell me."

It wasn't too difficult for the Jets and Nicholas to argue that someone with a knee missing as much cartilage as Klecko's left knee had no business on an NFL football field. Interestingly, the Jets never mentioned the five-inch bolt holding Klecko's knee together. That might have raised questions about the degree of "concern" they had for his health in the first place when they gave him the clearance to return. If he could help them, no one needed to know about the bolt, and if he wasn't the old Klecko, it would be easy enough to explain the decision to discard him in terms of age and missing parts.

But Klecko surprised the Jets' medical team in many respects, forcing Nicholas to go back on the understanding Klecko believed he had that he would be allowed to continue playing if there were no complications from the operation. "They talked about the knee blowing up and getting hot; that never happened," Klecko said at the time of the phone call from Walton. "I wear a brace. They told me when I played against Pittsburgh in '86 after I had arthroscopic surgery that nothing else worse could happen in a brace. I never had any serious pain or swelling. There were no 'maybes.' I never missed a day of practice or a game after I came back. Anytime you have reconstructive surgery and the knee doesn't come out completely tight, you can raise questions, but the brace does support it.

"Bart Nisonson, who performed the surgery on my knee, feels I still can play. I spoke to him the day after Walton called, and he said I'm fine."

The risk of permanent physical damage is a fact of life in the NFL, and one that Klecko always accepted willingly. After playing seven games with no swelling in his left knee, he was convinced that another season of play would not make his health at the age of fifty significantly worse than he already expected. In a prepared statement issued by the Jets, Nicholas mentioned "bone-on-bone changes that will worsen rapidly should he continue to play . . . accelerating the chances of arthritis."

But Nisonson said the bone damage that will lead to the onset of early arthritis was present before the operation. If he never injured the knee, Klecko still would have had an arthritic condition that would grow worse with continued play, a common situation throughout the NFL.

Nisonson characterized Klecko's decision to continue playing as a personal value judgment, saying, "The concern I had was that, in spite of the fact he was doing well, the repair didn't leave him with a perfect knee. He has significant looseness in parts of the knee. Part of the ligament repair didn't turn out as optimum as you would like. If it were up to me, I'd say, 'Joe, you're thirty-four. Your knee isn't a hundred percent. Does it pay to put yourself at risk?' "

It was a logical question, but it didn't mean Klecko was medically unable to continue playing. Both Nisonson and Jets trainer Bob Reese admitted Klecko could keep playing with full knowledge of the degree of risk.

Jack Foley, the head trainer at Lehigh University in Bethlehem, Pennsylvania, began designing training programs for Klecko in 1984. He is considered one of the foremost authorities in sports medicine, particularly in the area of rehabilitation and conditioning. When the Jets released Klecko after failing him on their physical exam, Foley laughed at the hypocrisy of the situation. There was absolutely no question in his mind that Klecko still was capable of playing.

"The X rays of Joe's knee show arthritis, bone spurs, calcification, and space in the knee," Foley says. "But probably seventy percent of all professional football players have that to some degree. It comes from hitting the turf for fifteen or sixteen years of their life, and they accept it. Truthfully, I didn't want Joe to go back when he did. I thought he needed a little more time. But he said, 'Jack, I've got to go.' He was true to Joe Walton and the Jets. He was determined to do it. He did certain things well, and he had some poor games, like the one in Miami.

"On a scale of one to ten, his knee was a twelve in the way it looked spaghetti-wise. But lots of athletes have bolts in a knee or a shoulder. The Jets copped out when they said he had to be released immediately. If that was the case, why didn't they release him before he came back and played? When they released him, Klecko met all the standards I set in testing his strength and movement. He still could play." And that is exactly what he intended to do.

After Walton's New Year's Eve call, the Jets had to wait until the day after the Pro Bowl more than a month later before they could make Klecko's release official. Walton still held out hope that Klecko would retire peacefully. He invited Klecko to come up to the Jets' complex for a face-to-face meeting to discuss the subject even though Klecko told him on the telephone that he refused to retire.

Walton had a surprise in store, but when Klecko arrived, he first asked Klecko if he had reconsidered his position on retirement. Klecko told him he still had something to prove about his knee. They discussed Nicholas's decision again, and then, Walton asked Klecko what he thought caused all the Jets' problems the previous season, as if Klecko were still his sounding board. Klecko expressed his opinion, but he sensed Walton wasn't really interested.

Finally, Walton said, "Joe, I'd really like you to coach."

At last, the purpose of the visit had been revealed. Without a second's hesitation, Klecko said, "There's no way. I'm not done playing."

Walton continued talking about the long hours assistant coaches put in for relatively low pay. He acted as if Klecko's answer hadn't registered.

"You're not telling me nothing," Klecko said. "I know all about it. I don't want to coach."

"Well, think about it. I don't want your answer now," Walton said. "But I'd like for you to say something. What do you think of the offer?"

"What do you want me to say?" Klecko asked.

"I hope you'd at least thank me," Walton said.

"Thank you?" Klecko said incredulously.

Klecko couldn't believe what he was hearing from the coach who was trying to force him into retirement. "He said it in such an arrogant way, like he was doing me a big favor," Klecko said of Walton's request for thanks. "Then, I saw the side of Joe Walton that says, 'I am the boss.' I was taken aback. He asked me to discuss it with Debbie, and I told him my wife didn't have anything to do with it. There was no question that I was going to play, and she supported me."

Klecko regarded Walton's job offer as little more than a face-saving gesture, a clever public relations ploy. But if he chose, Klecko could have shocked the Jets by taking it. "I think everyone knew Joe wasn't going into coaching, but the job was his with no conditions," Carson says. "I thought that was the best thing the Jets did. The other things were maybe not so good."

Walton called back to see if Klecko was interested in the coaching job, and when he said no, the Jets released him on February 8, 1988, the first day NFL teams were allowed to put players on waivers. They cited his failure to pass the postseason physical administered by Nicholas as the reason for Klecko's release.

After the announcement was made, none of Klecko's teammates, other than Fields, bothered to make a telephone call to wish him well. He hoped it would be different, that it wouldn't feel so lonely at the end, but he wasn't surprised.

Thinking of the closeness he often had felt with his teammates in the locker room and in the trenches, Klecko said, "The great thing about being a football player is that you don't usually find forty-five guys who do the same thing on the same days in the same place and are fighting for the same cause. That's what makes a football team such a close-knit group. But that's just part of the year. The rest of the time, it's not that way.

"I understand it. Sometimes, I know I don't want to get that close. I'm not that kind of guy. I don't have a lot of friends at home, either. Fields has a lot of friends he pals around with at home. I don't have one guy I can call up to go drinking. Not one guy. I don't like to be so involved with other people."

It wasn't a question of outgrowing the game—Klecko would never do that—it was a matter of growing out of the game. He lived it to the hilt for as long as it lasted, but when they turned on the lights and began collecting the glasses, Klecko looked around and saw that he and Fields were the only ones left. What happened?

"Toward the end, it was just Joe and Joe," says Debbie Klecko. "There were less and less people they hung out with. They lived with each other the last few years, but nobody on the team ever invited them to dinner. When it was the opposite, when other guys were living alone, they would always come to our house for dinner or just to spend the evening and watch TV, eat popcorn, and play games and stuff. When the tables were turned . . . Well, they were respected, but they weren't liked."

Fields was aware he rubbed some players the wrong way. There were times when he could be hard and simply ignore someone he didn't like. He made no pretense of friendship. Klecko helped draw him out; he made the eternal pessimist laugh. Still, Fields always maintained a cynic's mistrust of people's words and judged them by their actions. He didn't expect much from most people, and they rarely surprised him. But in Klecko, he found a man he could respect unreservedly.

"You're not going to leave this game with many friends that last," Fields said when Klecko was released. "It's a transient game. Klecko and I are very lucky in that way. We'll always be close."

For almost six weeks after the 1987 season ended, Fields's telephone was quiet, as far as news from the Jets was concerned. He was on a business trip to Buffalo in the middle of February when he phoned home to Kay. She told him Walton had called and wanted to see him as soon as possible. On the appointed day, Fields put on a business suit instead of the flannel shirt and jeans he ordinarily wore during the season, and he drove to Long Island. He said he wanted to look nice for his funeral after thirteen seasons as a Jet.

On the drive up, Fields thought of a thousand things he wanted to say to Walton. He was bitter because he knew what was going to happen. When he walked into the complex, Fields passed punter Dave Jennings, who was on his way out of Walton's office after receiving his release. Walton got up to shake his hand, and they both sat down.

"You're the hardest one of all," Walton began.

Fields thought to himself, "Yeah, sure."

"We're going to go another direction," Walton continued. "I think you should retire."

"I'm not going to retire," Fields said curtly.

"Well then, we'll put you on waivers," Walton said.

Fields rose to leave, and Walton reached over and shook his hand again.

"I wish you luck," Walton said.

Fields's reply came straight from the gut and crossed his lips before his brain had time to form a thought.

"I don't wish you any," he said. Turning his back on Walton, Fields walked away.

On Their Own Terms

The first line of the biographical sketch of Jets owner Leon Hess printed in the club's media guide is: "It all starts at the top." There was a certain irony in that for Joe Klecko. His Jets career *ended* "at the top" with a visit to Hess at his stately office in Manhattan, where the two of them had a long, comfortable conversation over lunch in a well-appointed private dining room with a view of the city. Hess was out of the country at the time of Klecko's release, so their get-together was more of a postmortem.

In sharp contrast to the shipbuilder who owns the New York Yankees baseball team and makes regular use of the forum available to him in the nation's media capital, the Jets' owner is an intensely private man. He became part-owner of the team in 1963 and sole owner in 1984 and held his first news conference on June 13, 1988. On rare occasions, he has talked to reporters while watching a practice session or in brief exchanges in the locker room after a game, but the conversations always are off the record and seldom about matters of substance. The chairman of the board of Amerada Hess, which is one of the giants in the oil and gas business, is one of the wealthiest men in America, but he has almost no public profile. It has been written of Hess that he is the most demanding of bosses, though not in a capricious way, such as the Yankees' George Steinbrenner. But those in the Jets' organization who have been permitted inside the layers of privacy surrounding Hess speak of him in tones of great respect and not a little awe.

Joe Klecko is one of those people. "I respect Mr. Hess on almost the same level as I respect my father," Klecko says. "I wanted to thank him for everything he had done for me and my family."

Although Klecko was at odds with most of the people running the NFL franchise owned by Hess, he still was concerned about preserving his relationship with the man at the top, who not only had paid Klecko well throughout most of his Jets career but also had shown him many personal kindnesses. Klecko and his younger son, Danny, once appeared in one of the commercials for the toy trucks sold by the Hess gas station chain. Their friendship really began during Klecko's hospital stay after he underwent surgery to repair the torn patella tendon in his right knee in 1982.

"Mr. Hess would come to visit me," Klecko says. "He usually came at one or two in the morning when he had finished working and no one else was around. I can hear that harsh, rough voice of his: 'Are things going good? They taking care of you? Do you need anything?' He'd always commend anybody else who was there for visiting me.

"Once when I was in the hospital, Don Schaeffer, who runs my fan club and used to be a New York City policeman, brought a couple of city cops with him for a visit late at night. Don went into the bathroom, and a few minutes later, he comes out wrapped from head to toe in toilet paper as a joke. Mr. Hess had just walked in. I said, 'Donnie, I want you to meet Mr. Hess.' Donnie felt like a fool. Mr. Hess saw him, said hello to me and left."

Great wealth is impressive by itself, but those who have had the opportunity to engage Hess in meaningful conversation about his experiences in dealing with some of the most important people in the world most often speak of the intellectual power of the man. "Mr. Hess is an intimidating person," Klecko says. "He reeks with confidence. I don't know Mr. Hess well enough to say that we're close, but the times I talked to him, he was a great guy. He has a heart, and he understands people. He notices every little thing. He astounds you with his knowledge of life and business.

"I went to see him after I was released to have a conversation with a great man and to say, 'Thank you.' I hope my relationship with Mr. Hess and the Jets will endure."

The feeling Klecko had for Joe Walton and Dr. James Nicholas was something else again. Klecko had something to prove about the condition of his knee, and he went to work with his personal trainer, Jack Foley, to get in shape to go job hunting. Five and, sometimes, six days a week, Klecko made the one-hour drive from his home to Lehigh University so he could spend two or three hours under Foley's supervision. For several years, Klecko had followed a total fitness and nutrition program designed by Foley. It included interval training to build his endurance, plyometric exercises to link his strength and speed for the explosive movements required of a defensive lineman, and exercises to increase the flexibility in his shoulders and legs. Klecko cut back on his consumption of alcohol and followed a diet consisting mostly of chicken, pasta, potatoes, rice, and salads, and he succeeded in lowering his body fat content to 7 percent by the 1986 season. To all that, Foley added hydrotherapy following the 1987 season because exercising in water reduced the stress on Klecko's knees and the water's resistance helped him make gains at a faster rate.

Foley was even more driven than Klecko, and there were times when he was pushing Klecko so hard that the exhausted player would playfully confront his trainer, saying, 'Do you know who I am? Do you know who you're ordering around?"

When he returned home, Klecko regularly did more lifting in the weight room in his house. Gradually, he reduced the strength deficit in his left leg compared to his right from 52 percent to 13 percent. Considering the strength in his right leg, Klecko had more than enough to support a bad knee and play in the NFL.

Whenever he was especially fatigued or felt like slacking off, Klecko says, "I thought about getting cut and how they did it. I thought about Walton being a two-faced son of a bitch."

That was sufficient to keep him going, and when he began entertaining offers from other teams, Klecko was ready for the physical testing to which each team subjected him. Denver was the first team to show an interest. Then, Indianapolis, San Diego, Seattle, the Los Angeles Raiders, and New England all contacted Klecko. San Diego and Seattle were early dropouts, but the other four teams brought in Klecko for testing. The results were a triumph for both Foley and Klecko.

"He went to these places, and they all passed him," Foley says. "He didn't have the pain in his knee that he was supposed to have. The important thing is that he has tremendous strength and power in his legs. The only team that didn't pass him on its physical was the Jets."

Denver, which showed the most early interest, opened the bidding, but the Broncos made just the one offer and stuck to it, saying they couldn't pay Klecko more than their highest-paid defensive lineman, Rulon Jones. Klecko flew out to Los Angeles, where he stayed with Raiders defensive lineman Howie Long and spent a day with owner Al Davis, whose contract offer was interesting but called for major concessions if Klecko didn't meet certain playing-time requirements. Patriots coach Raymond Berry was keenly interested in signing Klecko, but general manager Pat Sullivan didn't support his coach on the business end.

"Sullivan made a ridiculously low offer," Klecko says. "My agent, Marty Blackman, said to Sullivan, 'Do me a favor. Tell Raymond Berry what you offered us.' Sullivan said he would. That was bullshit. I called Eddie Khayat, the defensive line coach. He said Sullivan had told Berry we were very close. I said, 'Very close! Eddie, we couldn't be farther apart. The guy's lying to you.' Eddie stood up for Sullivan's integrity. I gave him the numbers for Denver, Indianapolis, and New England. The Patriots' offer was a joke. I talked to Raymond Berry when I went up there and told him Sullivan was telling him fairy tales."

Ultimately, Klecko signed with the Colts for a guaranteed base salary of $500,000 with incentives that could increase the value of the contract to the $800,000 range. Owner Robert Irsay had a reputation as a meddler and a tyrant, but Klecko's experience with the Irsay family was a pleasant one. General manager Jim Irsay had engineered a trade for superstar running back Eric Dickerson the previous season when the Colts won the AFC East title, and he was trying to build a team capable of reaching the Super Bowl.

"Jim Irsay was nothing but good to me," Klecko says. "The Irsay family gets a lot of criticism, but they treated me like a professional and they treated me with respect. I went there because they had Dickerson, and I really thought they had a chance for a Super Bowl ring."

When Klecko reported for the Colts' minicamp for veterans in May, he astounded the coaching staff with his performance in all the physical tests. He couldn't wait to share the news with Foley in a telephone call after the tests. "Joe blew everybody away," Foley says. "He was telling me about his vertical jump and his bench press, and then, he said, 'Jack, I know I'm not supposed to do squats, but I squatted seven hundred pounds once.'" Squats, a lift in which the bar is positioned behind the neck while the lifter drops into a squatting position, put a tremendous strain on the knees. Klecko squatted more weight than any player on the Colts, proving that his left knee and leg were in top condition.

While Klecko was training for his comeback, Joe Fields was settling into his life after football and working hard to start his own business as a food broker. He worked out all of February but soon found less and less time to go to the gym. Finally, in June, he got a call from Jim McNally, the offensive line coach in Cincinnati, asking if he still wanted to play. Fields said yes, but he didn't hear from Bengals head coach Sam Wyche until July. Wyche said he was going with younger players, but his last words to Fields were: "If I were you, I'd get in shape and stay in shape."

Resigned to the idea his career was over, Fields virtually stopped working out. Training camps opened around the NFL, and Fields watched a couple of exhibition games on television. He was learning what it was like to be on the outside looking in. Now and then, one of his friends would call up, claiming to be Don Shula or Dan Reeves looking for a center. One night in August, a reporter from the New York *Daily News* called to ask if Fields had heard from the Giants, and he said no. Early the next morning, Kay answered the telephone and, handing it to Joe, said, "It sounds like a football coach."

The voice on the other end said, "This isn't a joke or somebody fooling around; this is Bill Parcells of the Giants." Fields recognized the voice because Parcells always had talked to him before the annual Jets-Giants preseason game. "Think you can still play?"

Parcells was looking for a backup for center Bart Oates, and he wanted someone with experience whom he could trust to perform for a team that had a chance to go back to the Super Bowl after winning it two seasons earlier. When Fields drove up to Giants Stadium to take his physical, Parcells was totally honest with him. The coach went over the depth chart and told Fields whom he thought he would keep and whom he planned to let go. Backup center Conrad Goode couldn't handle the long snapping. If Fields could get in shape, the job was his. It was a perfect situation because Fields could commute to work from home part of the week and stay in a hotel on Wednesday and Thursday nights after practice. After talking it over with Kay, he signed for $200,000.

Parcells told Fields, "I'm not going to kill you in camp. You play twenty or twenty-five plays in two preseason games and tell me if you think you can do it. But be honest. God gives it to you, and God takes it away. If you can't do it, that's all right. You had a great career."

"I went in and almost died," Fields says. "I was so stiff after the first day of camp that I couldn't bend over far enough to touch my knees. But I told him after we played Pittsburgh that I thought I could do it. Our last preseason game was against Cleveland. I only played three or four plays, and I was on the roster."

When the Jets released him, Fields was afraid he had crossed the River Styx as a player, but it turned out he merely had crossed the Hudson. On his first day with the Giants, one of the trainers gave him a hat that was half Jets and half Giants. "Guys like Bart Oates and Billy Ard from the offensive line were really good to me, and nose tackle Jim Burt helped me out," Fields says. "They made me feel comfortable there even though it was strange to play for a new team. It was like *The Twilight Zone*. Everything was the same—I was playing football at the Meadowlands like I had before—but everything was different."

Klecko's training camp was not nearly so relaxed. In fact, he almost didn't make it to training camp because of an accident that nearly ended in tragedy. Three days before he had to leave for the Colts' camp, Klecko hosted a pool party for the softball team on which he played each summer. His buddies were playing touch football in the pool, and they began yelling for him to find someone else to serve the hamburgers and the beer and join the game.

Making a grand entrance, the 263-pound Klecko ran and dove in the shallow end of the pool, where the water was three feet deep. It was something he had done many times before, but someone threw the football at his face as he dove. Ducking his head just before he hit the water, Klecko crashed headfirst into the bottom of the pool.

"I paralyzed myself from the neck down," Klecko says. "Under the water, I saw my left hand drift up in front of my face. I concentrated as hard as anyone can concentrate and tried to move it, and I couldn't. As I was sitting there under the water, honest to God, I was thinking. 'Who can I get to kill me? I'm not going to live like this.' "

At first, everybody was laughing and telling Klecko they didn't buy his act. Then, one of the wives said, "He's not kidding around. He's really hurt." Hearts suddenly began pounding and stomachs knotted up in fear as his friends brought him to the surface. Klecko told them to move him to the side of the pool and keep him floating there while one of the wives, who was a nurse, told the others to find a board to which Klecko could be strapped. Debbie, Michael, and Danny were scared as never before in their lives.

"It seemed like an eternity while it lasted," Klecko says. "It was the scariest thing that ever happened in my life. But after about a minute-and-a-half, I got a tingling in my hands, and then, all the feeling came back."

Klecko was taken to a hospital, where he was examined and tested thoroughly by a neurosurgeon, who concluded that only the immense strength of Klecko's neck muscles allowed him to survive the compressive forces and prevented him from becoming a quadriplegic. Foley was infuriated by the accident because it was a major setback after all the training they had done to prepare Klecko for his new life with the Colts.

"We worked so hard to attain a goal, and we felt it was going to happen for him," Foley says. "Then, he made a stupid mistake. It happened on a Saturday evening, and he left on Tuesday for camp. When he got there, he was in therapy for ten days, and he couldn't make an immediate impact. He produced on all the physical tests, but he had residual pain. The Colts were saying, 'What's wrong with Joe Klecko?' "

The effects of Klecko's neck injury lingered all season. "My neck muscles were contused, and the ligaments in my spine were stretched," Klecko says regretfully. "There was no way I could be right all year. I got a lot of burners, which cause a tingling and burning sensation in your arms and shoulders when you get hit a certain way. You lose all your strength, and you're helpless when that happens. It was really bad at the end of the season."

To anyone old enough to remember the sight of Raymond Berry hooking his toes on the sideline and extending his body to make a fingertip catch of a pass from Johnny Unitas, the words "Indianapolis" and "Colts" never will sound right together. They're the "Baltimore Colts." In that same vein, the sight of Joe Klecko wearing the Colts' traditional white helmet with the blue horseshoe on the side and a blue stripe down the middle had a jarring effect on everyone who knew him as a Jet.

Like Fields, Klecko felt like a stranger in a strange uniform. A couple of days before the regular-season opener, Klecko received a call from someone who well understood the feelings he was experiencing.

"Joe Namath called just to see how I was doing," Klecko says. "He was getting ready to go up to New England to announce the Jets' season opener for TV, and he just called to shoot the breeze. We never talked about what happened to him and me, but I sort of sensed there was a bond. In my last days with the Jets, I always told people, 'They cut Joe Namath, and he meant a hell of a lot more to this fucking team than I ever did. What makes you think they won't cut me?' I didn't know Namath that well, so, his call came out of the blue. He called to wish me luck."

In a town that didn't have a pro football team until 1984, Klecko's reputation didn't carry much weight with the fans in Indianapolis. He was as much a stranger to them as he was to many of his teammates, most of whom were younger. It helped that he knew veteran linebacker Barry Krauss, who had played for Alabama at the same time as Klecko's old Sack Exchange buddy, Marty Lyons.

"Barry kind of adopted me," Klecko says. "The Colts trained in Anderson, Indiana, which is Podunk, USA. It was desolate. Barry demanded that I come home with him to Indianapolis on weekends. I was used to the fast life of New York, and Indianapolis is a slow, midwestern town. I felt like I didn't fit in.

"I was going from an atmosphere where I had been the honcho to a place where I was going through a rebuilding process for myself, not the team, but myself. It was do or die because they weren't going to wait for me to learn their system. The respect I got from some of the older offensive linemen, like center Ray Donaldson and guard Ben Utt, was great. They would tell stories about playing against the Sack Exchange and how hard it was. They were a great bunch of guys, but I just wasn't one of them. I was a New York Jet in a Colts uniform."

Separated from Debbie and the kids for longer periods of time, missing the camaraderie with Fields, and struggling because of his neck injury, Klecko felt a loneliness for which he was unprepared. He found a good New York-style deli in downtown Indy and Colts strength coach Tom Zupancic invited him to dinner with his family several times, but Klecko simply was out of time and place.

"Joe would call me up and talk for about an hour every week," Foley says. "He was very lonely and despondent. The Colts never got the total defensive package together around Joe Klecko."

The neck injury was a big part of the problem because he got off to such a slow start, but Klecko also had trouble developing a good relationship with Colts defensive coordinator George Hill. Klecko was allowed to line up at nose tackle in the cocked position that he had learned from Bud Carson, but he was restricted in Hill's defense in a way he never had been under Carson. The one redeeming factor in the situation was the way he was handled by Colts head coach Ron Meyer, who had been highly unpopular with his players when he coached at New England from 1982 to 1984.

"Ron Meyer and I really got along well," Klecko says. "Ron doesn't care about going out on Saturday night as long as you play on Sunday. We didn't even stay at a hotel the night before a home game. He's a hell of a motivator. The first time I met with him, he said, 'I'm sure you heard a lot of bad things about me when I was at New England. They wanted a disciplinarian. I played that role, but that wasn't me.'"

The Colts got off to an even slower start than Klecko, losing five of their first six games. They were involved in contract squabbles with several players. It was the price they paid for their success the previous season and the big contracts they handed out to the new players they brought in. Just before a home game against Tampa Bay that began a five-game winning streak, Meyer called Klecko in and said, "We've got to get more out of you."

Hill was using Klecko strictly in the Colts' basic defense on first and second downs and pulling him out of the game in most pass-rushing situations. "Tell me to play the way I want," Klecko told Meyer.

"You've got it," the coach replied.

Although he continued in the same role, Klecko began his most productive stretch of the season to contribute his part to the Colts' winning streak. Still, he wasn't the dominating force he had hoped to be. "Hill didn't know how to use me," Klecko says. "He was no Bud Carson. I've never been so humiliated in all my life as I was platooning."

From his vantage point in New York, Carson felt that Klecko needed more guidance and less freelancing. Ironically, Carson suggested that Klecko would have been better off playing head-up on the center like a traditional nose tackle. "Joe got carried away with trying to do too many things on his own," Carson says. "That was his only problem. If they had played him head-up on the center, it would have been harder for the guards to come down on his knees because they would have had to go too far to get him. Klecko still was strong enough to clog up the middle."

Life with the Giants was a far more pleasant and rewarding experience for Fields. Parcells warned him that he might not be comfortable as a backup player, but that wasn't the case at all. After the turmoil of the strike and his unhappy ending with the Jets, he wanted just one more season with a winner. Parcells essentially asked him to play the role of elder statesman, and Fields slipped neatly into the position.

The only hint of discomfort on Fields's part was the fact that he wore his green-striped Jets shoes for the first four games. The fans behind the bench at Giants Stadium stayed on his case, yelling for him to get blue-striped shoes, and Fields finally gave in and broke his last tie with the Jets.

"I didn't do anything but sit on the sidelines for the first two games," Fields says. "In the third game, I became the short snapper for placekicks, and that was my job all year. I had no difficulty in adjusting to that role. There's a lot of pressure when you're playing. I had done that for thirteen years, and I wasn't there to prove anything."

One of the interesting footnotes to his year with the Giants was the number of ex-Jets Fields ran into during the 1988 season. Previously, the Jets always had taken pains to point out how few of the stalwarts cut by Walton over the years had ever played football again, as if to say he always recognized the end of a player's usefulness. But Fields saw cornerback Jerry Holmes and fullback Tony Paige when the Giants played Detroit, and he said hello to safety Lester Lyles before a game against Phoenix. Safety Harry Hamilton found a home in Tampa Bay; the Raiders picked up cornerback Russell Carter and moved him to safety, and defensive lineman Barry Bennett caught on with Minnesota after making a one-game comeback with the Jets the week that Mark Gastineau deserted them to pursue his actress girlfriend.

An aspect of the game that few people understand is the difficulty of moving from one team to another in the NFL because so many coaches are committed to developing players over a period of time to fill a specific role in their system. That may change with modifications in the free-agent system, but it always will be harder for a football player to switch teams than, say, a baseball player, who does basically the same thing in a batter's box or in the field no matter what uniform he's wearing.

The fact that both Klecko and Fields played reduced roles with their new teams doesn't mean they couldn't have been as effective as ever in their old jobs with the Jets. It just means that Joe Walton didn't want them around anymore.

Bill Parcells didn't really have much of a job opening for Fields as a player, but over the years, the Giants coach had come to appreciate qualities in Fields that he felt could add a little something extra to his team. To Parcells, the presence of Fields in the locker room and on the practice field was more important than his ability as a snapper.

"Bill told me I had been one of his favorites over the years," Fields says. "He wanted me to pass on my experience to the young guys. Bill was in the locker room every morning. I'd get there early, and we'd talk for thirty or forty-five minutes. We just talked football. I didn't always agree with everything he said, but he didn't want a 'yes man.' He wanted you to tell him what you really thought. He really liked to talk to his players.

"At the end of the season, he sat down at my locker and told me I did a good job and that he appreciated it. He said, 'You were just what we needed.' "

As the schedule would have it, both Klecko and Fields got the opportunity to play against their old team. The Colts are in the same division, so, they played the Jets twice, which was one of the reasons Klecko considered when he signed with Indianapolis. In a way, he was lucky Fields was released at the same time so they didn't have to face each other, but Jim Sweeney, who lived with Klecko and Fields in their last season with the Jets and was a close friend, moved from tackle to center after Fields left.

The first time Sweeney and Klecko lined up across from each other was in the tenth week of the season at Indianapolis. On their first play, the Jets ran straight at Klecko. The message was: "Greetings from Joe Walton!"

"It was tough playing against Sweeney, real emotional," Klecko says. "I felt very close to him. Before the first play, I wanted to nod to him, but he wouldn't look at me. He was ready; I could tell he was a ball of fire. They ran at me, and Jim came off the ball hard. I sidestepped him, and he went right by. It was super physical playing against Sweeney. I was relieved when it was over. I felt I played okay but not great."

The Colts won their fourth straight game to even their record at 5–5. When it ended, Klecko and Sweeney met at midfield with their helmets off. Blood was trickling down from the open wound on the bridge of Sweeney's nose. That raw spot is an offensive lineman's trademark. It's created by the constant grinding of the front of the helmet on the nose, and it means he's driving his head into the defensive player's numbers in textbook fashion. Klecko and Sweeney each threw a meaty right arm around the other's neck and pulled their heads together so they were standing there holding the same nose-to-nose pose in which they had spent the game.

"We hugged and cussed at each other," Klecko says with a fond smile. "There was a lot of feeling."

The return bout was not as evenly played. It took place in the next-to-last week of the season when the pain in Klecko's neck had become more like a pain in the butt. The Jets scored a convincing victory, and Klecko left the game in the second half because of a burner.

Just making it to the fifteenth game of the season was a triumph for Klecko. It was considered a longshot by many at the start of the season that his knee would be healthy enough for him to play his return engagement at Giants Stadium. Klecko's introduction was expected to be an emotional moment, but there were more than thirty thousand no-shows because the Jets came into the game with a 6–7–1 record. Jets public relations director Frank Ramos did his part to drain as much of the drama as he could from Klecko's moment in front of the fans who knew him best.

"The Colts wanted to introduce me last on the defensive team," Klecko says. "The Jets' PR people refused to do it. They said, 'We don't think Mr. Irsay would like it if we did something like that at your stadium.' It was a typical Frank Ramos move. I was introduced second, which is the regular order, and defensive end Jon Hand was right behind me. They ran right over my name: "JoeKleckoandJonHand." They wouldn't even give me an 'adieu' like I deserved."

The loss ended the Colts' playoff hopes, and they returned to Indianapolis that night without Klecko, who went to his Long Island night club to spend the evening with old friends. His brother Jimmy was there along with Sweeney and Dan Alexander and Marty Lyons and Tom Baldwin and Pat Leahy and several other Jets.

"Joe Walton would have fired half the players if he knew they were with me," Klecko laughs. "It was a sentimental night."

It was obvious to his friends that the season had not been an easy one for Klecko. "Joe was getting a bit nostalgic," Leahy recalls. "He really missed his friends on the Jets and was glad his stay in Indy was almost over. He said it really wasn't fun for him anymore."

That game against the Jets was the last of Klecko's twelve-year NFL career. His neck injury prevented him from playing the final game of the season. Ironically, Fields's fourteen seasons also came to an end against his old team the next week. The Giants needed a victory to win their division and qualify for the playoffs, so, Parcells asked Fields to keep a low profile, in contrast to the hype for Klecko's return, to avoid giving the Jets any more incentive than they already had.

"The Giants had a lot of respect because they knew how explosive the Jets could be," Fields says. "But the Giants were different in the sense they had been to the Super Bowl and won two years earlier, and that breeds confidence. They felt somebody would pull it out."

The Giants fell behind, 20–7, in the third quarter, but quarterback Phil Simms played heroically to lead them on two touchdown drives, the second of which covered 80 yards and gave them a 21–20 lead with just under five minutes left to play. But the highlight of the Jets' season came when quarterback Ken O'Brien came through under pressure to throw the winning 5-yard touchdown pass to Al Toon with thirty-seven seconds left in the game. Their 27–21 victory enabled the Jets to finish with two big wins for an 8–7–1 record that was much better than expected, and it knocked the Giants completely out of the playoffs.

"I've got to admit I'm a Jets fan after thirteen years with them," Fields says. "But I was a Giant, and they stood in our way. I really wanted to beat them for no other reason than to go to the playoffs. The one thing I never got was a Super Bowl ring, and the Jets ruined my last chance."

When the final NFL season for Klecko and Fields ended, a funny thing happened. Unlike their last year with the Jets team on which they left their imprint, they discovered that football wasn't quite ready to let go of them. There still were people who valued their talent and knowledge. Bud Carson was one of the candidates for the vacant Cleveland head coaching job, and he let Klecko know that, if he got the job, he wanted Klecko to join him with the Browns. Then, Fields got a call from Bill Parcells, who offered him a job as an assistant working with offensive line coach Fred Hoaglin.

In making the offer, Parcells made a comment that would live with Fields long after he was through with the game, sincere words that helped restore whatever measure of self-worth was stripped away by the Jets at their parting. "Bill said, 'When you know a guy is your type of player, that's the type of guy you want to surround yourself with,' " Fields recalls with pride. "He thought I would fit in well on their staff. I told him later that I didn't want to coach, and he said he might need me for another year as a player. But in my mind, I felt I was done playing.

"My year as a backup was an easing away from football. It wasn't as abrupt as it was with the Jets. Maybe the way it ended with the Jets is why I felt haunted and wanted another year. Now, I'm very relaxed about the idea of not playing anymore. I have no qualms about the terms I'm going out on."

Fourteen years in the NFL was enough. While he was there, Fields devoted himself completely to his job, and if he were to continue as a coach, he knew it would consume him as playing had. More than anything else, he wanted now to focus that same energy and dedication on the children that were the product of the love he and Kay shared.

Christopher and Sean have the power to transform Fields from the eternal pessimist into a blind and unrepentant optimist. Their delight in his presence is Fields's escape from the pressures that always have driven him. He never had that before.

"My two boys really enjoy having Dad at home," Fields says with paternal feeling. "I work with Christopher on his leg. In your mind, you're always optimistic. You don't say there's nowhere to go. You feel there's always a place to go. I look at Christopher and think, 'There's something I can do that will help him.'

"What I'd like to do someday, if the boys play Little League or start to play some kind of sports, is coach on that level. I'd like to watch them do those little things; I'd like to watch them grow up."

Leaving the game was not quite the same gentle process of easing away for Klecko as it was for Fields. Yet, he was able to quit when there still was an opportunity to play on, and that had to be considered an upset. As long as he could limp on to the field, Klecko always found a way to play. But when it was time for the end, Klecko recognized it, just as he said he would in the days leading up to his separation from the Jets.

By the end of his year with the Colts, Klecko knew he didn't want to return to Indianapolis. There were indications that the Colts were considering releasing Klecko if he didn't want to retire, but Ron Meyer never reached a final decision. "I think they would have let me come back," Klecko says. "But I told Ron I'd make it easy for him; I'd retire."

Not even the chance to play in Cleveland, where he could get his uniform dirty and feel at home on a natural grass field in a defense coached by Bud Carson, could change Klecko's mind. He had called Carson on New Year's Eve, one year to the day after Walton called to tell Klecko the Jets were releasing him. Klecko just wanted to wish Carson a Happy New Year. The news that his old coach was a candidate for the Browns job hadn't hit the papers yet. Carson told Klecko he believed in Klecko's ability to play more football.

"I said, 'Joe, I may have a shot at this job, and if I get it, I want you to finish it the way you intended,'" Carson recalls. "Joe said, 'No, I'm finished.' I knew by the way he said it that he was. It was a completely different Joe Klecko.

"I was very definitely interested in signing him. I knew he had the neck injury and burners in his shoulders with the Colts. But he contributed, and I thought he could be a legitimate player on first and second downs and have a great 1989 season. I thought there was still gas in the tank. Joe was a warrior. When he thought he could do something, I knew he would put an unbelievable effort into coming back.

"But I could hear something different in his voice. He said it very quick, like there wasn't anything that could change his mind. It was over. As soon as he said he didn't want to play, then, I knew he couldn't play because he had to *believe* he could play with that knee."

When Carson landed his long-awaited job as an NFL head coach at the age of fifty-eight, Klecko called again to congratulate him. Carson said the offer still stood, but Klecko said, "Yo, Bud. Forget it. I just called to tell you I'm happy for you. You're going to be the best."

The decision was easy—if you didn't count everything Klecko went through after knee surgery at the end of the 1986 season to reach it. All things considered, his knees felt good, so good that he didn't find it necessary to wear a brace on the knee with the bolt in it when he played softball. Debbie and Michael and Danny were happy to have him home and to know there would be no more of the kind of pain he endured during football seasons, which always was a hard thing for them to watch. His future with Jet-group, Inc. was mapped out. It was time.

"Football wasn't fun for me anymore; the thrill of playing the game was gone," Klecko explains. "I spent two years of hell compared to the times I had earlier in my career. I was always so happy playing football, whether we won or we lost. But my last year with the Colts was totally anticlimactic to my career."

Klecko belonged with the Jets; they were like home and family to him. His anger when Walton kicked him out was such that he swore, "I'll never get over it. I understand it, but I'll never get over the bitterness."

One year later, he was surprised to find even the bitterness was subsiding. It took two years, but he and Fields managed to work through it together as they reviewed their careers so they could put it down on paper exactly as it happened. The process seemed to have a cleansing effect.

Reflecting on the end of his life as a professional athlete, Klecko says, "I think Joe Walton was vindictive toward me and did things that weren't in my best interests. He did it because he felt he was losing control. But there's no reason to think of my relationship with the Jets as a bad one because I had ten good years with them and one bad one. Right now, I'm so happy with my life that it would be meaningless for me to carry a chip on my shoulder forever because of the way it ended with the Jets.

"I wish other people could have what I had the chance to enjoy. Being in the limelight of professional sports was a godsend, and I'm grateful. The times we had, nobody can take that away. The things I had to prove, I felt I did. The things I did in the last couple of years, I felt I had to do for my own sanity."

If their end wasn't everything Klecko and Fields had hoped it would be as far as recognition and glory, neither was it the dark vision that many who knew them and understood their passion for the sport would have forecast. No one had to pry them from their lockers and escort them, kicking and screaming, to the street, nor were they carried out on their shields. Joe Walton's Jets may have abandoned them, but Klecko and Fields had enough respect from others in the game to earn the chance to walk away with dignity and to retire on their own terms.

Index

279